D0207747

LIBRARY
VISTA UNIVERS
WEST FOURTH
TORM LAKE, IA

# RATIONAL WOMAN

To feminists and some postmodernists reason/emotion and man/woman represent two fundamental polarities, fixed deep within Western philosophy and reflected in the structures of our languages, and two sets of hierarchical power relations in patriarchal society. Raia Prokhovnik challenges the tradition of dualism and argues that 'rational woman' need no longer be a contradiction in terms.

Prokhovnik examines in turn:

- the nature of dichotomy, its problems and an alternative
- the reason/emotion dichotomy
- dichotomies central to the man/woman dualism, such as sex/gender and the heterosexual/ist norm.

She argues for new 'relational' conceptions of all the terms involved, emphasizing the relationship or interdependence of reason and emotion, man and woman, rather than placing these terms at opposite poles. Prokhovnik then moves from the abstract to the practical by placing her thesis in the context of recent feminist theory and practice, including the backlash against feminism. She concludes that the second wave of feminism was still tied to a mind/body dichotomy, but that a third wave of feminism is emerging, bringing with it a relational non-dichotomous alternative.

*Rational Woman* offers a clear survey and evaluation of epistemological and ontological debates, but more importantly shows how these debates pertain to current political developments. This work makes a significant contribution to the literature of gender politics, political and feminist theory, sociology and philosophy.

**Raia Prokhovnik** lectures in Politics at Royal Holloway, University of London, UK. She has written on feminist theory, the concept of sovereignty, Hobbes, Spinoza and early-modern political thought.

# ROUTLEDGE INNOVATIONS IN POLITICAL THEORY

1 A RADICAL GREEN POLITICAL THEORY
*Alan Carter*

2 RATIONAL WOMAN
A feminist critique of dichotomy
*Raia Prokhovnik*

3 RETHINKING STATE THEORY
*Mark J. Smith*

# RATIONAL WOMAN

## A feminist critique of dichotomy

*Raia Prokhovnik*

London and New York

First published 1999
by Routledge
11 New Fetter Lane, London EC4P 4EE

Simultaneously published in the USA and Canada
by Routledge
29 West 35th Street, New York NY 10001



Typeset in Garamond by Curran Publishing Services
Printed and bound in Great Britain by Biddles Ltd, Guildford and King's Lynn



*British Library Cataloguing in Publication Data*
A catalogue record for this book is available from the British Library.

*Library of Congress Cataloguing in Publication Data*
Prokhovnik, Raia.
Rational woman: a feminist critique of dichotomy / Raia Prokhovnik.
208 p. 156 x 234 mm.
Includes bibliographical references and index.
1. Dualism. 2. Reason. 3. Emotion. 4. Feminist theory.
I. Title.
BB12.P77 1999
305.4'01——dc21 98—47963
CIP

ISBN 0-415-14618-6

For Kathy, Anna and Rona
and to the memory of Simon

# CONTENTS

# PREFACE

Some books bite so deep that their impact becomes almost invisible. It then becomes difficult to acknowledge their significance through specific references. Genevieve Lloyd's *The Man of Reason*, Elizabeth Grosz's *Volatile Bodies*, and Moira Gatens's *Imaginary Bodies* have been like this for me. My work is greatly indebted, not just to these three books, but to all the work of these three outstanding Australian feminists. These three splendid, robust, sound and imaginative thinkers make me feel that my birthplace has something to offer after all. They almost make me regret having left Sydney behind twenty-three years ago.

My interest in feminism derives from a background of strong but unreflective demotic egalitarianism, imbibed in a Marxist family upbringing with strong European and Yiddish, along with Methodist, cultural ties, set in the context of Australian 1950s suburbia, juxtaposed with the gradual realization of the insidiousness of the English class system which still ensures that the notion of privilege maps on to and so reinforces a range of power inequalities in British society.

This book also owes an enormous intellectual debt to Conal Condren, Michael Oakeshott and Quentin Skinner. My interest in dichotomy stems from the analysis of the presuppositions upon which the history of political thought rests, and the examination of its rhetorical dimensions in styles of argumentation and uses of language, which Condren developed in undergraduate lectures and seminars at the University of New South Wales. Oakeshott's seminars at the London School of Economics in the late 1970s, on the character of the philosophy of history, gave me a sense of the way in which a broad range of intellectual inquiry is susceptible to the principles of historical *understanding*, as opposed to the encroachment of scientific *explanation*. Quentin Skinner's in my view marvellous subversiveness, particularly in his brilliant *Reason and Rhetoric in the Philosophy of Hobbes*, in championing the value of ancient and medieval rhetoric against modern scientific rationalism, is a constant source of pleasure. The faults which the present book contains are in no way attributable to either Lloyd, Grosz and Gatens, or to Condren, Oakeshott and Skinner, and the responsibility for them is wholly mine.

I am grateful to the University of Southampton Social Science Faculty for a grant in 1996–7 to develop the idea of *Rational Woman.*

To Gary, Eleanor and Conal Browning I am deeply grateful, for their indispensable support and encouragement, and for their confidence in me, especially during the completion of this book. Gary's careful listening, acute comments and invaluable suggestions, engaging critically and openly with the ideas in the book, were always of positive benefit, and our wide-ranging intellectual discussions are the best I have encountered. I would also like to pay tribute to the sustaining warm friendship and wonderful individuality of Lucy Brookes, Ann Marie Legge, Lorraine Foreman-Peck, Angela Radcliffe, Ashka Beckerman, Gabriella Blakey, Caroline Thompson and George Farrelly.

I am also very grateful to Ian Forbes, John Horton, and Noel O'Sullivan for their support and encouragement, and to members of the Citizenship panel at the Bern conference of the European Consortium for Political Research in May 1997, including Birte Siim and Jet Bussemaker, and particularly Johannes Andersen for articulating the role of the family in providing the irreplaceable forum for learning love and hate, the crucial elements of care, attachment and independence. It is also a pleasure to record my thanks to colleagues at Southampton – Yvonne Marshall, Waltraud Ernst, Simon Blyth, Pauline Leonard, Sandra Wilkins, Vicky Preece, and Caroline Thomas – who have provided intellectual stimulation and support.

# INTRODUCTION

The title of this book invokes two implied contrasts. 'Rational' suggests a comparison with 'emotion', and also with 'body', 'intuition', 'passions', 'nature', 'experience' and the 'irrational'. This book is primarily concerned, in this first comparison, with the contrast between reason and emotion, and more particularly with the role of emotion in rationality. The second tacit comparison in the title refers to how the term 'woman' is the intimated opposition from 'man'.

Feminists and some other writers make a strong case that reason/emotion and man/woman are not simply innocent contrasts. As Gatens observes, such dichotomies are 'not a neutral way of dividing up the world into categories'. These dichotomies 'contain a set of implicit assumptions that assign a prominence and a dominant value to the term in the position of A at the expense of not-A' (Gatens 1991: 93). Dichotomies such as reason/emotion and man/woman represent fundamental polarities, fixed deep within Western philosophy and reflected in the structures of our language. The two polarities also represent two expressions of hierarchical power relations expressed in social practices in patriarchal society. It is crucial in feminism's commitment to praxis to bear in mind both the philosophical and political aspects at work in the operation of these polarities. According to the logic of dichotomous thinking in the Western cultural tradition the term 'rational woman' is a disjunction resting on a confusion of categories. The idea of 'rational woman' is, in terms of our inherited and still vital cultural assumptions, a paradox. But these cultural assumptions, such as the priority given to mind over body, upon which the self-contradictory nature of the term 'rational woman' rests, are not necessary features of the logic of concepts. This book explores the idea that 'rational woman', formed linguistically from the valued element of the reason/emotion dichotomy bracketed with the 'other', subordinate, element of the man/woman dichotomy, invites a reconceptualization of both sets of terms, to express not just a plausible idea but a coherent and fruitful conjunction.

Genevieve Lloyd's classic work of historical recovery on gender and reason provides the starting point for this book. Her central thesis is expressed in the recognition that 'the maleness of the Man of Reason . . . is not [a] superficial linguistic bias. It lies deep in our philosophical tradition' (Lloyd 1993: xviii). Lloyd and other writers have noted that there are also latent *conceptual* connections in the dominant Western cultural tradition which can be explored between reason, masculinity, truth and intellect on the one hand, and sense, femininity, error and emotion on the other (Gatens 1991: 94–5). The argument outlined here is framed to support the thesis that dichotomous thinking in which woman is seen as a subordinate term can be identified historically and is not a necessary feature of the logic of concepts. It is an important theme of the present book to examine some of the consequences of this thesis. Thus the following chapters explore some of the implications of Gatens' statement above and seek to engage in a sustained reconceptualization of reason and emotion, man and woman.

Underpinning the argument of the book is the strongly-held view that, faced with the legacy of the dominance of dichotomous thinking, the most effective way forward is neither to seek to abolish the terms held in the dualisms nor to revalorize women by inverting the dualisms, both of which are strategies that have been entertained by feminists. Rather, the present work agrees with an important aspect of Hekman's view that 'feminists will not succeed in privileging the female over the male because they have not attacked the dichotomy that constitutes the female as inferior' (Hekman 1990: 6). However, while endorsing Hekman's identification of the 'dichotomy that constitutes the female as inferior' as the critical locus of theorizing, it is clear that her further recommendation, the 'affirmation of the 'feminine' (ibid.), is discounted on the grounds that it would involve, this time in reverse, the same covert and exclusionary mapping of gender-character on to social behaviours and values as occurred with the range of modern dichotomies. For, as Lloyd cogently and crucially demonstrates, 'the symbolic content of maleness and femaleness cannot be equated with socially produced masculinity and femininity' (Lloyd 1993: ix).

The most effective way forward is to recognize the extended meanings of the terms reason and emotion, man and woman, extensions which occur when relations other than dichotomous ones are conceptualized. Indeed the meanings of reason and emotion, and man and woman, are very differently understood when the terms in each pair are conceptualized as interrelated and interdependent. Joan Cocks proposes a similar strategy in dealing with the dualism between theory and practice. She characterizes her approach as 'neither to snap nor to collapse the distinction' captured in the dualism (Cocks 1989: 2), but to probe the relationship they posit (ibid.: 6).

This introduction contains a brief synopsis of the argument developed in the four chapters of the book, considered under the headings of dichotomy, reason and emotion, sex and gender, and rational woman. The introduction also outlines some important general material which helps to establish and highlight the framework of the argument.

## Dichotomy

The argument concerning the two specific polarities of reason/emotion and man/woman which are the subject of Chapters 2 and 3, engages with feminist and mainstream theory to discuss some of the repercussions of these polarities for feminism as well as their consequences for mainstream political theory.[1] Before the argument concerning the two specific polarities is outlined, attention is directed to the general character of dichotomous thinking, the subject of Chapter 1. It is clear that the two dichotomies are interconnected and interdependent, in that 'reason' has helped to define 'man', 'man' has helped to define 'reason', and both definitions by their dichotomous nature have contained a subordination and exclusion of 'woman' and 'emotion'.

While modest practical gains have been made for some women, especially in the areas of education and work opportunities, at a conceptual level the dichotomies of reason/emotion and man/woman have proved extremely resistant to reform. Indeed it is partly due to the persistence of the dichotomous connection at the conceptual level, sustaining exclusionary social norms and practices, that it has proved so difficult to extend genuinely equal opportunities to women. Only when, amongst other things, the damaging effects of conceptualization in terms of presupposed but unthinkingly applied exclusionary dichotomies are recognized more fully, can the reconceptualization of reason/emotion and man/woman be conducted and realized in a positive sense. There is thus a necessary element of indeterminacy in this book, in that the positively realized conception and diversity of expression of 'rational woman' can only be advanced through concrete embeddedness in the normative language and practices of particular societies.

This book concentrates on the acute undertheorization of the conceptions of woman and reason. It argues that a coherent perspective can be articulated in which the conception of 'rational woman' is not a contradiction in terms. 'Rational woman' need no longer strike a discordant note, disclosing a disjunctive coupling of the superior component of one dichotomy with the 'other', subordinate, component of a related dichotomy. Neither need 'rational woman' be reconstructed by extending the meaning of one of the terms, 'rational' or 'woman', leaving the other to be defined in the light of a traditional dualism. Such a reform would lead only to either the notion of the rational housewife and mother (an absurdity in patriarchal culture) or the masculine-woman stereotype illustrated by Mrs Thatcher as prime minister. 'Rational woman' is best to be understood and achieved by a transformation of both reason/emotion and man/woman which reconceptualizes the components of the pairs in non-dichotomous fashion and so allows for the internal relationship and interdependence of the components in each pair to be explored.

Thus the general conclusion that is drawn from this argument concerns the polarities, the dualisms themselves. There is a strong case for the contention that Western philosophy and language, especially since the Enlightenment, has been characterized by a whole set of hierarchical oppositions, all allied to a primary elevation of 'man' at the expense of, and by excluding, 'woman'. However there are open to us possibilities for open-ended and non-dichotomous thinking and for relational social practice which values difference and diversity.

The general features of dichotomy, the problems with the dichotomous mode of thinking, and the character of the relational alternative are explored in Chapter 1, and in the subsequent chapters the value of a relational over a dichotomous theory and practice is proposed and analysed. It is worth emphasizing that what is proposed is not the replacement of the dichotomous with a relational mode, but the recognition of the dominating force and homogenizing effect of the authority attributed to the dichotomous mode, which has excluded other modes including the relational from serious consideration. Furthermore, while the continuing persistence and dominance of the dichotomous mode may lead the reader to assume that in this book dichotomous equals patriarchal and relational equals feminist, this is not the case. This book does not set up another dichotomy, of dichotomous/relational, or rather of relational/dichotomous. This book does not 'gender' modes of thinking, but seeks to explore the utility of one of the many possible non-dichotomous modes for feminist theory.

There are sound grounds for arguing that reason/emotion, sex/gender, and man/woman are dichotomies which have dominated the structure of our thinking and social practices since the Enlightenment. Moreover this dominant explanatory framework involves a process of mapping or patterning, whereby each of these pairs of categories have been mapped on to an underlying and fundamental source of meaning in the mind/body dichotomy. The force of the mind/body dichotomy has been that mind is 'naturalized' as free to construct and produce by artifice, while body is 'naturalized' as merely biological and tied to diurnal rhythms. Consequently, under the influence of the dominant dichotomous outlook the manner in which we achieve coherent cultural understandings of reason, emotion, sex, gender, man, and woman, has been through the mediation of the social meanings of the mind/body split.

The dominant understandings in Western philosophy (in being, knowledge, science), and the placing of value in social practices (of culture, society, politics, sexuality, work, family), and the ways these things are related to each other, follow as extensions of the logic of the mind/body dichotomy. Merchant's historical work is valuable in describing the cultural coherence that this kind of overall intellectual metaphor has provided when she examines the way in which the scientific revolution of the seventeenth century effected a 'transition from the organism to the machine as the dominant metaphor binding together the cosmos, society, and the self into a single cultural reality – a world view' (Merchant 1983: xxii).

Another important theme of the book has been the development of a view of partial historical and social construction which seeks to provide a plausible alternative to inappropriate determinist explanations, whether essentialist or fully socially constructed, that are thrown up by the debates on reason and emotion, man and woman, sex and gender. According to the view developed here, we inhabit a world of socially constructed practices along with explanations of that world. Our mind-set is derived partially from this inherited construction, as it interacts with our genetic predispositions and capacities, early experience, individual adult experience and circumstances, and sense of agency. Social and individual practices are affected not only by theory but also by the mediation of this theory through historical practices and social norms. In attempting to understand our inherited construction, we may exercize our critical capacities in particular upon the perceived incoherences in that inherited view. In reflecting upon its disjunction with our individual view, we display a capacity for agency, both individually and collectively. On the question of agency, it is clear that the kind of agency captured in the social engineer's blueprint is a rationalist fiction, but that a recognition and valuing of difference is crucial to the fostering of social diversity, inclusionary practices and social cohesion.

This view of partial historical and social construction is developed in each of the two central chapters of the book, with respect to reason and emotion and to sex and gender as a major locus of the man/woman dichotomy. It follows from the view advanced here that none of the meanings of the terms in these pairs of categories need be taken as simply 'given'; none have inherent or essential meaning; none are either biologically or socially determined without the mediation of historical and social meanings and individual understandings. The form of social construction developed here is designed to counter prevalent foundationalist determinist and essentialist theories, which naturalize particular biological explanations as given.

This insight goes some way to breaking down the force and potency which the dominance of the mind/body dichotomy has exercised over intellectual life and social relations over the past two hundred years. One of the strengths of the view of social construction recommended here is that it challenges the mind/body dichotomy posed between two major forms of explanation: a social constitutionalist form of social construction and the determinism of socio-biology. In other words this is the dualism between culture (nurture, agency) and nature. In contrast to the dichotomous cast of the dominant set of options, the view proposed here presupposes the interaction and interdependency of the material element, social norms and practices, and agency and reflection. All these three elements are mediated through social understandings. Furthermore when they have been 'denaturalized' all these categories (reason, emotion, sex, gender, man, woman) can be seen to be subject to contestable constructed understandings, to 'systems of cultural meanings' (Grosz 1990: 4). They are given by our capacity for interpretation and understanding within specific contexts, which has within it the possibility of revising those meanings. All of this involves the fluid and flexible mediation of language.

In this respect Grosz makes an important case for recognizing the impact of the metaphorical nature of language and thinking, on the production and reception of knowledge. She describes the process in terms of 'the two poles of linguistic functioning [which are] metaphor/condensation and metonymy/displacement' (Grosz 1990: 4). At an important level, these two poles necessarily have a relational rather than a dichotomous relationship. The primary way in which metaphor has operated in characteristically 'modern' knowledge, where 'knowledge' refers to ideas which are socially sanctioned as crucially significant and explanatory, is through dichotomy and through the mapping of central dichotomies on to other couples of categories seen as pairs. In this way mind/body and culture/nature have provided fundamental social evaluations for man/woman, reason/emotion, sex/gender, self/other, objective/subjective, exclusive/inclusive, justice/care, white/black and so on.

## Reason and emotion

One of the major conclusions of the current work will be that, rather than throwing out 'reason' altogether as a 'male' construction, the most conceptually plausible way for feminists to move forward from the exclusion of women from rationality, and the identification of women with irrationality, is to recognize that the notion of reason has been very narrowly defined and can be extended to take into account its immanent element of emotion.

The background to this conclusion involves a particular perspective on the 'modern' understanding of reason. Lloyd's book, *The Man of Reason*, has been central in recognizing that in modern European philosophy, science and culture, the term 'reason' has had a male character. Indeed Lloyd's book goes further than this, and argues that this identification of reason with masculinity goes back to the Greeks. Through the 'expression of values' by which reason has been tied to maleness, the 'equation of maleness with superiority goes back at least as far as the Pythagoreans' (Lloyd 1993: 103–4).

A pivotal feature of the argument is her demonstration that the claims of philosophers throughout our tradition to measure up to the philosophical virtues of universality and gender neutrality have been persistently unrealized. Lloyd sums up the point in the following terms: while '[p]ast philosophical reflection on what is distinctive about human life, and on what should be the priorities of a well-lived life, has issued in character ideals centred on the idea of Reason', the 'supposed universality and neutrality of these ideals can be seriously questioned' (ibid.: xviii). In consequence, Lloyd maintains, '[o]ur trust in a Reason that knows no sex has . . . been largely self-deceiving' (ibid.: xix).

Many feminists have contributed to elucidating and illustrating the male character of the Western intellectual tradition, especially since *The Man of Reason* was first published (Coole 1988, Jaggar 1989, Kennedy and Mendus 1987, Shanley and Pateman 1991, Evans et al. 1986, Nye 1988, McNay 1992, Battersby 1989, Fraisse 1994, Le Doeuff 1977, Okin 1989a). However Lloyd's delineation of the terms of the argument remains its classic statement. It is the most effective and far-reaching account because it combines an engagement in a highly-informed manner with our philosophical tradition, with an imaginative articulation of the feminist intervention at a conceptual as well as historical level.

Lloyd also contends that the history of the conception of reason, as the rational faculty responsible for the growth of what counts as knowledge in our society, demonstrates not only how it was denied that women had this faculty or were capable of exercising it, but that the conception of reason was actually *built upon* the exclusion of women from rationality. Lloyd argues a convincing case that the very *definition* of reason entailed not only the *omission* of women, but the expulsion, banishment and exile of women, to the realm identified with nature, emotions, passions, body, disorder, formlessness, subordination, passivity, otherness and danger. Many feminists (including Hekman 1990, Fraser 1989, Hartsock 1983, McMillan 1982) have recognized Lloyd's work as of crucial importance, not only in highlighting the historical identification of reason with masculinity, but also in reinforcing feminist arguments challenging the historical relegation of women to the 'private' realms of the domestic, the family, reproduction and sexuality. These are all seen to be governed by 'natural' rhythms, rather than being fit subjects for liberal rights, liberties, citizenship and justice.

Lloyd identifies a gendered reason/emotion dualism going back to the Greeks, though she also registers the particular contribution of Descartes to the modern entrenchment of this dichotomy. 'Neither the alignment of reason with maleness nor the opposition of the sexless soul to "female" sex difference was of Descartes's making', she notes. However, she adds, 'his influential dualism [the polarization of mind and body] has interacted with and reinforced the effects of the symbolic opposition between male and female' (Lloyd 1993: xiv).

Chapter 2 takes its bearings from the significance of the subsequent difference between pre- and post-Enlightenment rationality. This evidence is based on a reading of modernity which highlights the importance in this story of the split between reason and emotion which occurred in the seventeenth century. As Cocks (1984) argues, for the Ancients, while only men could be fully human, this understanding was not identified with rationality at the expense of emotion. The process by which reason was split from emotion occurred in a crucial sense with the development of modernity.

Lloyd's delineation of 'rational man', and Cocks's aim of showing that there is nothing inherently male about reason, both involve historical evidence that can be criticized. However, it is clear that in the seventeenth century, notwithstanding the underlying male/female dualism, philosophy and science still contained a legacy of an integrated notion of reason and emotion. It is with the reception of Enlightenment values that science really takes on its male journey. Notwithstanding alternative views put forward by writers such as Spinoza and Hume, a paradigmatic viewpoint was built upon the work of Descartes and Kant.

Modern empirical science as the exemplar of knowledge took an interpretation of Descartes's and later Kant's philosophies, and developed the idea of a strict separation between 'reason' as the logical cognitive faculty of the mind, which gives rise to knowledge, and 'emotion'. In consequence emotion, along with embodiedness and the passions, was associated with the realm of irrationality, from which 'knowledge' could never accrue. This development was furthered by the French Enlightenment writers in particular, who saw in the French Revolution the opportunity to sweep away not only the old feudal hierarchical political, social and economic order, but also all authority based on tradition, prejudice and irrationality, and to replace all such 'prejudice' with an all-powerful cognitive universal reason, divorced from the messy context of body, emotions and community ties.

In this context, Hobbes is a crucial figure on the cusp of the change, combining an acute awareness of the modern notion of reasoning with an inherited understanding of how reasoning utilizes emotions and passions. Merchant (1983) also recognizes the significance of the intellectual revolution that began in the seventeenth century for the development of modern dichotomous thinking, in her detailed historical work on the formation of the modern gendered nature/culture hierarchical bipolar opposition. Hobbes's thinking in *Leviathan* (1651) certainly exhibits a self-conscious and reflective attempt to use an up-to-date scientific method, replacing Aristotelianism not with a Baconian empirical methodology but with a deconstructive scheme of hypothetical resolution and composition, in the manner of Harvey's deductive theory of the circulation of the blood.

But Hobbes's *Leviathan* also exhibits (Prokhovnik 1991, Skinner 1996) an understanding of reason which can be seen as arising from an older, medieval tradition of viewing knowledge as entailing an element of communicative rhetoric. In particular, in his theory of language and speech, Hobbes argues that thinking depends upon trains of connections which are driven by the passions (including the passion to know). Thinking and emotions are inseparable for Hobbes. He concludes that for stable social and political life, only by a strict process of naming, of language defined by the public designation of the sovereign, can the naturally rhetorical aspect of speech be controlled.

The inherited understanding of reason is also present in the structure of *Leviathan* as a text. *Leviathan* is a very carefully written and systematically-ordered work, characterized by its sequence of cumulative definitions, and this is the aspect of the text most easy for a modern reader to spot. But it also contains a wealth of metaphor, creating correspondences between the natural person and the artificial person of the sovereign, as well as a comprehensive allegory of the Leviathan figure. This is expressed visually in the engraved title-page as well as verbally, in the philosophical argument in the body of the work. All of this non-rationalist material is vital to a full understanding of the significance of Hobbes's theory.

The import of this reading of *Leviathan* for the concerns of this book lies in the argument that Hobbes and others represent a threshold, after which reason and emotion were regarded as radically divorced. The split between reason and emotion persisted throughout the nineteenth and well into the twentieth century, despite the efforts of the Romantics and indeed Hegel to challenge the sterility of the supremacy of abstract reason and the consequent exclusion of the emotional and the subjective. At the end of the twentieth century, however, the dominant grip of these dualisms, and of the universalistic grand narratives of 'true' knowledge they spawned, seems to be to some extent receding. The reading of *Leviathan* sketched here thus represents an example of the suppressed existence in the history of philosophy and political theory of the importance of analogical reasoning, metaphor, and communicative rhetoric. Indeed in this reading *Leviathan* expresses a style of thinking that pre-dates the 'modern' extension of and intensification of the dichotomization of reason and emotion under the mind/body split.

Another text from which the current work takes its bearing is Grosz's *Volatile Bodies* (1994), in which she directly challenges the mind/body dualism by reinvesting the body and the mind/body relation with philosophical meaning. Part of the objective in this book is to reinstate the value of emotions from their suppressed position as relegated to body. Emotion is located principally in the mind (part of the body), and only secondarily in the senses or affects in the body. Thus this book aims to undermine the mind/body dualism by a different means from that employed by Grosz, by recalling the significance of emotion with respect to mind. Like Grosz's recent work, this book seeks to represent a challenge to the priority given to a narrow cognitive understanding of the mind as separate from lived and inscribed corporeality. The heart of Chapter 2 is a section which explores some of the ways in which emotion plays an important role in knowledge and theorizing, in salience, in accompanying and driving theorizing, in language, in underpinning the development of reason, and in the intellectual virtues.

## Sex and gender

One of the central claims of the book arises from the understanding that reason and emotion, and sex and gender, are all socially constructed in the sense that they all contain elements of materiality, partial social construction, and agency, which 'act in concert' (Gatens 1996a: 111). Gatens advocates not the obsolescence of either feminism or philosophy, but the transformation of both, based on the recognition that the 'notion of the socially constructed subject is absolutely central to feminist theory' (Gatens 1991a: 98). She identifies the vital consequence that the stable conceptions of human nature upon which much mainstream political thought rests are disclosed as essentialist. The coherence of much traditional political philosophy, taking its bearings from foundationalist categories, is thereby undermined.

The argument of Chapter 3 takes the arguments for social construction one step further. It contends that once the logic of the argument for the social construction of sex as well as of gender is taken seriously, and once it is recognized how the distinction between sex and gender has operated in a dichotomous fashion, then the basis of an important challenge to a cluster of dichotomies is established. The objection to gender divisions is that they express a difference which is not innocent; it is not an innocuous contrast but a dichotomized difference characterized by opposition, hierarchy, and the devaluation of the 'other' term. The sex/gender rubric contains three dichotomous pairs, and it follows not only that the sex/gender dichotomy is redundant, but that the bipolar male/female and heterosexual/homosexual dichotomies cannot be sustained in their present form either. What is proposed instead is a reconceptualization of the many things that the terms 'sex', 'gender', and 'sex/gender distinction' stand for, in terms of a relational view of the options and identities that are available, but which are not 'merely discursive' within the constraints of a given culture and the imperatives of materiality.

Chapter 3 is crucially concerned with developing, in the light of the man/woman dichotomy, a non-essentialist view of 'woman' which increases her visibility in both theory and practice. Carver makes a convincing argument that what is needed in the gender debate is not a degendering of women, to go alongside the degendered (male) 'man' of political theory, but more attention to self-expressed difference, particularly sexual difference, for both men and women (Carver 1996: 682). What is required is the combined recognition of sexual difference and specificity. No fully persuasive proposition for how this might be achieved has yet been developed in the feminist discourse, but in Chapter 3 the argument is proposed that two steps are vitally involved. The thrust of the thesis is that what is needed for a non-dichotomous man–woman distinction is more recognition of differences, not less.

Thus another important conclusion of the book will be that the man/woman dualism needs to be, and can be, recast to take account of the further implications of the work of feminists and others who have examined the way in which sex as well as gender is socially constructed. The two-stage process that is proposed moves from gender-blindness to gender visibility, and from there to the recognition of corporeal subjectivity.

The conflation of 'male' and 'human' that we have inherited in 'modern' philosophy and 'modern' social practices is not just a historical anachronism that is contingent and changeable at a legislative stroke. For that conflation, the mapping of 'male' on to 'human' that occurs through the privileging of male over female in the male/female dichotomy, is entrenched by the mind/body dichotomy that establishes the mind-set for policy and normative values in our thinking and social practices. The two-step process that is described here as a means for ending structures of inequality and discrimination, is designed to contribute to the challenges made to the conflation of 'male' and 'human'. The first step is based on the need to increase women's visibility rather than to attempt to degender women, and the second step is based on the construction of a relational mind–body connection, which will be expressed in the recognition of corporeal subjectivity. Once gender divisions are de-dichotomized there remains no significant foundation for preferring the notion 'gender' to the notion 'corporeality'.

Some important feminist debates are reassessed in the course of delineating the two steps involved in this process. For instance, it becomes clear that it is self-defeating to set up an opposition between equality and difference as goals for feminist theory. It is futile to portray equality and difference in a 'binary opposition' of choices, because the 'antithesis itself hides the interdependence of the two terms' (Scott 1988: 38), or to identify one rather than the other as the step which would bring about the emancipation of women. The dichotomous pairing of demands for equality and affirmations of difference creates impossible choices, and as Scott notes, the only response 'is a double one: the unmasking of the power relationship constructed by posing equality as the antithesis of difference and the refusal of its consequent dichotomous construction of political choices' (ibid.: 44).

Chapter 3, on sex and gender, explores the full implications of the social construction of sex and the dependence of gender on a biologically-defined bipolar sex assignment. It argues that these things make the distinction between sex and gender untenable, and develops a theoretical case for corporeal subjectivity as the result.

While the mind/body dichotomy remains in place in our thinking and in our practices, the primary and important task is to make gender inequalities visible. While the mind-set established by the mind/body split remains in place in thinking and practices, it is not possible to advocate corporeal subjectivity on its own, without being misunderstood as saying only that women ought to be recognized as autonomous and rational agents (that is, essentially mind and not body after all) in the way that Rawls would propose. That resolution is deeply flawed because it reinforces the current devaluation of the corporeality of all of us, women and men. The second task is to reconfigure our understanding of a mind–body distinction on relational terms. Only then can the force of the suggestion for corporeal subjectivity be understood.

This point can be illustrated by the way in which many women in Western societies currently face difficult and unsatisfactory choices in accommodating work and family. The lack of extended family support networks aggravates the problem, but more comprehensive child-care is not a satisfactory answer. Institutional care is geared towards satisfying needs concerned with the physical well-being and educational level of the child, and rarely provides the vital emotional continuity in which essential moral and emotional development can take place, nor the 'mental work' (Walzer 1996) necessary to the formation of stable and loving attachments. That it is mostly women who face this dilemma is owing to the continuing entrenchment of the mind/body split in our society. Work is identified primarily with mind and the public realm, while children and child-care are associated with reproduction and body and women, all located in the private sphere. Until the imbalance between men and women in facing this problem is made visible, and it is recognized as a form of inequality (or inequity), it is not possible to recognize that what is needed is a wholesale change, not so much in child-bearing and child-care practices, but in work practices. This must be seen as a problem for all, and not just as a problem for women on an individual basis, or there is no chance of taking the next step and acknowledging the implications of the corporeal subjectivity of all. Furthermore, the effective reform of work practices requires that the conceptualization of 'work' be extended, to fully value the work that is undertaken in the private sphere and to instantiate a flexibility with respect to paid work that encompasses the responsibilities of family life.

Ultimately the narrow conception of work with which we currently operate deserves to be recognized as a problem which derives from a mind/body split. It is a problem for all and not just for women, because we all have bodies. The recognition that we all have bodies, that follows from overcoming the mind/body split, is more important than the sex (that is, biological 'natural' sexual difference) of those bodies. The mind/body split encourages us to deny the diversity of our bodies, and to overlook the significance of our bodies in affecting both theorizing and social practices. It also encourages us to identify women's bodies as sexed and men's as neutral. In other words, the mind/body split provides a mind-set which denies the significance of corporeality for a range of activities including work practices.

## Rational woman

In an important sense, 'rational woman' cannot be delineated clearly prior to the diversity of realized expressions in concrete practice. At the same time, 'rational woman' cannot be recognized without a language which can describe her as such. The development of such a language requires at least three things: the acceptance of an extended conception of reason which encompasses its emotional element; an understanding of a corporeality which overcomes the inner/outer dichotomy of the mind/body approach to the world and to knowledge; and a recognition that specific relational connections of interdependence can provide as fruitful and valid a mode of thinking as can the dichotomous mode. The final chapter is concerned to outline some of these possibilities in the context of a third wave of feminism.

One of the strengths of the position outlined here is that it overcomes some of the problems associated with those writers who retain an ambivalent relationship with the dualism of Western philosophy. For instance some French feminist writers (Irigaray 1993, Cixous 1981, Le Doeuff 1989) fragment the notions of 'man' and 'woman' but at the same time regard them in essentialist terms. That is, they do not fully challenge the 'either/or' basis of the terms 'man' and 'woman'. There are also those postmodernists who subscribe to Lacan's view that these polarities are fixed and unalterable estrangements within the paternal law of the 'Symbolic Order' (Lacan 1977). This view is vulnerable to the charge of determinism, in the explanatory power given to the connection between the alleged unalterable Symbolic Order and the alleged deep structures of language.

An argument running through this book is that neither the idea of the presence of a Symbolic Order, nor the idea of the fragmentation of the self and its knowledge, impairs the cogency of the potential of 'rational woman'. The relational mode of theorizing discussed in the first chapter argues for the intellectual and social benefits of recognizing that within each dualism, that is, within the pair reason/emotion or man/woman understood as an either/or, the relationship, the connection, the interdependence between the two parts is crucial to the character of both parts.

The term both–and (Tavor Bannet 1992) enriches and captures the significance of both parts, in a way that either/or cannot do. Similarly Gatens proposes a critique of mainstream philosophy, in which the 'disjunctive relations internal to the reason/passion, mind/body and nature/culture dichotomies must be eroded' (Gatens 1991: 99). The elucidation of the relational mode needs to be careful and detailed, since the authority attributed to the dominance of the dichotomous mode of thinking has suppressed the serious consideration of any other mode of thinking, and has led to a climate which promotes social exclusion.

The central aim in writing this book was to challenge by means of a theoretically reasoned argument the continuing and deep-seated prejudice in theoretical disciplines, and the only partial acceptance in more practical areas, against recognizing that 'rational woman' is not a contradiction in terms. It seemed that there was a need still to argue the case, and that the case needed to be expressed in terms that bite deep into established assumptions. Although it may seem to some readers that what is being challenged is a straw man, or a set of straw men, the enterprise is important because there are still many, many of those men (and women) out there, trailing their straw.

This book is a feminist project in several senses. First, it is a feminist work because the feminist literature is the richest source for this debate. Second, this book supports the feminist commitment to political change as a crucial aspect of reconceptualizing values. Braidotti succinctly describes the commitment of feminist theory to changing concrete practices, and the crucial role of 'reason' and sexual difference in this story, when she commends the way in which 'feminist critiques of theoretical reason as a regulative principle, by paving the way for the deconstruction of the dualistic oppositions on which the classical notion of the subject is founded,' have 'resulted in approaching the notion of sexual difference as laying the foundation for an alternative model of female subjectivity'. In other words, 'the specific feminist approach to the question of modernity consists in the evaluation of the links or complicity between knowledge and power, reason and domination, rationality and oppression, and of them all with masculinity' (Braidotti 1992: 181).

This is not, however, a feminist book in the sense of excluding men. The focus of the book is on women, and on the situation of women, as a necessary step toward rectifying a form of unfair discrimination and the unequal treatment that follows from it. Rectification enables both sides to be recognized in self-identified ways, rather than through the process of stereotype and opposition which is damaging to both. However, the difference remains that these things are more damaging to the side without the power.

Third, the discourse of feminist theory, upon which this book largely but not wholly draws, contains many diverse contributions from the whole range of philosophical, theoretical and empirical backgrounds. It has been important and stimulating to engage with all these contributions, which nevertheless have a common thread of being addressed to a shared feminist project.

In the fourth place, in the course of writing the book it became clear that the argument is located within a broader context of feminist debate. Thus reflections on central feminist issues are incorporated at several points in the book. In particular the book develops a distinctive approach towards the issues of essentialism, gendered subjectivity, and equality and difference. The final chapter discusses the future of feminism in the light of the non-dichotomous relational alternative advanced through the earlier chapters, and links that discussion to the development of a new perspective on feminism's history.

Philosophy and politics have traditionally been male preserves, bastions of power and knowledge. Marilyn Frye (1993), Rosi Braidotti (1986) and Janice Moulton (1989) identify the case in respect of philosophy, and Wendy Brown makes the point about politics explicitly and convincingly when she observes that, '[m]ore than any other kind of human activity, politics has historically borne an explicitly masculine identity'. She argues that politics 'has been more exclusively limited to men than any other realm of endeavour and has been more intensely, self-consciously masculine than most other social practices' (Brown 1988: 4). This book considers topics at the heart of this bastion: rationality, the relegation of women to the private realm on the basis of a biologically 'given' sex difference, and the dominance of dichotomous structures framing thinking in Western philosophy and politics.

Before these introductory observations about 'rational woman' are concluded, the discussion will benefit from being placed more fully in the context of the political and philosophical framework of modernity. Specifically there are three points to make, concerning the term 'feminism', postmodernism, and the rationalist character of feminism.

One of the problems that has bedevilled feminism since the beginning of the second wave concerns the relationship between feminist theorizing and feminist practice, and the confusion between two equally valid meanings of the term 'feminism'. We need to distinguish between the very real, specifically gendered, subordination faced by women as a group at the practical level, which has been socially constructed in patriarchal society, and the theoretical level at which the previously suppressed potentialities of women (what might be called their both–and potentialities) can be explored. Both of these can be, and are, called 'feminism'.

Thus while feminism is undoubtedly a set of beliefs and values attached to an emancipatory political programme, allied to other attempts to specify a politics of democratic inclusion, and as such is characterized by fruitful praxis, there has also been a confusion in feminist theorizing between accounting for how things are and discussing how things could be. On the one hand, feminists have highlighted and criticized the power relations which characterize contemporary societies, which result in entrenched inequalities and unjustifiably different treatment. On the other, feminists are concerned with the theoretical exploration of women's (and by implication men's) potentialities, a project which is most cogent when it leads to an understanding of potentialities which are extended, diverse and interlinked, rather than unitary and narrow and built upon an excluded 'other'.

The dilemma of modern liberal political philosophy, the dominant theory and practice in Western societies, is to be marooned on the beach of impartiality, unable to embrace effectively gender, colour and class differences as important aspects of subjectivity and as sources of discriminatory practice. Liberalism's dilemma is owing in part to its commitment only to 'thin' theories of the individual and of the 'good', which regard differences of gender, colour and class as morally irrelevant. This predicament is a classic illustration of the poverty of the narrow and unitary sense of potentialities. Feminists seek to redress this as a matter of urgency. The detrimental consequences that follow from some liberal values, and the reach of their pervasiveness, have been even more extensive than previously documented.

It is clear that the ambiguity in the aims of feminism – where the conclusions reached from the commitment to critique can diverge from those reached from the commitment to reconstruction – is in part owing to the manner in which patriarchal society and Western philosophy have reinforced each other. Together they have perpetuated the hierarchy and polarity between masculine and feminine in social roles, language and philosophy, in a way that seriously constrains the available choices in thinking and reconceptualization.

While language expresses our contextual values and reflects our inherited norms, we do not have to accept, as do some postmodernists, that language also determines our values. Fraser identifies the problem neatly as the continued 'structuralist reduction of discourse to symbolic system' (Fraser 1997c: 157). To the same end, Gilligan (1993: xiii, xix) notes that the explanatory choice given in the nature/culture distinction presents a false and narrow pair of options, for it overlooks the role of 'voice' and agency. Humanism, in the specific sense of knowledge understood as produced crucially by individuals, is not incompatible with the recognition of knowledge produced within contextual languages, discourses and power relations. This understanding informs the view of social construction articulated here in the discussions of reason and emotion, and man and woman.

A second criticism of some, but not all, postmodernist theorists concerns competing conceptions of the term 'difference'. Grosz analyzes the pitfalls following from the presumption of Western reason of 'a unified, rational and self-knowing or conscious subject' (Grosz 1990a: 72), and she pays tribute to Le Doeuff's insight that male philosophy's exclusion of metaphor is part of its inability to recognize its reliance on textuality and language (ibid.: 163–5). Postmodernist theorists such as Braidotti (1991) go further. They perceive reason as complicit in the sexual power structure, and argue for a nomadic post-crisis epistemology characterized by the non-unity of the subject and pure difference. It has been plausibly suggested by Sabina Lovibond (1989) that such theorists go too far in rejecting all rationality. Most do in fact retain criteria of rationality such as a distinction between adequate and inadequate argument, and non-arbitrary value judgment.

There is another, more convincing, idea of difference. Gilligan, for instance, proposes a notion of difference which while not producing an anything-goes relativism, implies a network of concrete relationships and connections with others. According to her view, the way we operate both as private individuals, and as citizens and employees, draws upon two moral senses, the sense of justice and the relational sense. Both the public and private spheres can be characterized by the 'interaction of multiple moral voices' and, as Hekman (1995) concludes, we can stop attempting to integrate all voices into a unitary pattern.

A common criticism of some postmodernist theories is that the fragmentation brought about by pure difference leaves no basis upon which the solidarity and common goals of political reform can be mobilized. The activity of politics, beyond resistance, would seem to be suspended. As Lovibond argues in an influential article (1989), postmodernism is not radical *enough* to accommodate the political programme required by feminism's aims of ending sexual oppression. Social reconstruction on a grand scale is rejected by postmodernism. Feminism as emancipatory politics is therefore still within the modernist agenda, Lovibond argues (Lovibond 1989, see also Nash 1994, Steinberg 1994: 300).

There is strong ground for reasoning that, notwithstanding the valuable insights which postmodernist theories have produced around the notions of anti-foundationalism and perspectival truth, some 'modern' aims and assumptions, in both their political and philosophical forms, neither can nor should be discarded. Whatever its faults, and inflated claims to universal truth, timeless and genderless reason and so on, the Western philosophical tradition has been and can continue to be an emancipatory philosophy. As Pauline Johnson (1993) contends, radical democracy has been central to the Enlightenment project, and feminism's concerns with extending democratic objectives are good grounds for recognizing its inclusion in this project. Furthermore, as Lloyd (1993: 109) notes, this philosophical tradition 'also contains within it the resources for critical reflection' on its own false and inflated claims. Indeed, as Johnson shows in particular, 'to suppose that the undermining of the role of the philosopher-arbiter has been accompanied also by the collapse of the need and the possibility of seeking rational assent for normative claims' would be 'to concede far too much to the self-aggrandising representations of modern philosophy itself' (Johnson 1994: 114). The strategic advantages of this approach, over one which forecloses discussion in 'modern' terms, are clear.

This leads to the third point, concerning the rationalism of feminism. Feminism is a classic 'modern' project, in two ways. First, it aspires to find a solution to a problem of inequality and lack of liberty. One of the aims of this book is to demonstrate how, on the basis of the understandings of reason, emotion, sex and gender outlined here, feminist theory may be in a position to resolve a puzzle at its core about essentialism and its own incapacity adequately to embrace difference. That is, while feminist politics will continue to address concrete examples of patriarchal structural inequalities in the name of the emancipation of women, feminist theory may be able to incorporate an understanding of difference which accepts that at some level the emancipation of women as an absolute aim is not possible, nor is it necessary to achieve this. The number of concrete meanings of emancipation and equality is infinite and ever-multiplying, and must involve the emancipation of other self-identified groups as well, including ethnic, racial, sexual and age minorities that comprize men as well as women.

Second, feminism is a classic 'modern' project in that it is confident of finding a solution through the exercise of reason, though now in two rather different senses. It now posits an extended conception of reason, incorporating its emotional dimensions and the experience of the recognition of gendered subjectivity and corporeality, rather than persisting with a narrowly cognitive view of reason which posits the omnicompetence of (narrowly-defined) reason and the finality of theory. And it recognizes that neither the political nor philosophical experience of the modern age can simply be discounted, such that some sort of blank sheet rationalist perfectionism could be embarked upon by feminists.

However feminism remains opposed to a rationalist perspective in an important respect. The liberal ideology which purports that we are all now free, rational, independent individuals, has currently largely been swallowed uncritically by yet another generation of young people in Western society. This widespread belief has the consequence that many young people greet as ludicrous the proposal that there exist structural inequalities, let alone the thesis that social practices have a normative dimension which generates and is generated by social values and assumptions in our society. The grip of an inflated, purely agency-directed individualism is so strong that many young people regard with outright disbelief the ideas not only that we are subject to psychological conditioning and socialization, but that it is part of our make-up to experience a mind-affected and value-affected mediation of the world, such that we would develop this kind of view even if it was not specifically provided. Indeed the difficulty for ideas of equal opportunity to find credence in our society is partly due to the way in which their application of a basically liberal feminist approach to an insight gained from outside the liberal conception of the world is regarded as fully persuasive to neither school of thought. In this sense liberal rationalism remains a serious obstacle to the recognition of the political and philosophical insights which feminism has developed, and to the further development of feminist aims.

The basis of the conception of 'rational woman' which the following chapters will explore is summed up well in Gross's statements that '[f]eminist theory today is not simply interested in reversing the values of rational/irrational or in affirming what has been hierarchically subordinated, but more significantly, in questioning the very structure of binary categories' (Gross 1986: 202), and that feminism 'attempts to develop alternatives to the rigid, hierarchical and exclusive concept of reason' (ibid.: 203). Like Gross's argument, though in a slightly different sense, the argument presented here is for extending the notion of reason, rather than rejecting it as a male category, as Cixous (1981) does when she argues that desire, not reason, provides the means of overcoming the constraining concepts of Western intellectual thought. Feminist theory which privileges a woman's standpoint based on woman's experience is essentialist, and reinforces and takes part in a 'curious collusion' (Cocks 1984) with the existing dualism between man and woman. And whereas some post-modern feminists advocate the proliferation of differences within masculinity and femininity, neither does this – possibly dangerous – fragmentation on its own overcome the polarity.

The two dichotomies, of man/woman and reason/emotion, have worked together, 'rational man' being a potent symbol of the modern age. But the definition of 'rational man' has depended upon 'emotional, that is, irrational, woman' as an inferior counterpoint. The narrow and exclusivist meanings of man/woman and reason/emotion have led to the rationalist myth that disembodied and disembedded reason is a higher faculty, separate and necessarily distinct from accompanying emotion, perception, reflection, memory, and deliberation upon felt experience. These narrow meanings have also limited the scope of traditional political theory, which seems unwilling and unable to deal with gendered political issues like pornography, and with those issues located in the so-called private sphere of the family, such as marital rape, domestic violence, the unequal division of labour in the family, and childcare.

Building on the historical recovery undertaken by Lloyd, Brown and others of the persistent association of man with reason and the devaluation of women upon which it has rested, the present book seeks to do for reason/emotion and sex/gender what Gatens, Grosz, Lloyd, and Butler have done for other aspects of mind/body, Pateman has done for public/private, Plumwood and Merchant have done for nature/culture, De Beauvoir began and others have developed for man/woman, Cocks has done for dichotomous power relations, and the Gilligan debate has done for justice/care. Underlying this work is the view that a relational rather than a merely inverted dichotomous mode of thinking is the most cogent (though not the only) way in which to contribute to the redress of inequality and the recognition of difference.

The term 'rational woman' incorporates a broader notion of rationality, a wider range of what counts as rational, along with the inclusive recognition of gendered subjectivity and a rich notion of corporeality, in the light of a more self-defining idea of woman that is not distinguished in an essentialist way from man. It is important to disclose the problems consequent upon the dominating effects of dichotomous thinking because of their pernicious and deep-seated impact on real social practices, in the workplace, in the family, and in social and political life. It follows that the significance of the relational proposal for 'rational woman' is not limited to a merely theoretical reconceptualization, but is about providing the vocabulary and the arguments to sustain political reform, where political reform is undertaken not just in the name of promoting individual self-realization and self-development, but also in the name of fostering social practices which affect positively groups of people and social relations between them. What is suggested here is that 'rational woman', understood in a non-hegemonic relational mode of thinking (that is, one which does not naturalize a dominance of any one form of relation) in terms of the connectedness of both–and rather than the opposition of either/or, represents a fruitful way forward for feminist theory.

# 1

# DICHOTOMY

## From the dichotomous either/or to the relational both–and

The argument of this chapter follows directly from the appreciation expressed in the Introduction for the work of Lloyd and others in explicating the negative role of dualisms in the Western intellectual tradition (Lloyd 1993; see also Flax 1992, Green 1995). Plumwood's work (1993, 1995) is also dedicated to documenting the important negative effects of dualism. She highlights the dualism involved in the specific opposition between 'human' and 'nature', leading to a whole series of dichotomous readings of the human condition.[1]

Against the viewpoint fostered by the dichotomous mould, there are strong grounds for holding that reality is a meaningful world in which things (objects, persons, concepts, events, practices, language) contain meaning partly through being understood in relation to one another. An example is Patton's description of the view that the 'virtual relations with other concepts constitute the "becoming" of the concept in question' (Patton 1997: 243). Dichotomy plays a part in a world of meaning, but only a part. While dichotomy is a useful tool amongst a range of tools in theorizing, in refining and sharpening distinctions and definitions, its scope has been sharply inflated. The role it has played in arresting the meaning given to persons and qualities, presented to us in A/not-A form, and consequently in systematically promoting the marginalization of both certain social groups and alternative modes of thinking, needs to be challenged.

This chapter examines aspects of the general character of dichotomy that provide the conceptual basis for that history of dualism identified by Lloyd and others, in order to demonstrate how dichotomous thinking has operated to dominate the construction of ideas. The chapter also seeks to argue for an alternative standpoint, one of the possible alternatives, to the stranglehold that has been sustained in the modern period by thinking in dichotomous terms.

The expression of the mind/body split in the philosophies of Descartes and Kant, and the subsequent dominance of rationalist philosophy, led to consequences (intended and unintended) which are now widely recognized as problematic. For instance it is now considered in several areas of political and social theory, international relations theory and post-analytic philosophy, that the impulse to define one's conceptions, oneself, and one's political community in opposition to, in rejection of, and in a hierarchy with something else, rather than in connection to it, entrenches division. While not all such attempts are or need be compatible, and not all attempts at an alternative approach achieve their aim, the recent contributions, for example, of Seyla Benhabib (1996) to the debate on subjectivity, of Allison Weir (1996) on identity, of James Tully (1995) on multiculturalism, of Rob Walker (1993) on sovereignty, and of Axel Honneth (1995) on the politics of recognition for citizenship, testify to the diversity of successful attempts to find workable alternatives to the dominant over-arching explanatory force of dichotomy.

Most recently the theory of decentred management, and the work of psychotherapists to overcome in different ways the inside/outside dualism upon which their profession has operated, represent two further examples of attempts in theorizing to overcome a Berlin Wall mentality, to break down the absolute priority given to one component of a pair over the other, and to reconceive richer possibilities for social and personal interaction. Of particular interest are the contributions of two psychotherapists. Susie Orbach (1998) calls for overcoming the split between the inner world and the body, and Adam Phillips (1998) seeks to overcome the Cartesian split between the world of the inner self and the outer world of politics.

Dichotomy forms the basis of one mode of thinking within a range of possible modes. The virtues of dichotomy are clear and can be defended.[2] What is at issue here is not dichotomy as one mode within a range of modes of thinking: it is the repressive effect on other modes of thinking that the dominance of dichotomy has exercised over the past two hundred years. This dominance is in urgent need of criticism and remedy.

The purpose of examining here the general features of dichotomy and some of the problems associated with it is thus threefold. The first aim is to bring to light the manner in which dichotomy's domination magnifies features of, and aggravates, its problems. The second is to help to understand the process by which dichotomous thinking, when mapped on to understandings of categories such as man, woman, reason, emotion, culture, nature, mind, body, leads to exclusion in real social practices, and naturalizes the marginalization that takes places in social exclusion. The third aim is to provide the basis for proposing an alternative mode of thinking, free from the naturalized assumptions within dichotomous thinking that would simply deny the value of alternative modes of thinking.

This enterprise inevitably builds upon the intimations of earlier theorists, in particular perhaps Hegel and Spinoza. Contemporary non-dichotomous alternatives involve recovery and recapture as much as exposition and explanation. The intellectual provenance of the idea of a relational alternative to dichotomous thinking goes back at least to Hegel's discussion of the relationship between master and slave, which centres on misrecognitions, relations, and the need for reciprocal recognition, as well as to Spinoza's holism which was framed to override dichotomy (See Lloyd 1994, Gatens 1996a, 1996b, Grosz 1994).[3] However, an intellectual pedigree does not explain the contemporary significance of earlier intellectual moves against dichotomous thought, nor the use to which they may now be put. Neither can an intellectual tradition in itself provide criteria for the selection of some of its aspects and the discarding of others (for example the misogyny of both Hegel and Spinoza). These crucial features of the current enterprise must be developed and justified in the present. It is also worth noting, to avoid confusion, that the argument pursued here occurs within a primarily Anglo-American theoretical context. As such it develops independently of, and only occasionally intersects with, the route taken by writers such as Irigaray (1993) and Cixous (1981) in their engagement with the legacy (not to mention intellectual baggage) of binary codes and the particular understanding of the role of language of Lacan, Derrida and others. Nor is it designed to chart the route they have taken.

The concern with dichotomy is not exclusively feminist, but it is the argument of this book that feminists have a particularly acute contribution to make to the debate. This is to be explained first by the coincidence between the historical treatment of women and the gender-coded character of subordinate terms in a range of interlocking dichotomies (Plumwood 1993: 427). Second, the wider feminist interest in dichotomy is closely related to the political feminist objective of social change, and so concerns what Jay refers to as the alignment of 'the insistence on A/Not-A dichotomy (associated with resisting change) and of abandoning dichotomy (associated with striving for change)' (Jay 1981: 52).[4] Thus the emancipatory aims of feminism are integral to Jay's well-substantiated point, that '[a]ttention to relations between conservatism and dichotomous thinking seems particularly important for feminist theory because of the great susceptibility of gender distinction to A/Not-A phrasing' (ibid.: 54). As she observes astutely, the 'exclusively binary structure of gender distinctions may explain this susceptibility, but not why women, rather than men, are so consistently put in the Not-A position' (ibid).[5]

A third related interest of feminists with dichotomy follows from the pioneering work of Lloyd (1993), Cocks (1989) and other feminist writers, in tracking the hierarchical element in modern dichotomous thinking, diagnosed as central to the repressiveness of modern rationalism. Feminists such as Grosz (1994) and Gatens (1996a, 1996b) are developing the implications and consequences of non-dichotomous, relational thinking in current theoretical debates.

This chapter analyses key features of dichotomy. It then considers problems involved in dichotomous thinking, before setting out the basis of an alternative to the paradigm of dichotomy.[6]

## The features of dichotomy

A dichotomy is a hierarchical opposition.[7] When it is analyzed, dichotomy can be seen to contain four important defining features, though these do not exhaust the analysis. The four features are an opposition between two identities, a hierarchical ordering of the pair, the idea that between them this pair sum up and define a whole, and the notion of transcendence.

### *Opposition*

Dichotomy takes the virtue of distinction, that is the capacity to distinguish between things, and extends it into opposition. Distinguishability is clearly essential to being able to make evaluations, and so it is easy to see why the notion of a distinction is synonymous with a virtuous attribute. It is therefore no part of the argument developed here to advocate the indistinguishability, or the conflation or merger of distinct categories. However, the presupposition that is habitual in dichotomous thinking leads in turn to the habitual and presumptive extension of distinction into opposition, to an 'alienated form of differentiation' (Plumwood 1993: 443). As Butler notes of dichotomous thinking, 'oppositions are, after all, part of intelligibility; the latter is the excluded and illegible domain that haunts the former domain as the spectre of its own impossibility, the very limit to intelligibility, its constitutive outside' (Butler 1993: xi).

This results in what Plumwood, discussing the conceptions 'human' and 'nature', calls the 'discontinuity problem' (the general form of which she explains in the terms coined by Rodman), that is, '"the Differential Imperative" in which what is virtuous in the human is taken to be what maximizes distance from the merely natural' (Plumwood 1995: 157, 156). In terms of the specific human/nature dualism with which Plumwood is concerned, she argues convincingly that the 'upshot is a deeply entrenched view of the genuine or ideal human self as not including features shared with nature, and as defined *against* or in *opposition to* the non-human realm', such that the 'human sphere and that of nature cannot significantly overlap' (ibid.: 157). Furthermore, she adds 'this kind of human self can only have certain kinds of accidental or contingent connections to the realm of nature' (ibid.).

It follows that the first defining feature of dichotomy is related, but not identical, to the notion of antinomy or contradiction. The distinction between dichotomy and antinomy helps to highlight the meaning of dichotomy.[8] There are two important examples of contradiction which are relevant to the discussion of dichotomous thinking: the contradiction between two equally binding laws, and the contradiction between conclusions which seem equally logical, reasonable or necessary; that is, a paradox. Antinomy describes the only possible permitted result of the tension between the two things, namely contradiction. It describes the mode of judgment where a contrast and comparison between two things cannot be allowed to rest, with its connections explored and articulated, but the two must immediately be seen instead as conflicting, antagonistic, contrary, competing, as rivals.

Thus antinomy and dichotomy share the feature of not only holding two things in tension, but holding them in rigid, fixed tension. Rogers provides a valuable definition of dichotomy which emphasizes this element of rigidity. She says a 'dichotomy is a polarization with discontinuity which ignores overlap. Differences are seen to be more interesting than similarities and there is a tendency to see these differences as absolute' (Rogers 1988: 44). Grosz refines Rogers's point in an interesting way. In the course of her discussion of feminist epistemology, she describes three kinds of 'male' knowledges, which she calls sexist, patriarchal and phallocentric. She argues that dichotomy is present, for example, in phallocentric knowledge, which is founded upon 'excluded, negative counterparts, or "others"' (Grosz 1988b: 96). However, what is particularly useful about Grosz's work here is the idea that the relation within the dichotomy is different in each kind of knowledge; her classification breaks down the assumption that there is only one kind of possible relation between a polarized pair.

Antinomy and dichotomy also have in common the significance placed on duality. Whereas contemporary theorists such as Iris Marion Young (1990a, 1990b) highlight the positive value of 'difference', contradiction and dichotomous thinking are both based on difference, now as a negative feature in the sense of things being incompatible, incommensurable and untranslatable. But in contradiction and dichotomy, difference is narrowed down to only two possibilities, and they are seen in terms of opposition. Difference here is always dual and always antagonistic. The equality of difference, which underlies the notion for theorists like Young, is something that in the dichotomous-thinking mentality must be overcome. Thus while a contradiction poses an opposition between two things held in tension which are equally valued (since if they were not equally valid, one would simply be considered 'wrong' and there would be no tension), a dichotomy describes an opposition between two things held in tension, only one of which can be right.

A second important difference between antinomy and dichotomy is that while both terms could describe special cases of two things which are regarded as polar opposites, antitheses, extremes, which are adverse, irreconcilable, or inconsistent, in a dichotomy these two things are characteristically thought to sum up the whole range of possibilities. The scope of antinomy – equally binding laws, equally valid conclusions – is more localized, open-ended, and does not contain this sense of closure. Thus for instance the dichotomies man/woman, reality/appearance, mind/body each between them define the universe as it exists through the lens provided by that pair. The oppositional feature of dichotomy is thus what Grosz calls a dualism, the 'assumption that there are two distinct, mutually exclusive and mutually exhaustive substances, mind and body, each of which inhabits its own self-contained sphere. Taken together the two have incompatible characteristics' (Grosz 1994: 6).

Thus an important aspect of dichotomy is that it entails an exclusive disjunction. Gatens (1991) highlights this feature of dichotomy, whereby the definition of the subject/scope of the object/world is either A or not-A. Not-A is anomalous with respect to A, the very antithesis of A. As Haste graphically puts it with respect to the man/woman dichotomy, 'A is defined as being not-B; it is defined as the negation of B. Women and the feminine, therefore, exist as *that-by-which-men-define-themselves-as-not-being*' (Haste 1993: 6). The consequent negative effects of dichotomy for philosophical thinking in general and feminist theorizing in particular are summed up by Grosz when she recommends Gatens's attempt to develop 'a philosophy that could articulate what cannot be spoken in philosophical paradigms derived from Cartesian dualism' (Grosz 1988b: 57). However the quality of exclusive disjunction that characterizes the two-fold nature of the element of opposition in dichotomy is not limited to the A/Not-A logical form; it applies also to the A/B form. So long as only two possibilities can be envisaged, the oppositional element of dichotomy has negative effects, in being unable to countenance heterogeneity.

## *Hierarchy*

Grosz identifies the central significance of the hierarchical feature of dichotomy when she argues that the 'bifurcation of being . . . [in] mind and body, thought and extension, reason and passion, psychology and biology . . . is not simply a neutral division of an otherwise all-encompassing descriptive field' (Grosz 1994: 3). For '[d]ichotomous thinking necessarily hierarchizes and ranks the two polarized terms so that one becomes the privileged term and the other its suppressed, subordinated, negative counterpart' (ibid.). Lloyd reinforces the point when she notes that 'the male-female distinction . . . has operated not as a straightforward descriptive principle of classification, but as an expression of values' (Lloyd 1993: 103). It also follows from the hierarchical ranking of dichotomy that so long as A represents what is socially and intellectually valued, then the same negative self/other effect occurs whether the logical formulation is A/Not-A or A/B.

The distinction between difference and dichotomy is important in elucidating the second as well as the first feature of dichotomy. For instance Young (1990b) contrasts the case in which difference is horizontally disposed and means heterogeneity, and has positive social effects, from the case in which difference is vertically ranked, such as when categories of dominant/subordinate, norm/deviant, internal/external, self/other, community/foreign, strong/weak, and male/female are introduced. In the latter case, not only is one side of the pair weighted, but also that side of the pair is defined and elevated by shunning, excluding, not being the other, and so difference has negative social effects. In the same way Plumwood notes with respect to the human/nature dualism, '[n]ature is sharply divided off from the human, is alien and usually hostile and inferior' (Plumwood 1995: 157). Grosz also draws out the negative social effects of hierarchical patterns informing thinking when she comments that, '[d]ichotomies are inherently non-reversible, non-reciprocal hierarchies, and thus describe systems of domination' (Grosz 1989: xvi).

Furthermore, as Lloyd (1989) and others have noted, the 'separate but equal' or 'separate spheres' formula for men and women, which has sought to legitimize dichotomy during the modern period, has negative effects not only in implying hierarchy behind the benign facade, but also in denying women self-determination of location between the two terms of the pair, denying them choice, and denying altogether a free play of differences.

However, on the positive side, hierarchical ordering in dichotomy is designed to promote at least two positive purposes. First, its aim is to be instrumental in overcoming an obstruction or obstacle to the emergence of truth. Second, hierarchical ordering shares with the feature of opposition a rigidity and inflexibility, the positive objective of which is to sustain order. There are two aspects of this: the truth is seen to emerge triumphant, and the truth is defined precisely in terms of the exclusion of the term which is subordinated.

But it follows that hierarchical ordering necessarily involves a form of oppression, through the necessary suppression of one term, and because of this element it can be argued that the positive purposes of the oppression are either self-defeating or achieved at too great a cost. An example with respect to the first aspect, the triumphant emergence of truth, can be seen clearly in the dichotomy man/woman. Although the dominance of the predominant term 'man' contains within it a promise of independence, autonomy can never be achieved. Because the winning term never breaks away from the vanquished one, the tension between them remains perpetually, perennially. In other words, this aspect of dichotomy 'results from a certain kind of denied dependency on a subordinated other.' Furthermore this 'relationship of denied dependency determines a certain kind of logical structure, as one in which the denial and the relation of domination/subordination shapes the identity of both the relata' (Plumwood 1993: 443). As Baier observes in taking issue with Davidson's either/or approach (with respect to motives, using the same logic), '[w]e rarely have to leave a felt motive entirely unexpressed when we act, even when it has been "defeated" by better reasons. There can be a lot of life left in defeated motives' (Baier 1985a: 130). In the history of modern patriarchal culture those promoting the winning term have had constantly to reiterate its victory and reinforce the suppression of the other term.

In this way a dichotomy, despite its imposition of rigid order through hierarchy, is unstable. Although, as Hartsock notes (1990: 162), '[r]adical dichotomy . . . functions to maintain order', the conceptual tie between the pair leads directly to the need perpetually to reiterate and reclaim victory. As the history of racism and colonialism evidences, this unwanted and unstable tie, together with the failure of the dominant term to achieve independence, also contains within it the threat that perhaps those thought to represent the subordinated term will gain ascendancy. This in turn leads to the fear by those promoting the winning term of those thought to represent the suppressed one.[9] The potency of the nineteenth and twentieth-century miscegenist fear of racial mixing and 'mixed marriages' resulting in 'half-castes' also illustrates this point.

The instability of dichotomy is also illustrated in the proliferation of heresies during the medieval Christian period, threatening the dichotomy which purported to explain the problematic relation between the perfection of God and the material human world. A third example of the instability of dichotomy is found in Dolar's reading of Foucault's interpretation of Kant. For Kant, according to this reading, the 'contradiction', the 'division [which] is basic and irreducible' between power and reason is unstable – 'constantly reproduced' – and leads to a 'split subject.' It cannot be resolved and only has 'consistence in division.' But while its maintenance ensures the continuing dominance of power, it also enables the expression of freedom. It is also interesting to note that, according to Dolar, the only alternative to unstable dichotomy that Kant could envisage was the frightening prospect that both sides 'dissolved' or 'evaporated' (Dolar 1995: 268–70).

The second aspect of the oppressive structure of hierarchy is the definition of truth in terms of the exclusion of the subordinate term. Indeed Grosz underlines that the secondary status of subordinate terms in binary pairs, 'is the *condition* for dominant terms, namely, reason, mind, culture, public' (Grosz 1988a: 56; emphasis added). The dependence of the dominant term upon its exclusion of the subordinate term has been famously expressed by De Beauvoir (1952). A powerful example of this second aspect comes from the observation that Freud's proposal of the normal could only occur because of what he posited as deviant/abnormal. His work was largely based on clinical practice involving Viennese women, who for him defined not the normal but the deviant and abnormal. Thus while the paradigm of psychological development in Freud's theory is derived from a model of male development (Lloyd 1993: 69), his theory relied heavily not only on evidence derived from case-studies of Viennese women, but also on the interdependence of the definitions of the terms normal and deviant. [10] Moreover, the recognition of the importance of women in Freud's theory does not rebut the view that the dichotomous nature of his theory, especially in the lower status of subordinate terms, is important for feminists to challenge and counter.

Hierarchy is also central to dichotomy in another sense. For instance there is a deeply embedded belief in the Western cultural tradition (in the dominant liberal tradition, but also subscribed to by the broadly Marxist tradition) that there are some activities (reproducing ourselves and ensuring survival through food, shelter, etc.) which are more primitive, foundational and fundamental than are intellectual, artistic, political, cultural, and linguistic practices. This view implies a hierarchy (to which Arendt also subscribes) from certain 'primitive' things (body, survival, the physical), ascending to things of the mind and to politics. This view sustains the extremely powerful and pervasive culture/nature dichotomy; a particular form of it (reason/emotion) is the subject of the following chapter. However there is a good case for arguing against a *hierarchy* between mind and body here, on the grounds that *all* these practices are discursively and socially constructed, and are practices whose meanings are interdependent. The hierarchical view, it is argued, is based on a biological myth about the natural being *necessary* to survival but theoretically uninteresting, while things of the mind are superior.

It also follows from the exclusive disjunction of dichotomy that it sets up inequalities of power through the hierarchical structure. It is clear for instance that the two polarities with which this book is centrally concerned – reason/emotion and man/woman – are not only of theoretical interest. Both imply hierarchical power relations in actual social and intellectual practices. Longino highlights the importance of recognising the power dimension of dichotomies. While some mainstream analytic philosophers have examined aspects of the mind/body dichotomy, she argues that their 'critiques have been limited, however, by their failure to comprehend the relation of these distinctions to gender distinctions and through those to power relations' (Longino 1995: 41).

## *Parts of a whole*

Dichotomy is a means of classification that involves a cutting in two. However, because it also involves the denial of an open-ended kind of difference or plurality, it may also imply the division of an entity, a whole, into two parts or sections. In other words, as Grosz observes, when a 'system of boundaries or divisions operates by means of the construction of binaries or pairs of opposed terms, these terms are not only mutually exclusive, but also mutually exhaustive.' Furthermore these term operate in such a way that they 'divide the spectrum into one term and its opposite, with no possibility of a term which is neither one nor the other, or which is both' (Grosz 1989: xvi). There are two important kinds of cutting in two to be examined here.

The first is the dualism, that is a twofold division in the sense of a system of thought which recognizes two independent principles. An example is the doctrine that mind and matter exist as independent entities, as opposed to both the doctrines of idealism and materialism, which hold that mind and matter belong to a single principle. A second example is the doctrine that there are two independent ethical principles, one good and the other evil. Good and evil are in this case understood together to sum up universal ethical possibilities, although in this case, as with the gender dichotomy Jay is concerned with, the A side can be defined whereas the 'other' side, whether it be Not-A or B, is characterized by the 'infinitation of the negative [which is, in turn, associated with] . . . the "contagion" of pollution' (Jay 1981: 44–5).

Another example, outside the conventional philosophical tradition, from grammar, may be useful in rethinking dualism and dichotomy. According to this example dualism, the fact of expressing two in number, is a form of plurality, a figure for the conception of plurality. Thus whereas in the Western philosophical tradition the dualism that underpins dichotomy is precisely opposed to the notion of plurality, there is a pedigree for dualism as plurality in an alternative Western discursive tradition.

Dichotomy can also mean cutting in two in the sense of the division of a class into two lower, mutually exclusive classes, as for example in the successively smaller branches of a tree or a root, or the circulation of the blood from arteries to veins to capillaries. This division into lower classes, and the consequent implication of a whole from which they both derive, is the second way in which dichotomy implies holism. However the emphasis on a more positive connection, in holism, that this third feature of dichotomy implies, is generally marginalized in analytical philosophy.

Thus while it is the case that the closed-ended dichotomies of modern philosophy rely upon contradiction, their very closed-ended character ensures the presence of the integrative function of holism, in two respects. First the relationship of contradiction between two things may logically only be recognized as a contradiction by seeing the two things and their relation in a wider context, where another or more comprehensive or inclusive element discloses a previously unperceived problem with the two things at issue. Even self-contradiction depends upon presence of a third term as context, since divergent things can co-exist without being in contradiction. Or second, a contradiction may occur not simply because of the presence of two things, but only when *a relation between* those two things is highlighted. The relation here is understood not as constitutive of either of the two things, but as an independent element whose force derives from another source. Both examples depend ultimately upon a coherentist theory of justification, the idea that 'all beliefs in the system are logically interdependent, for their justification depends upon their coherence with the rest of the system' (Fricker 1994: 196).

The paradoxes which follow from the view of autonomy as radical independence, which is a defining feature of the dominant liberal intellectual tradition, arise from the denial of the importance of context and relation. Bernstein is concerned with one of these paradoxes, which neatly sums up the point. As modern agents, he says, the ultimate barrier to our self-recognition is 'formed by our understanding of ourselves as autonomous moral beings.' The problem is that if 'we are autonomous, then nothing on heaven or earth can tell us what is right other than our conscience; but then *my* conscience cannot be an absolute touchstone of rightness if yours is too.' In other words, if 'I uphold the dictates of my conscience, then I cannot recognize myself in your conscientious claims. Conversely, if I surrender my conscience to the dictates of yours then I surrender my pure self-recognition; I become your moral beast or slave' (Bernstein 1994: 55).

### *Transcendence*

The fourth feature of dichotomy is the notion of transcendence. Transcendence is the sole mechanism by which, in the Western intellectual tradition, access from the inferior term to the superior term can be made. Thus there is a sense of movement upwards, of ascendance, between the pair. But in the Western intellectual tradition, in the many uses of dichotomies for distinguishing between groups of people, this transcendence can typically only be achieved by one category of people, defined by their *not* being the other kind.

This feature of dichotomy is closely connected to the role of transcendence in the Western philosophical tradition in general. Nussbaum argues cogently that '[p]hilosophy has often seen itself as a way of transcending the merely human, of giving the human being a new and more godlike set of activities and attachments. The alternative I explore sees it as a way of being human and speaking humanly. That suggestion will appeal only to those who actually want to be human' (Nussbaum 1990: 53).

It is ironical that with respect to the man/woman dichotomy the criterion for inclusion in the privileged category is physical difference. For while the general mind/body dualism gives priority to the explanatory force of the mind, it is important to recognize that the association of man with mind and woman with body rests on a biological rather than a mind-based assumption. Men, by virtue of 'natural' sexual difference, have typically been regarded as having exclusively the capacity for reason, culture, and the life of the mind. As Grosz notes on this point, '[t]he role of the specific male body as the body productive of a certain kind of knowledge (objective, verifiable, causal, quantifiable) has never been theorized' (Grosz 1994: 4). Skin colour, disability, age, and same-sex sexual preference, which are also based on biological anatomy and physiology, have all also been used to differentiate dichotomously, between those with a fully human capacity and those without it.

Plumwood examines how transcendence implies both an 'overcoming of self' – that is detachment – and the achievement of an abstract and universal impartiality. She comments that the discarding of 'our own particular concerns, personal emotions, and attachments' is associated with 'the familiar emphasis on the personal and the particular as corrupting and self-interested'

(Plumwood 1995: 163). In this crucial sense the aim of transcendence is the wholesale denial of particularity. In Jay's terms, '[e]xcept that it is not A, Not-A, is wholly undefined and undefinable' (Jay 1981: 45).

## Problems with dichotomy

### *Instability, internal irreconcilablity*

One problem with dichotomy has already been outlined. In the discussion of the hierarchical feature of dichotomy, an instability was noted, arising from the ongoing tie of the dominant term to the subordinate one, which threatens the order which dichotomy is designed to establish. Grosz describes another serious problem with dichotomy, in that 'Descartes instituted a dualism which three centuries of philosophical thought have attempted to overcome or reconcile.' The 'major problem facing dualism . . . has been to explain the interactions of these two apparently incompossible substances, given that, within experience and everyday life, there seems to be a manifest connection between the two' (Grosz 1994: 6).[11]

Apart from this problem, which is internal to the history of modern philosophy, and the problem of instability in the hierarchical tie, four other conceptual problems with dichotomy can be identified.

### *The detrimental effect of dichotomy as a dominant metaphor*

The first problem relates to a broader point about the role of metaphor in thinking and language.[12] In a very general sense theory and practice are integrated, in a culture, by the presuppositions involved in a dominant metaphor, through which ideas, actions and practices (and the connections between ideas and actions and practices) are seen as meaningful and understood and coherent. Dichotomy, and in particular the mind/body form of dichotomy, has been a potent metaphor in the modern period, instrumental in setting out the conditions and structure of thinking, and of 'possible' thoughts. It has acted as a paradigm though not determinant for our whole mode of thinking. Dichotomy is one of the many possible metaphors that can be used to *explain* the world as well as the relations of things within it, account for our categories and understand our thoughts. Thus dichotomy contains inherent explanatory force which, if naturalized and used unselfconsciously, can operate to predetermine the meaning of the *nature* of A and Not-A, *and* the relation between them.

Thus the first problem with dichotomy concerns the manner in which this metaphor of the mind/body split has become in our culture the *dominant* metaphor of thought and action and practice. Indeed the heart of the problem lies in the uncritical and unreflective, and so *indiscriminate* usage and blanket coverage of dichotomous thinking that has followed from the resolute devaluation of the significance of metaphor in thinking since the inauguration of Enlightenment rationality. As Plumwood indicates, dichotomies proliferate: the process by which the human/nature dualism operates, 'closely parallels the formation of other dualisms, such as masculine–feminine, reason–emotion, and spirit–body' (Plumwood 1995: 156). Similarly Jay comments on the 'peculiar affinity' of A/Not-A distinctions with gender distinctions (Jay 1981: 47). Likewise, Little notes the 'association' of men with reason and women with emotion (Little 1995: 119). Grosz also builds on the idea that the 'mind/body opposition has always been correlated with a number of other oppositional pairs. Lateral associations link the mind/body opposition to a whole series of other oppositional (or binarized) terms, enabling them to function interchangeably, at least in certain contexts.' Further, Grosz observes that 'the correlation and association of the mind/body opposition with the opposition between male and female, where man and mind, woman and body, become representationally aligned . . . is not contingent or accidental' (Grosz 1994: 4. See also Grosz 1993: 195).

But the manner with which dichotomous thinking has had a licence to operate can be put more strongly than the 'parallel logic' Plumwood refers to, Jay's 'peculiar affinity', Grosz's 'lateral associations', 'representational alignment', or 'correlation', or Little's 'association.' With such licence the logic of dichotomous thinking means that it systematically *maps on to* the rest of the world and our thoughts about it. By this metaphorical process – because we understand things in terms of others we feel we know – dichotomous thinking defines a whole set of specific dichotomies (for instance mind/body, man/woman, reason/emotion, self/other, inclusion/exclusion, public/private) which have had very divisive concrete effects, in the form of anti-Semitism, racism, sexism, homophobia, disablism, fear of the foreign, a hostile mentality towards immigrants, and insoluble multicultural problems, to name a few. Rob Walker, in *Inside/Outside* (1993), makes the same important point with reference to nation-state sovereignty. Helen Haste cogently sums up this line of argument when she proposes that '[w]e have a deep predilection for making sense of the world in terms of either/or, in terms of polarities. But most significantly, we map the polarity of masculine versus feminine on to other polarities' (Haste 1993: 3).

This mapping process of dichotomous thinking has characterized the 'modern' period. Mind/body has mapped on to reason/emotion, objective/subjective, universal/particular, culture/nature, man/women, human/nature, and more recently sex/gender. The process of mapping occurs through the action of the complex metaphorical process of likeness and so analogy between mind, reason, objective, etc., as well as likeness between dichotomous structures. As Grosz explains, 'metaphor, in breaching the barrier . . . makes what was once a signifier into a signified. Metaphor requires two hierarchically distinguished orders or levels, generating a signified by replacing it with another which represents it' (Grosz 1990b: 103) to form a chain of dichotomies.

This metaphorical method is served by what Plumwood calls 'linking postulates', that is, 'assumptions normally made or implicit in the cultural background which create equivalences or mapping between the pairs.' For instance, 'the postulate that all and only humans possess culture maps the culture/nature pair on to the human/nature pair' (Plumwood 1993: 445). Plumwood notes two further characteristics of this mapping process. First the number of pairs of dichotomies is endless since 'any distinction can in principle be treated as having the structure which characterizes a dualism.' And second, through the mapping process, dichotomies of ancient origin do not 'fade away because their original context has changed, but are often preserved in our conceptual framework as residues, layers of sediment' (ibid.: 443). In exploring the conception 'rational woman', this book seeks to go against the grain of the implicit pattern of mapping which evaluates this term as a disjunction and so potently disbars the conjunction it contains from serious consideration.

## *Adversarial style of argument*

The second problem with dichotomy concerns the rhetoric of the style of reasoning it recommends. Dichotomous thinking is reflected in an advocacy of an adversarial style, which rests on the belief that through confrontation the truth emerges, in philosophy, in practical politics in the House of Commons, and in legal argument. It holds that only under hostile pressure can the basis of an argument be brought to light and evaluated, and that the objective of reasoning is for a clear winner to emerge. It also maintains that the soundness and effectiveness of an argument is best established through the process of an intellectual duel, by seeing how hard one needs to push before the argument buckles.

Adversarial argument operates on a zero-sum assumption based on a very 'modern', or pre-postmodern, conception of truth; not only that through this method will 'the truth' be established, but also that only one party can be right, and if one party is right then the other must be wrong. If one argument is right, then that is taken to prove that the other must be wrong. An argument could be made that the adversarial style has at least some plausibility in the example of the rule-bound framework of the law, where conflicting claims and conflicting interpretations of applications of the law to particular cases are the basis of legal practice. Mansbridge (1996) and Connolly (1993) consider its use in relation to political theory.

Mansbridge uses the adversarial conception to typify representative democratic politics legitimated by 'fair aggregative' procedures, and to discuss the merits and shortcomings of this 'adversary tradition' in comparison with deliberative democratic political procedures (Mansbridge 1996: 51–2).

Connolly (1993) argues that the use of counterexample, which characterizes the adversarial method, is very destructive specifically in debate about political concepts, because it seeks to suppress their essential contestability. Concepts used in political practice and whose definitions are subject to political debate, will always be and remain necessarily contested. No absolutely coherent account of a concept will ever be found, for there are no absolutely superior grounds, no ultimate 'truth', no 'right' explanation to be found. This need not lead to relativism, for reasons still need to be advanced to demonstrate that one formulation of a concept is more adequate or stronger than another. As Connolly concludes, *that* is politics; we are not neutral observers, but are involved in the process of debating the concept (Connolly 1993: 22–41).

Moulton goes further and makes some convincing points in her critique of the adversary method in the dominant, deductive, form of philosophical reasoning. According to this style of reasoning, she observes, '[g]eneral claims are made and the job of philosophic research is to find counterexamples to the claims'. The 'philosophic enterprise is seen as an unimpassioned debate between *adversaries* who try to defend their own views against counterexamples and produce counterexamples to opposing views' (Moulton 1989: 9). The adversary method operates in philosophy on the assumption that 'the only, or at any rate, the best, way of evaluating work in philosophy is to subject it to the strongest or most extreme opposition'. It 'is assumed that the best way of presenting work in philosophy is to address it to an imagined opponent and muster all the evidence one can to support it' (ibid.). Justifications for this method, she goes on, are first that 'a position ought to be defended from, and subjected to, the criticism of the strongest opposition', second 'that this method is the only way to get the best of both sides', third 'that a thesis that survives this method of evaluation is more likely to be correct than one that does not', and fourth 'that a thesis subjected to the Adversary Method will have passed an "objective" test, the most extreme test possible' (ibid.).

One of Moulton's aims is to analyse critically the claim of adversary reasoning that 'its evaluation procedures are exact and value-free' (Moulton 1989: 18). She finds that, in the light of the number of shared assumptions which are required for the shared grounds of debate, a condition of the effective working of the adversarial method, the method is often self-defeating or ineffective in establishing anything in any positive sense (ibid.: 10–11). Moulton sees that adversarial counterexample has a certain value, in that a 'good counterexample is one that illustrates a general problem about some principle or general claim' (ibid.: 17). But she shows that the value of counterexample reasoning is limited, for it 'can be used to rule out certain alternatives, or at least to show that the current arguments supporting them are inadequate, but not to construct alternatives or to figure out what principles do apply in certain situations' (ibid.). Moreover, 'counterexamples can show that particular arguments do not support the conclusion, but they do not provide any positive reason for accepting a conclusion, nor can they show how a conclusion is related to other ideas' (ibid.). Moulton also points out that it 'has mistakenly been assumed that whatever reasoning an adversary would accept would be adequate reasoning for all other circumstances as well' (ibid.: 15).

Moulton's discussion of the crucial importance of analogy in the adversarial method (ibid.: 15), also raises the question of the interdependence of deduction with other, unacknowledged, forms of argument. Thus another of her pertinent aims is to show that the idea that any other form of evaluation is weaker is mistaken (ibid.: 10). Her major objection to the adversary method, then, concerns its false exclusion of other methods of reasoning, and so 'its role as a paradigm. If it were merely *one* procedure among many for philosophers to employ, there might be nothing worth objecting to' (ibid.: 9–10). Moulton also indicates that in contrast with the situation in science, in philosophy the paradigmatic status of adversarial reasoning could easily be given up, for it 'is not that we have to wait for an alternative form of reasoning to be developed. Nonadversarial reasoning exists both outside and within philosophy but our present paradigm does not recognize it' (ibid.: 10).

Moulton's conclusion provides strong support for the view commending the virtues of a both–and position over an either/or position, and she recognizes that 'one of the best ways to reduce [the adversary method's] paradigm status is to point out that it *is* a paradigm, that there are other ways of evaluating, reasoning about and discussing philosophy' (ibid.: 18).

Plumwood presents a useful account of the problematic dominant conception of logic, proceeding according to a method which 'naturalizes an account of the other in terms of dualism and domination' (Plumwood 1993: 442). The problems which her account identifies closely resemble those which Moulton elucidates in the adversary method. Plumwood's argument is also helpful here in making explicit the connection in the Western intellectual inheritance between this dominant form of logic and the definition of rationality.

Baier also criticizes the adversarial method in philosophy, on the grounds that it gives an exaggerated importance to the role of justification in argument. She argues that often it is sufficient to support an argument by giving reasons, a process which falls short of full justification. When philosophers in ethics and epistemology 'force all considering of reasons into this adversarial and officious mold . . . the [legitimate] difference between having grounds for one's belief and having justification gets blurred.' However she shows that, '[m]oral beliefs often have good grounds, but . . . they rarely can be given successful justification.' For such philosophers, to show that an action is justified, she contends, 'it is not enough to show that there were good reasons for it, one must also show that it broke no authoritative rule, or that, if it did, there was nothing better one might have done'. But, Baier convincingly concludes, '[t]his legal or quasi-legal structure of accusation, defense, and judgment does not normally apply to ordinary action for reasons' (Baier 1985a: 122).

Another problem with the adversarial style of reasoning is that it does not recognize the effect of its own intervention. The adversarial style is held by its proponents to be neutral. However as Nussbaum recognizes so well, 'if one is pursuing understanding . . . is, in that sense, a philosopher . . . Style itself makes its claims, expresses its own sense of what matters. Literary form is not separable from philosophical content, but is, itself, a part of content'. Nussbaum's insight refers to verbal debate and defence as well as to written texts. In other words, literary form is 'an integral part, then, of the search for and the statement of truth' (Nussbaum 1990: 3).

The relation between form and content, along with the full understanding of the role of metaphor in theorizing (not as ornament, but as a means of structuring and expressing discourse), and the understanding of ambiguity as a discursive virtue, was another of the casualties of the development of the 'powerful currents of scientific and philosophical reason', as Condren points out. The construction of the dichotomy between form and content was an 'abstraction from the mutually informing aspects of discourse' (Condren 1985: 172). The danger and problem with the work of some contemporary French feminist theorists is that the accentuated role accorded to language and texts and symbols, signs and chains of significance, again undervalues the relation between form and content, and so perpetuates the mind/body split.

The adversarial style of argument does not warrant the dominant status that has been accorded to it. As Tully outlines, our historical legacy provides us with a range of different forms of undertaking critical reflection. Among others, the 'reflexive concepts of deconstruction, evaluation, explanation, genealogy, interpretation, interrogation, justification, representation, survey, validation, verification', all 'have distinctive grammars and complex historical genealogies as established practices or language-games of critical reflection.' Moreover Tully shows convincingly that 'no type of critical reflection can play the mythical role of founding patriarch of our political life presumed of it in the debate' (Tully 1989: 198, 199).

### *Hard-shelled holism*

The third problem with dichotomy arises from it being closed-ended rather than open-ended. The hard-shelled holism implicit in dichotomous thinking means that the two opposed positions of a dichotomy between them sum up the extent of the range of possibilities. Dichotomous thinking thus closes off other potential resources, thereby denying a prospect of heterogeneity, by forcing any possibility into an established polar opposition, in which any particular choice involves the rejection, refutation, repudiation, exclusion, disapproval or rebuff of another, now an 'other'.

Baier provides a clear example of this process and its damaging effects when she concludes her discussion of reasons for action and feeling by indicating that, '[p]hilosophers of action, in the analytic tradition, have introduced a grossly oversimplifying *either/or* structure into their account of our intention-formation, by ignoring all the ways we can and do fit our actions to our mixed and conflicting motives and reasons' (Baier 1985a: 130). One of the consequences of this either/or mentality is, as Joan Scott highlights, that '[o]pposites conceal the extent to which things represented as oppositional are interdependent' (Scott 1988: 35).

## *Denigration of women*

The fourth problem with dichotomy is that it leads specifically to the denigration of women. Plumwood notes that the 'exclusion of the natural from the concept of the properly human is not the only dualism involved' (Plumwood 1995: 157). She identifies the way in which what is involved in the construction of this 'dualistic conception of the human is the rejection of those parts of the human character identified as feminine – also identified as less than fully human – giving the masculine conception of what it is to be human' (ibid.). Indeed '[m]asculinity can be linked to this exclusionary and polarised conception of the human, via the desire to exclude and distance from the feminine and the non-human' (ibid.). Plumwood concludes convincingly that the 'features that are taken as characteristic of humankind and as where its special virtues lie, are those such as rationality, freedom, and transcendence of nature (all traditionally viewed as masculine), which are viewed as not shared with nature'. As a result, '[h]umanity is defined oppositionally to both nature and the feminine' (ibid.).

It follows that the devaluation of women has been caught up in this dichotomous mode of thinking, through the notion of transcendence discussed earlier. One consequence is that feminism cannot effectively challenge male dominance, and the 'disavowal' (Grosz 1994: 4) of the subordinated term, only by liberal feminist means (legislation, institutional change, implementation) and radical feminist means (political campaigns, separatism). To be effective, feminism also has to challenge the validity of the dominance of dichotomous thinking in our culture and propose a viable alternative. For the dominance of dichotomous thinking which underlies social practices and cultural values renders the devaluation of women not simply contingent but inherent. Grosz underlines this point when she notes that in patriarchal theories, the 'feminine may function as metaphor or image, necessary for the theory's foundations, but is incapable of being accepted by it' (Grosz 1988b: 94). The problem with the polarities is not just that their hierarchies subordinate women and maintain the dominance of men. They also 'separate but do not fully divorce' pairs of things which are interconnected, so that the positive senses of connectedness of the terms cannot be recognized and therefore neither of them can be adequately understood or operative. This is the key point developed in Chapters Two and Three on reason and emotion, and sex and gender.

## An alternative to dichotomy

A range of feminists are already making important contributions to the theorization of non-dichotomous ways of thinking, arguing for what Jane Flax (1992: 196) refers to as 'thinking in relations', Sonia Kruks (1995: 16) dubs 'relations of reciprocity', and what Carol Gould (1993: 411) calls 'individuals-in-relations', together with the idea of an open-ended distinction, or recognition of (more than twofold) difference, rather than closed-ended dichotomy. Fraser (1995) provides an example of the gains of practising relational rather than dichotomous thinking. Joan Scott (1988: 33) also calls for a way of theorizing 'that will let us think in terms of pluralities and diversities rather than of unities and universals . . . without either simply reversing the old hierarchies or confirming them', and Val Plumwood (1993: 458, 459) proposes a 'critical reconstruction of dualised identity' which is different from the simple reversal of dualisms; a 'logic of mutuality'.[13] Elizabeth Grosz (1994: 24, 21) puts forward a strategy to go beyond 'oppositional categories' and the 'impasse posed by dichotomous accounts'. And Glennon ( 1979: 27) ridicules the view that the members of dichotomous pairs represent 'incompatible ways of acting', a view sustained by the belief that 'it must be "either–or", or disaster will follow'.

Minow and Shanley (1996) propose a theory of relational rights and responsibilities, to rectify the shortcomings of the contract-based, community-based and rights-based models of the individual's relation with the state, a particular aspect of which is taken up by Gail Weiss's (1995) relational approach to abortion. Caroline Whitbeck (1989: 63) advocates 'the self–others relation [which] generates a multifactorial interactive model of . . . reality'. Hekman (1990: 16, 17), pointing to the value of Gadamer's work, argues that '[f]eminists have shown that Enlightenment thought has identified the values Gadamer is rejecting – rationality and abstraction – as masculine and those that he espouses – contextuality and relatedness – as feminine', and she contends that the 'fact that contextuality and relatedness have been associated with the feminine through the misconceived dichotomies of Enlightenment thought is part of the problem that would be overcome should these dichotomies be displaced'.

The present work can do no more than sketch out seven of the important relational features of a both–and mode of thinking as an alternative to the dichotomous mode. These are: that the character of the relation is not a given; dynamic movement; open-ended relation; relation as inclusive; the role of a self-conscious commitment to change; ambiguity; and the 'broken middle'.

It is important to stress three points at the outset of this discussion. First, the relational logic of both–and proposed here is put forward neither as a general but uncritical panacea equivalent to a weak variant of liberalism, nor as an apology for vacillation. Second, the relational logic of both–and represents no more than one alternative explanatory metaphor. (Others include harmony, evolution, organism, mechanism, cyclical rhythm, process.) Like dichotomy, and like all such metaphors, the relational metaphor contains inherent explanatory force in thinking, action and practice. The aim is not to prescribe a substitute for all dichotomous thinking, nor a monopoly over all possible explanatory metaphors, but simply to attempt to counter the dominance which the dichotomous mode has exercised over the last two hundred years by pointing to the utility of one of the possible alternatives. It should also be noted, third, that the relational alternative to adversarial reasoning envisaged here does *not* involve a view of reasoning for theorizing analogous to the models of deliberative reasonableness sometimes suggested for political decision-making.

The conception of relational thinking proposed here is a positive and critical assertion that follows from the view that 'the middle and the extremes exist concurrently' (Tavor Bannet 1992: 10). The relational conception of thinking advanced here also draws in other important ways upon a contextualist view of how meaning is generated. It holds that the meaning of concepts, and the stability of the components of a concept, always arise within particular social and cultural contexts. It also seeks to develop some of the consequences of the general view of the meaning of concepts as arising from their relational dimension, as described by Patton. According to this view, concepts are 'understood as a certain kind of "rendering consistent" of their components', such that the 'components and their consistency in a particular concept are two distinct dimensions of the concept, but they are related in that the consistency is established only by means of the existence of a certain "communication" between the components' (Patton 1997: 244).

Part of what is meant by the relational alternative to dichotomy in thinking is well envisaged by Fox Keller when she says, describing the work of the geneticist Barbara McClintock, '[i]n this world of difference, division is relinquished without generating chaos. Self and other, mind and nature survive not in mutual alienation, or in symbolic fusion, but in structural integrity' (Fox Keller 1985: 165). Morgan and Radden, in work that has a direct bearing on a relational alternative to dichotomous thinking, both convincingly argue for the merits of a relational conception of different aspects of the self–fetal personality, and therapy respectively. Radden puts forward a strong argument for understanding the autonomy of the self as occurring at 'the mean of relational individualism', and illustrates that 'an oppositional portrayal' of relationality and autonomy 'as contraries' is misleading (Radden 1996: 86–7). Morgan emphasizes the importance of three aspects of relationality: its diversity, its non-denial of individuality, and its dynamic character. She clarifies the way in which there are 'different kinds of relationality', and argues persuasively that 'relationality and individualism coexist as interdependent aspects' of social practices, and that '[r]elationality (like individualism) is a socially dynamic process; its parameters are set within historical and political contexts. The focus must turn, then, to social practices and contexts' (Morgan. 1996: 64).

### *The character of the relation is not a given*

One of the very important points which Morgan is highlighting here is that the relational alternative to dichotomous thinking challenges the uncritically-held assumption that the specific hierarchical and oppositional relation posed, for example between nature and culture, is the only way of considering nature and culture. Even more important is Morgan's point that the relational alternative asserts that no relation between nature and culture (for instance) can be taken as a given. There is no warrant for naturalising a connection between nature and culture.

The view that there is some sort of essential basis or innate significance for thinking about nature and culture in the same breath also seduces some feminists. For example, Plumwood's important work (1995) on relational modes of thinking about nature and culture, risks falling into this trap of taking nature and culture as a given universal pair. Glennon (1979), while seeking to consider the range of different ways in which members of dichotomous pairs can be related, and to develop a relational view of the connection specifically between (male) right-side rational instrumentalism and (female) left-side expressivism, falls into the trap of considering instrumentalism and expressivism as given alternatives, a pair fixed by biology. Thus one of the major aspects of dichotomous thinking that must be challenged is the way in which it not only implies that only one kind of relation (dichotomous) is possible, but also naturalizes the terms of the pair themselves. We can argue in contrast that while nature and culture are an important pair, the fixation on this pairing masks the importance of the relation each has with other categories.

Developing this feature, an important difference between the dichotomous and relational modes of thinking can be framed in terms of, respectively, the certainty and the initial uncertainty of the character of the relations posed in each mode. In the dichotomous mode, the character of an unknown is already given, for if it is not a self, it is an other. In the relational mode, in contrast, the character of an unknown is not given, and has to be established in each concrete case. That is, in the relational mode the character of the relation is not known in advance, and so cannot be assumed at the beginning. The relational mode therefore encompasses a much wider scope of possible kinds of relations, whereas in the dichotomous mode the character of the relation is always a given because it is *always* either identity (with self) or opposition (with other) (Whitbeck 1989: 62).

The contrast at stake here can be expressed in two meanings of the interestingly ambiguous term 'identity'. In dichotomous thinking, identity in the sense of sameness defines the designation of something as either self or other. It either absorbs something into itself or banishes it to the other. In relational thinking however, identity in the sense of constructed meaning (as in the sense of achievement captured in phrases like 'personal identity' and 'identity politics') must be established through the concrete terms involved and the specific relation envisaged between them. In this second sense an identity is constructed as particular and unique among a multiplicity of identities, and requires reciprocal recognition in order to be visible.

Allison Weir's thought-provoking critique of 'sacrificial logics', by which she means systems 'predicated on a logic of exclusion of nonidentity or difference' (Weir 1996: 184), resembles in important respects the critique of dichotomous thinking outlined here. Weir argues that this logic of domination and exclusion, 'the repression of otherness by the logic of the Same' (ibid.: 5) has characterized not only traditional discussion but also much feminist discussion of self-identity, collective identities and the identity of meaning in language. It is too often and mistakenly assumed, she says, 'that any concept of self-identity necessarily represses the fragmentation of multiplicity of the self, or the connectedness or relationality of the self to others', and as a result 'feminist theory has become caught in a series of impasses, produced by a failure to theorize nonoppositional, nondominating relationships between identity and difference' (ibid.: 3). Thus, 'rather than simply rejecting identity in the name of difference, or accepting it as something oppressive but inevitable, we need to develop alternative theories of universality and of individual identity which do not exclude but include difference and otherness' (ibid.: 7). Weir seeks to elucidate 'a shift from a sacrificial model to a model of self-identity as a capacity for participation in a social world' (ibid.: 8). She outlines an interesting concept of self-identity 'as the capacity to experience oneself as an active and relatively coherent participant in a social world', as 'capacity for meaningful interaction with self and others' that involves 'reflexivity and intersubjectivity as essential components of self-identity' (ibid: 185).

### *Dynamic movement*

The *dynamic* aspect of relational thinking, the many kinds of continuity between objects in thought, contrasts strongly with the one-way transcendence which is seen as the sole mechanism for positive movement within a dichotomous pair. This dynamic aspect of relational thinking is well captured by Honneth describing one of the possible outcomes of relational thinking, breaking down the dichotomy between subject and object. He reasons that 'the connection between the experience of recognition and one's relation to self stems from the inter-subjective structure of personal identity'

(Honneth 1995: 173). In consequence it becomes clear that, as Scott (1988: 44) puts it, 'the oppositional pairing misrepresents the relationship of both terms.'

The ethic of care can also be read as a complex example of relational thinking, in which the dynamic aspect features in at least two different ways. For the ethic of care not only emphasizes the significance of connectedness and interdependence, but is also a 'morality of seeing "both" and "and", of grasping two points of view simultaneously', and so 'is at home with the discomfort of ambiguity' (Dimen 1989: 47). An understanding attuned to relation and context is able to transform the meaning of single identities in a manner that dichotomy cannot do. As Bernstein makes explicit with respect to his reading of Hegel, 'the features of conscience that lead it to realize itself only within a community of conscientious selves equally means that conscience itself changes its meaning from its initial self-understanding' (Bernstein 1994: 56).

### *Open-ended relation*

A critical analysis which employs a relational perspective operates with an open-ended view of the relation between the terms at issue. The opposition between two terms is thus reined back from the fixity of extreme polarization, to the point of being a distinction whose basis has yet to be established. For instance in evaluating the claims of the Enlightenment versus Counter-Enlightenment, or of modern and postmodern philosophy, under a relational perspective, the object is not to see which of two terms *wins out*. Rather it is to suspend that kind of judgment and consider instead a range of judgments concerning such questions as, for instance, *how* they are related, or the character of the ambiguity for the self-term's autonomy or independence or superiority, inherent in the 'other' term being tied to the definition of the 'self' term, or what is going on *between* them. The judgment of which of two terms wins out, as in a competition, is thus not the only important kind of evaluation that can be made.

The example of the Enlightenment and Counter-Enlightenment is an interesting one, in that the Romantic reaction against Enlightenment rationality is often regarded as a wholesale challenge to Enlightenment values. However mainstream Enlightenment figures like Diderot clearly share the presence of dichotomous thinking with the rebel Rousseau as well as with the eighteenth-century German Romantics. In this sense such thinkers perpetuated the self/other mentality of the Enlightenment.[14] The example of modernity/postmodernity is also one of a constructed dualism at another level. In the debate on postmodernity the interesting relational questions have been dwarfed by the priority accorded to the dichotomous question. But a good case can be made not only that the question of 'deciding' which is more important is sterile, but also that to explore the tensions and continuities between them, and to see why that relation is interesting, is a fruitful enterprise (Mangena 1994).

In a thoughtful essay, Dolar makes a similar point in reviewing Foucault's reassessment of the Enlightenment. For Foucault in the late essay 'What is Enlightenment', Dolar says, the 'rehabilitation of the Enlightenment depends on the possibility of not taking the Enlightenment en bloc, wholesale'. That is, it depends upon 'not falling into the trap of choosing between alternatives: *either* the defence of the principles of reason, progress, freedom, etc., *or* their rejection as insufficient, the highlighting of their hidden repressive character, etc.'. Foucault's new non-dichotomous approach is contrasted with those who questioned and criticized the Enlightenment, who 'have themselves fallen into the trap of believing the Enlightenment's myth about its own nature as a coherent, unitary project, which can only be either accepted, or questioned in toto' (Dolar 1995: 263). Dolar also makes an interesting case that Foucault's new approach also contrasts with his own previous understanding of the Enlightenment, in which 'the universal principles of reason and freedom were underpinned by their very opposite – a tightly knit system of discipline and control' (ibid.).

It is clear that the claims made by Enlightenment thinkers for the ability of abstract universal principles to supersede and sweep away the hierarchies of the medieval period and the Christian church (dismissed as based on nothing more than prejudice and irrational custom) could not be sustained. In practice such principles became devalued as they were mapped on to the stubbornly intransigent pattern of dichotomies of inclusion and exclusion. For example 'modern' reason was held to be universal, abstract, without history, untainted by particularity, and all of this was felt to be liberating; yet some individuals and groups of persons were seen as outside or below this 'universal', for instance the working class, 'primitive' peoples, women, disabled persons, and children.

Another example of the fruitfulness of relational over dichotomous thinking is found in contemporary attempts to theorise democratic politics. The history of democratic theory is often portrayed as giving us two broadly opposed views: democracy as the representation by means of a normatively-neutral aggregation of individual autonomous self-interested personal preferences, and democracy as the collective combined moral deliberation and agreement as to what is in the interests of the whole group. The most fruitful contributions to current debates however, while recognising the major tension in democratic theory, seek in various ways to find an accommodation or balance between these two competing claims of democracy. Contemporary democratic theory is no longer preoccupied with advancing the claims of one view and rejecting those of the other in the way that characterized for instance Berlin's tremendously influential dichotomous statement, 'Two Concepts of Liberty'.

Furthermore, what is being envisaged in setting out the relational features of the both–and mode of thinking needs to be distinguished from the kind of holism sometimes thought to characterize the theory of, for instance, Hegel, and the coherence theory of truth to which the British Idealists subscribed. Holism may be regarded as providing knowledge with closure, a fixed and closed-ended and completed whole through which the parts are understood, which defines the relation of the parts to each other and to the whole, a sealed unit of meaning. But what is envisaged here is an open-ended or loosely-knit structure, whose aim is not to adduce a grand narrative of the whole, but to provide the basis on which relational work can be undertaken.

Holism is also criticized on the grounds that it may effect 'a resolution of contradiction into a third term' (Derrida 1972: 43–3, quoted in Grosz 1994: 211n), but this is certainly not advocated here. It is clear that the logic of thesis–antithesis–synthesis, particularly when the synthesis forms a new thesis, operates as a dichotomous chain. It is also holistic in the sense of being closed to anything outside the dichotomous pair, and absorbing the entire range of difference within a closed-ended synthesis. Instead the current proposal points to the important knowledges to be gained by exploring relations between opposites, tensions, and ambiguities, knowledges recognized as dynamic, irreducible and uncompleted. The relational perspective thus seeks to give authority to the process of opening up the range of interpretation and understanding in the vast middle ground between the integration of holism and the idea of transgression. This is taken up for instance in queer theory, and is examined in Chapter Four. In the field of interpretive possibilities, integration and transgression (a form of trespass only) represent the narrow poles which for the most part offer too much and not enough.

Relational thinking also lends itself to the recognition of the importance of the historical perspective and of metaphor in thinking and in theorizing. History is important to relational thinking because it stresses the importance of the *provenance* of ideas, that ideas, concepts and theory occur in situated contexts of meaning, not in an abstract and universal realm. Babich supports these ideas in her reading of Nietzsche's understanding and use of metaphor, and his criticism of the grasp of 'modern' scientific rationality over thinking and theorizing, specifically through the logical notion of 'identity'. Her starting point is that 'Nietzsche argues that logical (or modern scientific thinking), follows erroneous patterns of largely *a-perspectivalist* conviction'. Nietzsche, she goes on, 'locates the principle of identity at the basis of logical and causal thinking, further articulated as the ideal of simplicity. Thus the axiomatic essence of logic is founded on the fiction that "*there are identical cases*"'. However, Babich argues convincingly that, '[s]trictly taken (i.e., in reality) identical cases are never identical but only similar cases. Similar cases insofar as they resemble one another, that is, insofar as they are only similar things, are inevitably unequal and as such exactly non-identical' (Babich 1996: 29).

This is evidence for the view that in thinking and theorizing, the role of abstract universal concepts is limited by their situatedness, not only in politics and ethics but *also* in philosophy. It is also evidence for the view that (even) philosophical thinking works by use of metaphor, by seeing similarity, resemblance, connection, rather than simply by logical identity.

## *Relation as inclusive*

Dichotomous thinking is based upon the 'principles of order' which we accept as defining the fundamental logical rules of thinking. As Jay puts it, they are the 'Principle of Identity (if anything is A, it is A); the Principle of Contradiction (nothing can be both A and Not A); and the Principle of the Excluded Middle (anything, and everything, must be either A or Not-A)' (Jay 1981: 42). The quarrel of the present work is not with these principles of order themselves, but with the way in which they are interpreted in a narrow and exclusionary fashion, such that two damaging and unnecessary consequences are held to be also fundamental. These are that the values of relation and connection are systematically overlooked, and that the value of the principles of order is extended to form, to prioritize and to naturalize dichotomous thinking.

Jay invokes Dewey to add weight to the idea of the paucity of logical principles on their own to account for meaning in the practical and political world: as a 'fundamental principle of formal logic, the A/Not-A dichotomy is wonderfully simple and supremely all-encompassing'. However 'it is necessarily distorting when it is applied directly to the empirical world, for there are no negatives there. Everything that exists (including women) exists positively' (Jay 1981: 48). But in making a case for the authority of a relational mode of thinking, it needs to be made crystal clear that a dichotomy between dichotomous and relational thinking is not being suggested. For it does not follow from the argument developed here that a relational mode of thinking is the only one which is seen as valid, or that only one form of relation is legitimate.

Moreover it is important to recognize that the relational mode of thinking carries no suggestion of dissolving the terms of the pair. One of the unsatisfactory aspects of dichotomous thinking is that its major proposal for bridging the gulf between an oppositional pair is by reductionism, as Grosz perceptively says, to 'leave their interaction unexplained, explained away, impossible.' Furthermore reductionism 'denies any interaction between mind and body, for it focuses on the actions of either one of the binary terms at the expense of the other.' Historically, '[r]ationalism and idealism are the results of the attempt to explain the body and matter in terms of mind, ideas, or reason; empiricism and materialism are the results of attempts to explain the mind in terms of bodily experience or matter'. But '[b]oth forms of reductionism assert that either one or the other of the binary terms is 'really' its opposite and can be explained by or translated into the terms of its other'

(Grosz 1994: 7). It is clear that attempts to abandon terms in the pair in this form of reductionism are ultimately unsatisfactory. What can be done positively, however, is to re-envisage the relation, as one among many possible kinds of connection rather than as an opposition.

The relational mode advocated here does not seek to banish the element of relationship between the pair (in the manner for instance of consensus politics and the notion of reconciliation), but to reinvest the connection between the pair with multiple possibilities. The relational presupposition places the either/or position, which implies dominance/subordination and self/other relationships, in the wider context of a both-and position which recognizes interconnection and interdependence.[15] While the dominant term of a dichotomous pair perpetually asserts independence, the relational mode of thinking involves the invitation to acknowledge interdependence.

An example of the difference between dichotomous and relational thinking in this respect comes from Bar On's discussion of the inappropriateness of the idea of epistemic privilege for feminists (and in regard to other socially marginalized groups). She makes a good case that '[a]lthough the claim to epistemic privilege as a tool may seem to be a claim of the oppressed, due to some of its history, it nonetheless reveals itself also as a master's tool' (Bar On 1993: 97). Her reasoning is that 'the Enlightenment subject of various forms of feminism . . . tends to be not an Enlightenment rational being, but a neo-Romantic subject . . . an emotional subject whose rationality is not formulaic'. Such a subject 'is not separated from its objects in a dualistic relation that gives the subject the power to dominate the objects' (ibid.: 95).

## *The role of self-conscious commitment in change*

In the face of the 'naturalization' (see Plumwood 1993: 436) of opposition and exclusion that underpins the dominance of dichotomous thinking, the kind of reform envisaged here cannot be undertaken by an ad hoc process. It involves changing the pre-eminence of the underlying *commitment* to thinking in terms of dichotomy, to a *commitment* to include thinking in terms of reciprocity and relation.

A range of contemporary political theorists have struggled to accommodate and account for their commitment to difference in social and political practices. Part of what underlies their work is the view that difference is important in politics because it embeds a non-hierarchical and plural conception of different groups and individuals. It follows that difference can only work in a relational, non-dichotomous atmosphere, and in this sense the relational mode underpins Habermas's commitment to the respect due to different voices in a public space.

Foucault's critique of a privileged, dominant knowledge can also be seen as a criticism of dichotomy on the grounds that such dominance excludes all other knowledges as 'other'. Nancy Fraser's view too can be seen as underpinned by a commitment to a relational mode when she argues that the 'long-term goal of deconstructive feminism is a culture in which hierarchical gender dichotomies are replaced by networks of multiple intersecting differences that are demassified and shifting' (Fraser 1997a: 30). Her view that cultural recognition and social redistribution must go hand in hand before democratic politics can operate effectively (Fraser 1997b: 187) again can be read as a demand for dichotomy to be replaced by relation in a thoroughgoing manner.

## *Ambiguity*

As Condren (1985: 171) describes, thinking which is clear and unambiguous has been a cardinal virtue of mainstream theorizing. Ambiguity is associated with vagueness and obscurity, lack of coherence, confusion and dissembling (ibid.: 174). Condren accounts for the poor reputation of ambiguity as resting on the assumption that all theorizing should be governed by the logical rules of conventional philosophy – 'clarity, consistency, and certainty of argument, which renders any hint of equivocation a sin' – as well as on the subscription to a 'heavy reliance on form/content distinctions' (ibid.: 175).

But ambiguity can also be a positive quality. For a start, the greatest texts in the canons of philosophy and political theory are those which outline a suggestive and original thesis which is open to a rich interpretive field. Condren shows how not only is there no 'correct' reading of a text, but that 'great books are not written, they are read, and it is a notion of ambiguity which helps draw the line between the recognition of this fact and the advocacy of a millennialist anarchy of interpretation' (Condren 1985: 251–2). Furthermore once the impact of form on content, the inherent instability of language, and the rhetorical and metaphorical dimensions of all discourse are recognized, then it is no longer possible to rule out of court the positive potential of ambiguity. This point may be more obvious with respect to theory with a political or social character, but holds equally with respect to philosophy (Prokhovnik 1991).

Ambiguity may indeed in some cases be a fault and a failing, but in other pieces of theorizing the recognition that an argument is ambiguous can be an invitation to 'restructure the world' (Condren 1985: 184), a dynamic to further theorizing. Neither is ambiguity a fixed quality of a piece of theorizing. Whether or not an argument is ambiguous will depend upon the conceptual framework in which it is assessed. For instance Hobbes's figure of the sovereign in *Leviathan* was considered by many of his readers in the political context of 1650s England to be ambiguous, showing a lack of decisiveness in specifying neither or both King and Cromwell. However in terms of Hobbes's philosophical argument the figure of the sovereign is clear and unambiguous.

One of the strengths of the relational mode is that it can listen to ambiguity without the need to expunge it by definitional fiat. The adversarial method fits the 'modern' view of truth as clear, singular, unitary, and certain. But for a postmodern perspectival view of truth, a relational method is more fitting, for it allows for more discrimination and judgment to be exercised. Furthermore, philosophies that deal with good and bad as absolutes and universals, with no middle ground and no connections between the poles, are not necessarily more constructive for arriving at understanding than philosophies that attempt to take into account ambiguity, struggle, fallibility, the validity of different perspectives, connections, the contingency of any particular problem, and its concrete embeddedness in a particular context of understanding. The relational conception of theorizing thus has strengths which the dichotomous adversarial mode does not have, for the latter polarises, creates a closed-ended dichotomy of a hierarchically opposed pair which narrows and limits the range open to interpretation, and forces all other arguments into the 'other' position. The strength of the adversarial mode is its capacity to refine a distinction and sharpen a definition; its weaknesses are that this capacity is a limited one in intellectual endeavour, and that it eliminates all ambiguity.

## *The 'broken middle'*

Many of the features of the relational mode are illustrated in Gillian Rose's important articulation of a conception of the 'broken middle', the idea of going beyond dualistic thinking and beyond the deconstruction of dualisms, to a more positive outcome which attends to the excluded middle. The notion of the 'broken middle' sums up the spirit of the relational mode, and Rose's use of the term to articulate a critique of postmodern responses to Hegel is the final point to be made in this chapter. The metaphor of the broken middle represents the construction of a politics in the relational ground suppressed (broken) by dualistic thinking.

Rose argues that 'our proud and deadly dualisms' (Rose 1994: 21) have brought about a modern history characterized by misrecognition. 'All dualistic relations to "the other"', she contends, and 'to "the world" are attempts to quieten and deny the broken middle, the third term which arises out of misrecognition of desire, of work, of my and of your self-relation mediated by the self-relation of the other' (ibid.: 20).

The strength of Rose's individual and 'comic' reading of Hegel's conception is twofold. It builds precisely upon a critique of dualism and dichotomy, and it provides a critique of some postmodern responses to Hegel. Rose compares dualistic and relational approaches to Hegel in the following way: '[o]nce the question of the relation to the Hegelian dialectic has been posed anew for our time, two responses . . . need to be distinguished'. One response 'has discerned the relation to the Hegelian dialectic on the part of a post-modern consciousness that restricts its operation to the dialectical oppositions of the Understanding, and proceeds dualistically and deconstructively'. The second response 'comprehends the dualisms and deconstructions of the first response as the dynamic movement of a political history which can be expounded speculatively out of the broken middle.' The first response Rose characterizes as 'tragic in the sense of the baroque mourning play, aberrated mourning,' while the second response is 'comic – the comedy of absolute spirit, inaugurated mourning' (ibid.: 17–18).

Rose also points to the theoretical poverty of the self/other construction of dualisms. To begin with, 'far from absorbing otherness back into self-consciousness or subjectivity . . . the presentation of otherness has a motility which the post-modern gesture towards otherness is unable to conceive.' The heart of her argument here is that 'the separation out of otherness as such is derived from the failure of mutual recognition on the part of two self-consciousnesses who encounter each other and refuse to recognize the other as itself a self-relation'. As a result 'the other is never simply other, but an implicated self-relation.' Moreover, she argues, this 'applies to oneself as other and, equally, to any opposing self-consciousness'. For 'my relation to myself is mediated by what I recognize or refuse to recognize in your relation to yourself, while your self-relation depends on what you recognize of my relation to myself' (ibid.: 19).

The value of Rose's contribution also lies in her concern with the importance of developing a politics out of the 'broken middle', a concern which relates closely to the idea behind the conception put forward in this chapter of a relational both–and. She argues that it follows from 'the anxiety produced by the self-opposition of subject to its substance, by the modern evasion of mutual recognition attendant on the separation of subjective rights from the law of the modern state, intensified by the individualism of post-modernity,' that 'to rediscover politics we need to reconfigure the broken middle, not to deconstruct static dualisms' (ibid.: 20).

Plumwood elicits a similarly positive relational potential, from the starting point of her observation that some other cultures consider that a *range* of 'genuinely human virtues' connects us to nature. This stands in contrast with the dominant Western view according to which nature is seen as 'sharply discontinuous or ontologically divided from the human sphere of reason'. The effect of the Western approach has been 'a view of humans as apart from or "outside of" nature, usually as masters or external controllers of it' (Plumwood 1995: 155). But 'on the divided-self theory it is reason, the essentially or authentically human part of the self, and in that sense the human realm proper, that is outside nature, not the human as a physical phenomenon' (ibid.). Thus Plumwood is able to identify what is lost by dichotomous thinking in this example, and what could be gained by a non-dichotomous mode of thinking, namely the possibility of recognising the distinctive quality of a range of 'genuinely human virtues', in place of the narrow scope of reason as the distinctively human capacity.

# 2

# REASON AND EMOTION

Haste's insight, that '[i]n the dualistic view of mind versus body, the tension between rational and emotional is closely interwoven with sexuality' (Haste 1993: 164), sums up some of the common ground in the subjects of this and the following chapter. This chapter seeks to identify a range of connections between reason and emotion which are undervalued and often unacknowledged in mainstream theorizing, in order to substantiate the claim for the recognition of a broader notion of rationality which encompasses emotion. In Chapter Three the double gendering of sexuality is addressed, in the dichotomies of masculine/feminine and heterosexual/homosexual.

The intellectual context in which the relational non-dichotomous view of mind and body is developed here owes much to Oakeshott (1933, 1975). According to this view, mind apprehends the operations of intellect and emotion, mediated by sensation, affect and desire, and body registers desire, affect and sensation mediated by intellect and emotion. The interaction between mind and body together is understood to contribute to experience of the world, which is perceived in the context of (but not determined by) social practices and language and the values expressed in them. Adapting a phrase from Jaggar, this non-dichotomous relational view of mind and body, reason and emotion and body, is crucially both 'nonhierarchical and non-foundationalist' (Jaggar 1989: 149). It is on the basis of experience (as an integrative faculty, but one which is conditional and open-ended) that action in the world is undertaken and that understanding is gained. It is through understanding that meaning is achieved.

Experience is a key and integrative fulcrum in this process, occurring at the point where inner and outer, internal and external, meet. In this sense feminist epistemology is not wrong to wish to focus upon experience as a key category in knowledge. Understanding is also a key part of the process, is also integrative, and is always the basis for socially-sanctioned meaning. The term 'meaning' refers to entrenched socially-valued understandings. In this perspective, the kind of cognitive (knowing) powers of the mind with which this chapter is primarily concerned are those cognitive powers utilized in theorizing which focus upon the interaction of intellect and emotion. While the body as the location of desire, affects and sensations is also a source of some kinds of knowing, this chapter concentrates upon the undervalued cognitive connection between intellect and emotion in theorizing.

The Introduction described some of the work which specifies convincingly the historical correlation of reason with maleness, and the way in which the dichotomy between reason and emotion emerged. (See also Okin 1979, McNay 1992: 91–7, 126–30, Haste 1993: 31–3.) Lutz's study of contemporary American society supports the case that this correlation continues to have resonance. She argues that while in contemporary American society emotion continues to be constructed as gendered, there is good evidence which contradicts 'some of the stereotypical beliefs about the relationship between gender and emotion' (Lutz 1996: 151–2).

Also relevant to this discussion is Little's unpacking of claims concerning the gendered association between reason and emotion as having been based on three broad grounds. Such claims consist of the idea that it can be empirically shown that women are more swayed by emotion and less by reason than are men; the idea that 'women *by nature* have less *capacity* for reason' and more for emotion than men; and the idea that it is socially '*inappropriate* to woman's role for her to cultivate and act from reason and *appropriate* to cultivate and act from emotion' (Little 1995: 119). Historically the dominant strand of at least Western philosophy has considered that reason and emotion are mutually exclusive, and that theorizing proceeds by the former and is impeded by the latter. This chapter seeks to show not only that the dominance of this dichotomous view has led to a misleading understanding of both of these terms, but that in a more broadly coherent understanding reason and emotion can be recognized as deeply implicated in each other in a positive manner.

The argument of Chapter One was concerned with the general character of dichotomous thinking, the problems associated with its operating as a paradigm for all thinking, and with eliciting the possibility of a relational mode of thinking which does not suffer from the drawbacks of holism. In this chapter and in Chapter Three, two specific dichotomies will be examined and challenged. This chapter demonstrates the crucial interdependence of reason and emotion, specifically with respect to the cogency of theorizing, and so calls for the recognition of an extended notion of reason which acknowledges some of the immanent elements of emotion. Chapter Three argues that the dichotomy between sex as biological and gender as social, upon which the sex/gender distinction rests, can no longer be accepted as tenable once the consequences of the social construction of sex as well as gender are fully explored. The overall point of these two chapters is that a fuller understanding of reason, emotion and body involves the recognition of their non-dichotomous tripartite connection. None of these three categories can be fully characterized independently of their constitutive connections with the other two. Thus according to the view endorsed here the subject is rational, embodied, and a subject with emotions. It is curious that no satisfactory adjective for emotion exists in this context. 'Emotional' carries the misplaced connotation of excess, and 'emoted' suggests only the actor's representation of emotion.

Within this tripartite connection, feminists such as Grosz, Butler, Gatens, Bordo and Brennan have produced important work undermining the mind/body dichotomy which has operated to devalue the *body* and its relation to mind. Advocates of the importance of *emotion* have a task which is in one sense easier and in another sense more difficult to accomplish. Mind, body and emotion are interconnected, but emotion, while lodged in the mind, straddles the mind/body dichotomy through its relation to affect. In one sense the task of reinstating the value of emotion is easier than reinstating the value of body because in the case of emotion the mind/body dichotomy is not being challenged directly. However, reinstating the value of emotion is also more difficult in the sense that challenging the oppression of emotion within the mind (part of the body), through the definition of a narrow conception of rationality and reason, strikes at the very heart of the mainstream understanding of mind.

A range of contemporary writing converges upon just such a challenge. Damasio for instance has recently made a strong case that emotions are profoundly implicated in the use of reason. To highlight the connection between reason and emotion is not to say that emotion highjacks judgment and decision-making, nor that we are not rational beings. It is to say, rather, that 'certain aspects of the process of emotion and feeling are indispensable for rationality' (Damasio 1994: xii-xiii).[1] Damasio's contention is that the evidence points to the necessity of revising the view that our lives are guided by reason, with emotions only operating to jeopardize and cloud rational action. At its best the alliance between reason and emotion leads to insightful, pertinent and perceptive practical and moral reasoning and theorizing.

The reason this chapter is necessary can be attributed to the stubborn persistence of three kinds of traces in our culture's approach to theorizing, namely a pre-postmodern view of reason as abstract and universal, a reductive biological view of emotion, and a pre-constructionist determinist view of both reason and emotion. Numbers of important books have been devoted to criticizing in a multiplicity of ways the first trace, the universalist claims of Enlightenment reason. However the consequences with respect to the second and third traces, the connection of reason with emotion, in the implication of emotion in the cogency of reason, have not yet been adequately spelled out. It is now widely accepted in the abstract that although our knowledge does not have foundations in a human essence or nature deriving from a grand narrative of reason, our knowledge is nevertheless not ungrounded. But the notion that the interplay of reason and emotion may perform an important part in grounding our knowledge is still regarded with suspicion. Thus despite the renunciation in the abstract of grand narrative reason, we seem reluctant to follow through the consequences of that disavowal. This chapter seeks to make a strong case for the role of emotion, experienced through the interaction of inner mental actions and social practices, in a conception of knowledge specifically concerned with theorizing, in which reason is grounded but not foundational.

One valuable strategy to this end would be to recover and reinterpret the links between reason and emotion acknowledged by Aristotle or Spinoza or to resuscitate those present in the 'recessive' Western tradition (Jaggar 1989: 150) that includes Hume, Nietzsche, Dewey, and James for example.[2] The strategy adopted here, however, is to draw upon a variety of pertinent current literatures: from the psychology of emotions, described by Harré, Greenspan, and de Sousa; from the philosophy of mind and ethics of Baier, Amelie Rorty, and Nussbaum; from the philosophy of Putnam and Nozick; and from the feminism of Grosz, Gatens, Lloyd, Whitford and others.

From these literatures the aim is to establish that reason and emotion are not just compatible but are important to the operation of each other in a positive way. The starting point is that contemporary philosophers of mind, philosophers of psychology, and psychologists of emotion all recognize as uncontroversial the important point that emotions are part of mind, rather than being primarily located in the body more generally as affects. See for example Arnold's explicit articulation of her aim to present 'emotion as experience rather than . . . [as] behaviour. Whether we like it or not, emotion is a "mentalistic" phenomenon' (Arnold 1968: 10). De Sousa's work is particularly important here because he supplies a persuasive extension of the notion of rationality to include the possibility of assessing the rationality of emotion, and also because he constructs a theory about the role of emotion in judging the salience of a belief, situation, action or want, which can be extended to refer to theorizing.

Although the argument of this chapter includes reference to the work of psychologists, it is important to emphasize that the argument is not thereby a reductionist one to psychological categories. While it is necessary to specify emotion with reference to psychology, the explanation that is offered here is focussed upon the knowledge that is produced in theorizing, and not on psychological states. Stocker makes the same point clear about his own project: in 'arguing that there are intellectual emotions, and that they are essential to intellectual activity . . . I have not "psychologized" such activity. I have not been at all concerned with traditionally so-called psychological reasons, influences, or causes of intellectual activity.' Rather, Stocker continues, '[w]hat I have tried to show is that there are and must be desires, goals, interests, emotions, and the like within and proper to the intellect, within and proper to intellectual activity, for there to be intellect and intellectual activity' (Stocker 1980: 333).

The major point of this chapter is that very important consequences follow from the widespread recognition of the cognitive nature of emotion

(McMillan 1982: 28–9). Because emotions involve cognition, located in the mind, as well as (secondarily) bodily affects, the strict separation and opposition between mind and body, on which the reason/emotion dichotomy rested, breaks down. This is shown in several different ways in this chapter: through demonstrating the cultural resonances or ambiguity (rather than clear universal definition) and the cultural particularity of definitions of reason and emotion; through showing how reason and emotion are both involved in knowledge of emotion; through specifying five particular roles for emotion in theorizing; and through proposing a relational social constructionist theory of emotion, to accompany the more readily accepted notion of the social construction of reason.

It is central to the argument of this work, which seeks to redress the exclusion of women from full rationality (see Pateman 1980, 1988) by extending the status of rational personhood to women, that the interdependence of reason and emotion in theorizing be recognized much more fully and explicitly than it has been. It is also vital to the argument of the present work that the complicity of the dominant 'modern' notion of reason in the systematic subordination of women be recognized and challenged by undermining the mapping of reason/emotion on to man/woman. This mapping is accompanied by the associated mapping of other dichotomies such as object/subject and abstract/concrete, as well as rational/irrational. While, as Worrall notes (1990), deviation from gender role expectation by females has often been interpreted as evidence of mental disorder, the current work advances the case that deviation from gender role expectation can lead instead to a richer understanding of rationality.

The argument developed in the chapter proposes an alternative to the line that women can share (male) rationality by casting off emotion and taking part in a 'sexually-neutral' realm of autonomous personhood, or the line that women's emotionality is a separate and independent good which the conception of rational autonomous and free personhood has systematically undervalued. Rather, the present work seeks a way forward from the dichotomous thinking that characterizes both these views. Similarly the chapter endorses neither of the alternatives for rationality presented by M. Walker (1993) as expressing the French feminist philosophers Irigaray and Le Doeuff. Walker criticizes Irigaray for reducing 'rationality to a masculine speaking position' and supports Le Doeuff's defence of rationality, 'at least in its future potential – as a gender-neutral practice' (Walker, M. 1993: 422).

Indeed the criticisms of Le Doeuff by Walker and Sanders perform a useful function in the context of the present work in helping to pinpoint a very different and more satisfactory conception of rationality. Sanders (1993) makes clear that while the notion of rationality is central to Le Doeuff's work it also has a paradoxical status. According to Sanders, Le Doeuff does not have an integrated and coherent concept of rationality; that is, rationality is for Le Doeuff both ambiguous and multiple. Instead of the two unsatisfactory positions represented in interpretations of Irigaray and Le Doeuff, there is the view pursued here of an extended conception of reason. Simply working to take out the gendered and hierarchical elements of a rational/irrational, reason/emotion dichotomy is not enough, and following Cocks's persuasive argument (1984) that there is nothing inherently male about reason, it is the aim of the present work to present a compelling view of rational, corporeal, and emotion-rich subjectivity.[3]

In particular this chapter concentrates on supporting the thesis that in specifically philosophical thinking, broadly understood, that is in theorizing, in theoretical critical reflection, there are important links between reason and emotion. These links fundamentally invite the revision of the definition and status of both terms.

The chapter is divided into two sections. Having considered the range of meanings of the terms 'reason' and 'emotion', it is concerned first and centrally to elucidate a series of connections which operate between reason and emotion in cogent theoretical critical reflection. The chapter then makes the case for the social construction of emotion. The aim is to establish that reasoning, in the use of the cognitive faculty to produce knowledge, has an emotional component, and to demonstrate the rationality of the emotional component of reasoning.

This chapter aims to add support to an alternative to the theory of reason pre-eminent during the modern period, taken in particular from Descartes and Kant, which devalues, excludes and denies the involvement of emotions. But it is important to make clear that in doing so it does not fall into either emotivism or several other conceptions of emotion. The present work is, thereby, definitely not setting up some sort of theory of emotivism, which as MacIntyre observes, is 'the doctrine that all evaluative judgments and more specifically all moral judgments are nothing but expressions of preference, expressions of attitude or feeling' (MacIntyre 1985: 11–12).

Based on a dichotomy between the realm of fact in which factual judgments (which are true or false) are made according to rational criteria, and the moral realm in which value judgments, being expressions of attitude or feeling, are not subject to rational criteria, emotivism asserts 'that there are and can be no valid rational justification for any claims that objective and impersonal moral standards exist and hence that there are no such standards' (MacIntyre 1985: 19). In the course of her criticism of Barry's notion of impartiality, Mendus (1996) highlights the way in which Barry uses a dichotomy between reason and emotion along these lines when he takes Popper's endorsement of this dichotomy in *The Open Society and Its Enemies* as the motto for his book, *Justice as Impartiality* (Barry 1995). According to Popper, '[i]f a dispute arises . . . [t]here are only two solutions; one is the use of emotion, and ultimately of violence, and the other is the use of reason, of impartiality, of reasonable compromise' (Popper, quoted by Mendus 1996: 319).

Jaggar however finds a 'grain of important truth in emotivism' which is worth examining. She identifies this grain of truth as 'its recognition that values presuppose emotions to the extent that emotions provide the experiential basis for values' (Jaggar 1989: 137). She continues, if 'we had no emotional responses to the world, it is inconceivable that we should ever come to value one state of affairs more highly than another' (ibid.). But while Jaggar's recognition of the connection between emotion and values is important, it is clear that her argument, framed in terms of an emotivist theory, is not necessary. Nor does it successfully undermine the Kantian argument for the generation of the moral categorical imperative (which supplies value) simply from the human capacity for freedom, autonomy and responsibility, which effectively sidesteps the need to derive value from emotion.

Neither does the present argument subscribe to Hume's subsumption of the emotions under empirical bodily states and affects, or his view that belief (knowledge) 'is a function of our sensitive rather than of our cognitive nature' (Lloyd 1993: 52). As Little points out, while Hume regarded passions and sentiments 'as indispensable to moral judgment', and considered that 'reason alone cannot yield moral verdicts, for such verdicts move us to act, and reason itself is impotent on this score', the result is that 'Hume's theory only reinforces the traditional view' that emotions cannot generate truth, for it is the very role of emotion in moral judgment that 'contaminates the moral verdict's claim to full epistemic respectability' (Little 1995: 135). Nor is the present work advocating Locke's empiricist view of the generation of knowledge based on reflection upon sense experience, through bodily sensation, of the world outside. For Locke knowledge is not gained through introspection; he is a philosopher of sensation, and it is important to clarify that sensation is not emotion. Emotion is primarily part of mind (the mind part of body) rather than of body directly, although often (but not always) having bodily affects accompanying it.

A further point of clarification is also in order, to contextualize the argument developed here. Criticism of the dominant modern notion of reason is not new, but began almost with the Enlightenment definition of reason itself. Part of that definition was the idea of reason not only as a secularized version of the capacity through which to see the natural law given by God, but also of reason elevated to the point where it could gain access to the inflated scope of God's boundless, infinite and true knowledge. The history of criticisms of reason takes in the eighteenth and nineteenth century Romantics, Hegel, Freud, Jung, Darwin, and latterly Kuhn, Feyerabend, Derrida, Foucault and others. Recently criticism has focused upon the status attributed to reason in the modern period (its inflated views of the autonomous individualized self, of truth, of knowledge, and of power). Feminists have been very active in this, especially in the manifold implications of the marginalization of the body.

However, an added complication in the history of the modern notion of reason and its reception is that both defenders and critics of modern reason have usually addressed a socially-powerful construct that is at variance with the philosophy upon which it was based. According to the socially-powerful construct, warrant for regarding reason and emotion as mutually exclusive and hierarchically ranked is found in the philosophies of Descartes and Kant, and according to critics of this construct the philosophies of Descartes and Kant are guilty of dichotomizing reason and emotion. But as Jaggar observes, 'Descartes, Leibnitz, and Kant are among the prominent philosophers who did not endorse a wholly stripped-down, instrumentalist conception of reason' (Jaggar 1989: 150). Thus what Descartes and Kant actually had to say is much more subtle than some of what has subsequently been both endorsed and attacked. As Little notes, Descartes, for whom emotions were 'simply confused beliefs', posed an injunction to 'transcend the particular, the parochial, and the perspectival', but this was 'quickly translated into an injunction to transcend inclination, emotion and desire' (Little 1995: 134). Similarly there are strong grounds for arguing that Kant did not necessarily belittle emotions but just considered them separately from reason. However, as Little argues, 'even where he does concede a role for affect [by which she means emotion] in moral life, it is only the role of helping us respond and act as we should (supplying motivation when the motive of duty fails us)' (ibid.). For Kant the role of emotions was 'not [in] helping us to discern what morality requires of us in the first place: that epistemological project is still the sacrosanct domain of reason' (ibid.).

Furthermore as Oakley notes, while according to Kant 'only acts which are done from duty have moral worth', Kant explicitly states that the exception to this, which can motivate moral good, is the emotion of respect for the moral law. For Kant respect in this sense 'is the only emotion which involves a recognition of the determination of the will by the moral law' (Oakley 1992: 86). Moreover, moral good and duty are closely tied to the rational and to freedom; for Kant, when we are acting from duty or reason we are acting freely, whereas emotions are beyond our control. However, if it can be shown that some emotions are *within* our control, taken with the now widespread acknowledgement that autonomy is always situated, the plausibility of Kant's case for the reliance on the notion of will is diminished and the argument for the social construction of emotions is strengthened. Then the ground is cut from under Kant's view of emotion and his strict division between the realm of reason, freedom and moral good on the one hand and emotion on the other.

However the current work is concerned as much with the socially-powerful construct extracted from Descartes and Kant as with what those writers intended to say or can be interpreted as saying. The current work is concerned to address the legacy of Descartes and Kant; to examine their work in detail would not provide an answer to the central question in this chapter. The current challenge to the dominant modern notion of reason is legitimized by the way in which social values based on and derived from Descartes and Kant in particular have mediated and been filtered through the intellectually entrenched and socially pervasive value-laden dichotomies of mind/body and reason/emotion. The current work challenges the enormous influence of such mediated values and entrenched dichotomies in the general currency we use, imbibe and are affected by, in theorizing as well as in real effects in practical life. Our conduct and practice are not based on pure Descartes and Kant, and are not completely resistant to the currency of social values. This much is inevitable since even in rational theorizing we are not immune from social values.

The focus here on emotion and reason is solicited by the almost general absence of an argument about emotion from current criticism of the dominant modern notion of reason. The absence of an argument about emotion is in turn due at least in part to the way in which emotion has generally but mistakenly been seen as within the scope of body, and in part because only an emaciated view of emotions has been recognized.

## The links between reason and emotion in theorizing

This section studies three aspects of the links between reason and emotion in theorizing. First, it examines the terms 'reason' and 'emotion', and it distinguishes between reason which here refers to the cognitive rational faculty, and the practical reason or reasonableness which might be appropriate to political deliberation. The first part of this section also stresses the important point that reason and emotion, while connected in theorizing, are nevertheless conceptually distinct and must not be conflated. Second, this section investigates the connections between reason and emotion in knowledge of emotion, in order to indicate the rationality of emotion and so undermine the devaluation of emotion in general. It is also preparatory work to investigating the connections between reason and emotion in theorizing, by clearly distinguishing the two kinds of knowledge. The core of the section considers the role of emotions in knowledge and theorizing, with the aim of submitting an expanded understanding of reason informed by emotion. The aim here is to demonstrate some of the ways in which knowledge is generated through the interaction of reason and emotion.

### *The terms 'reason' and 'emotion'*

Lloyd's book *The Man of Reason* is the soundest and most convincing treatment of the historical elevation of reason in line with the dominant sides of a range of other dichotomies.[4] In order to develop the challenge to the hierarchical ordering established in these dichotomies, the terms reason and emotion can also be shown to be conceptually compatible and important to each other in the production of knowledge. First it is important to indicate the wealth and ambiguity of usages of the terms reason and emotion within our intellectual legacy, as a basis upon which to make some positive links between the two. The importance of this task is not diminished by Longino's accurate stricture that '[f]ar from being a neutral distinction . . . the distinction between reason and feeling is itself a highly politicized one', and so 'the very concepts upon which philosophy constructs itself rely upon and reinforce a distinction between the domain of reason, the world of philosophy, and the domain of feeling and passion, the domain of political movements such as feminism' (Longino 1995: 22).

The understandings of the terms reason and emotion concern on the one hand the cognitive capacity for reason, for reasoning, for rational argument, the rational faculty, the practice of making conceptual connections, and on the other hand the immanent emotional dimension of all experience, thus including thinking, deliberating, shared deliberation, reflection and theorizing. The exploration of the terms reason and emotion is not designed to solve the question of what reason is in any ultimate sense, because the meanings of reason (and emotion) are necessarily found in the meaning of the concrete and embedded socially-constructed *practices* in which they operate (and are contested). The exploration of the terms reason and emotion is proposed to highlight the *scope* of their meanings, and to lay the basis on which to elucidate some of the connections between them that are suppressed by the reason/emotion dichotomy.

The term 'reason' has accumulated, even just within the Western intellectual tradition, a wide range of different meanings, associations and resonances, expressed in different conceptions. Six of the most influential, which are not necessarily mutually exclusive, are picked out below as a point of departure for the discussion of reason. The first three of these meanings have been thought to exist independently of the definition of subjectivity, indicating reason as having a supposedly objective character, and one independent of a need for empirical verification, while the latter meanings are tied to selfhood, crucially located in and not just apprehended by the mind.

The purpose of describing these six meanings is not to specify a 'correct' meaning of reason, nor to seek to establish from conceptual clarification alone what reason means. Rather, it is twofold. First it aims to identify the indebtedness of the understanding of reason in the present work to a meaning of reason which is more than simply a functional rationality or one which refers to rational justification. The understanding of reason in the present work acknowledges that in our culture reason is constructed as a special *human* capacity. The second purpose is to indicate that while some meanings seem to exclude a role for emotion, others in principle do not. As Nozick argues, rationality does not have to exclude emotion; and even the notion of rationality given in decision theory can pursue emotion (Nozick 1993: 106). Indeed the case for an extended conception of reason, beyond the dichotomous stranglehold, is well envisioned by Nozick. He argues that '[p]hilosophers who write about reasoning tend to concentrate upon an exceedingly narrow range of thinking as the sole legitimate mode of reasoning' (ibid.: 164). Sometimes, he adds, 'writers on rationality treat it mainly as an exclusionary device, whose main purpose is to disparage something as "irrational", rather than as positively marking an efficient and effective vehicle' (ibid.).

Baier's description of reason points immediately to the plurality of its meanings. She also sums up the way in which a narrow deductiveness has been regarded as the dominant form of rational argument in our intellectual tradition: she notes that '[d]emonstration, or reason in the strict sense, traces logical links, where reason in the improper sense traces causal consequences or causal ancestry' (Baier 1980: 420). The scope of reason, then, could be explored by considering more widely the different kinds of argument that can count as rational. Thus induction as well as deduction is a form of rational argument: so are modelling, argument by analogy, thought experiment, transcendental argument (a regressive argument on the basis of what is implied in the conditions of experience), and argument from laws.

In the first of the six principal meanings of reason, reason has been identified with universal abstract principles, expressed either as the thin rationality of tests or as instrumental rationality. Instrumental rationality is a crucial meaning of reason, containing much internal diversity. It can be employed in arguments of justification, but also covers reckoning, evaluating or calculating the necessary means to achieving a (rational self-interested) goal, hypothesising by induction or deduction and examining consequences, or providing a motive for a course of action. For Hobbes, rationality was instrumental because it was purely concerned with calculation and could not operate as a motive for action in its own right.

Reason has secondly been equated with logical principles such as noncontradiction, consistency and comprehensiveness derived from the Western (initially Greek) exposition of the discipline of logic, and with the ability to make valid inferences, and so in this sense with the conformity of an argument to the dictates of reason. 'Is it rational?' here means, 'Is it consistent?' As Jaggar observes, the validity of logical inferences, 'from premises established elsewhere . . . [involved] the ability to calculate means but not to determine ends', and it 'was thought independent of human attitudes and preferences; this was now the sense in which reason was taken to be objective and universal' (Jaggar 1989: 130).

A third meaning of reason refers to the Greek *logos*, pure objective reason as expressed in (and so discovered through the use of?) language. This is an interesting meaning and one which perhaps deserves to be recovered further, straddling as it does the notion of pure cognitive ability with a recognition of the expressive and rhetorical nature of language. (See Haste 1993: 9, ch.2.)

Reason can fourthly refer to a substantive and normative conception that distinguishes humans from beasts (and so is contrasted with instinct), necessary for the exercise of active agency in freedom, equality, independence, autonomy, and moral choice. This is a conception of reason as the 'sovereign human character trait' (Lloyd 1993: 37). It is characteristic of the 'modern' intellectual project, closely intertwined with the notion of 'modern' scientific rationality.

Berlin sums up an influential version of this view when he asserts that the 'exercise of "mind over body"' distinguishes mankind from beast, rendering the individual worthy of respect and responsible for his or her choices and actions' (Berlin 1969: 134). Furthermore in Locke, as Berry notes, 'the freedom and equality of individuals stems from their possession of reason (s.63). It is by the use of their reason that individuals are able to act as independent agents'. For Locke, once 'the "age of reason" has been attained, every individual is a free, equal and independent agent able to make their own decisions' (Berry 1988: 3). It follows for Locke that '[f]or some other person to take a decision on the part of another who is rational is to abrogate the latter's freedom and equality' (ibid.).

In Kant this meaning of reason is captured in the power by which first principles are grasped a priori (as distinct from mere understanding), producing clear and distinct ideas, as well as in the resulting responsibility of individuals for their own actions and for the consequences of those actions. For Kant it is only when a person is motivated by reason (as opposed to motivation from fear, reward, another agency acting through them, or nature) that their actions can be undertaken in an autonomous and so free manner. Reason is here identified with the moral imperative to treat others as ends in themselves and not as means to one's own end.

Reason can, fifthly, indicate (as in psychology) the cognitive faculty, the faculty of knowing. Cognitive powers are thought to refer to such things as apprehending, observing, awareness and perception.

A sixth meaning of reason refers to the Cartesian cogito which explicitly fused rationality and (an abstract and universalized) subjectivity. It follows from this meaning that, as Berry puts it, because 'Man knows himself to be an animal . . . he ceases for that reason to be an animal . . . To say that Man alone can think is also to say that Man uniquely is free' (Berry 1988: 15). Here rationality is deeply implicated with consciousness and self-consciousness. Rationality on this basis has also been the criterion by which some individuals and groups have been, spuriously, denied subjectivity.

Two further elements influencing the meaning of the term reason need to be registered. Not only has our inherited view of reason contained an implicit or explicit rejection of emotion, where emotion stands for unruly passions, affect and sense experience, lack of objective and dispassionate impartiality, and lack of control, foresight, and predictability. The rejection of emotion has also been combined with the potent fear especially in the nineteenth century of a 'confusion of sexual identities' and racial pollution: the idea that sexual difference, along with racial mixing, and emotion (itself gendered) all need to be kept at bay to avoid the chaos and contamination that would certainly follow from the recognition of heterogeneous difference.[5] Second, our inherited view of reason has also contained a secular colouring. The secular nature of reason, particularly since the Enlightenment, has contributed to the legacy of its character as an autonomous, self-contained faculty independent of any higher power, associated with human freedom and therefore the highest source of moral judgment.

Another important aspect establishing the plurality of meanings of 'reason' concerns how and if reason establishes certainty. Baier introduces three shrewd questions on this point, which challenge assumptions about the unity and so universality of the meaning of reason by pointing to 'the variety of what makes reasons better or worse reasons'. She wants to know 'just what reasons *are*': whether, 'as Davidson supposes, for action they are desirability judgments, a psychological or social-psychological reality if a reality at all, or whether they are the *content* of those judgments, the recognized desirability itself, rather than just the imputation of it' (Baier 1985a: 132). Her second question concerns reductive chains: 'whether reasons can always have reasons, and what different sorts of *chains* of reasons we get' (ibid.). Baier's third question revolves around the discussion of whether a reason is a rational cause, and what it means to hold this view (ibid.: 127). Baier's questions also raise the important related point that 'reasons' are not, after all, monolithic. For the criteria for reasons for action may be different from those for reasons for feelings (though Baier's point is that they are not), which may be different again from those that count for reasons for holding the outcome of a piece of theorizing.

All these points suggest further reasons why the stubbornly lingering traces of the pre-postmodern view of a reason insulated from emotion cannot be sustained in the light of the evident dependence of its meanings and criteria on situated practices and norms, and on contextual understandings. Grosz identifies another important strand of the dominant 'modern' notion of reason when she indicates how it derives from 'Descartes' conflation of consciousness with subjectivity' (Grosz 1990b: 2), together with the expunging of emotion from mind. While some postmodern thinkers have effectively challenged the claims of reason to produce abstract, certain, and universal knowledge, the notion of reason as not only located in, but as defining, and *exclusively* defining, the superior part of the mind/body dichotomy is still very potent.

Thus while the core of this chapter is concerned to identify the often unacknowledged but important connections between reason and emotion in theorizing, it is worth considering briefly why this task is required. For along with the definitions of reason given above, there has also been a 'crisis of reason'. As Grosz astutely puts it, 'Descartes and Hume represent rationalist and empiricist approaches to knowledge; neither they nor the traditions they founded have been able to resolve the insecurities and doubts that both imply.' For Descartes, 'this crisis consisted in the fact that knowledge lacked secure foundations.' For Hume the crisis is that 'universal natural laws – the laws it is the task of science to discern – are unable to be rationally justified.' And for a range of postmodern theorists the crisis lies in 'reason's inability to rationally know itself . . . know itself from the outside' (Grosz 1993: 188–9). Braidotti goes further and argues that the 'crisis of rational thought is nothing more than the forced realization, brought about by historical circumstances, that this highly phallocentric mode of thought rests on a set of unspoken premises about thinking which are themselves non-rational' (Braidotti 1992: 183).

Nozick also acknowledges a crisis of rationality, though 'without a solution to propose' (Nozick 1993: xvi). His framing of the crisis identifies the way in which 'many of philosophy's traditional problems have turned out to be intractable and resistant to rational resolution'. He contends that this is the outcome of a disjunction between an understanding of rationality as 'an evolutionary adaptation with a delimited purpose and function' and philosophy as an 'attempt of unlimited scope to apply reason and to justify rationally every belief and assumption' (ibid.: xii).

Le Doeuff also identifies an important problem with our notion of reason: that it is neither simply common property nor individually defined. She seeks to recover a conception of reason between these two points: '[i]f everything rational were always already held in common, we would have nothing to tell each other on that score. If what is not held in common had the status of a purely personal opinion, everyone would only engage in monologues' (Le Doeuff 1990: 10). She analyzes how the conception of woman as a non-rational being is the 'offspring' of the mainstream tradition of philosophy, a 'sort of "second best" system sometimes produced by the very same authors who might already have produced much better work elsewhere' (ibid.: 12). In her enigmatic article, the course that Le Doueff seems to be suggesting is that the notion of rationality, as exemplified for instance in Kant's *Critique of Pure Reason*, can be detached from the exclusion of women from rationality (ibid). However, this conclusion would be very problematic, for it would leave intact the mind/body split which underpins this traditional view of reason.

Now that the diversity of the meanings of 'reason' and its crises have been identified, it follows that the aim of this chapter could never be simply to choose one of the above six definitions of reason and explicate its connections with emotion. Any plausible contemporary understanding of reason needs to be extended to overcome the central crisis of reason which results from the exclusion of body and emotion from the definition of reason.

Another important factor in understanding reason is the publicity of reason, which applies both to practical reason and to theorizing. While this author does not agree with the covert objective/subjective dichotomy present in Beiner's formulation (1983: 8–9), his point that we release ourselves 'from the confines of private subjectivity' when we 'support our judgments with publicly adducible reasons or grounds' is a good one. It follows that the products of reasoning, in knowledge, do not have universal validity, and even the meaning given to the formal criteria for theorizing such as noncontradiction lies in the conventions of application, which vary across cultures. Putnam takes the publicity case a step further in his formulation that we rightly attribute to humans in the past *vis-à-vis* ourselves, 'shared concepts, however different the *conceptions* that we also attribute' (Putnam 1981: 119).[6] That is, what is shared across time is not commensurable substantive conceptions of knowledge and rationality, but translatable concepts of knowledge and rationality. But what we also share, in an interesting way, in values and moral principles, is defined by and challenged within a particular society's social and cultural practices. The use of reason is to give reasons for, and the test of rationality is the ability to construct an argument recognized by others as rational.

Reason and the exercise of rational freedom, furthermore, always take place within practices. As MacIntyre argues, any sufficiently circumscribed and purposeful human activity requires that the practitioner submit him/herself to the rules and constraints central to that practice (MacIntyre 1985: 187). Putnam supports the same viewpoint when he says 'Wittgenstein argued that without such public norms, norms shared by a group and constituting a "form of life", language and even thought itself would be impossible' (Putnam 1981: 107). For Wittgenstein, 'it is absurd to ask if the institutionalized verification [whether logical positivist or other] I have been speaking of is "really" justificatory' (ibid.; see also Tully 1989).

On the basis of the foregoing discussion of 'reason', in the present work 'reason' (which involves emotion) means the verb to reason – to develop a reasoned, rational argument – but not the noun 'reason' as a substantive normative conception. Moreover reasoning is considered as involved (with emotion) in knowledge seen as contextual and grounded, not abstract and universal. This position does not entail a vicious relativism, for while reason operates within social practices and conventions, these are not arbitrary, and are subject to critical reflection. As Putnam (1981: 137) notes, the notion of rational acceptability (that is, what is rational) needs to include adequacy and perspicuousness as well as being a standard of whether or not we should accept a statement as true. Furthermore, he demonstrates that 'it is not possible both to have standards of rational acceptability and not to accept them . . . The kind of scepticism which consists in refusing to have any standards of rational acceptability commits one to not having any concepts at all' (ibid.: 147). At the same time Putnam makes a good case that this position does 'not . . . reject pluralism or commit oneself to authoritarianism' (ibid.).

The term 'reason' here contains four parts. It includes a functional non-relativistic rationality along Putnam's lines; a limited element of instrumental rationality arising from the awareness of one's own self-interest; plus a more substantive sense as an irreducible human faculty. The fourth part has to do with having a moral capacity, not in the sense of an objective universal abstract object, but in the sense of an ability consciously to reflect and see as rational a viewpoint outside one's own self-interest. This fourth part is related to Macmurray's definition of reason as 'the capacity to behave consciously in terms of the nature of what is not ourselves', which is in a way a 'capacity for objectivity' (Macmurray 1962: 7).

The fourth part also implies that very often the 'ascription of the rationality' or otherwise of actions, beliefs and ideas can only be made by reference to a wider context of actions, beliefs and ideas. Griffiths for instance gives the example of the set of grounds for the rationality of a hungry person's holding back from finding food to eat. According to a definition of rationality in terms of narrow self-interest, the action seems irrational, but it may well be rational when seen as the outcome of 'dieting, [being] busy, observing a religious fast, looking forward to having a meal out later' (Griffiths 1995: 110). What is rejected here, however, is the rationalist view articulated and criticized by Hekman, that there is 'an Archimedean point from which knowledge is acquired. The existence of such an Archimedean point that abstracts the knower from the known is, for rationalism, definitive of truth' (Hekman 1990: 12).

The way in which reason has, in the dominant 'modern' tradition, been regarded as sovereign, and as juxtaposed to an inferior 'emotion', as part of the mind/body split, is well described by Baier when she lists the 'prejudices acquired during my philosophical unbringing'. The primary prejudice she identifies is the idea that '[i]ntellect or reason, rather than any other human capacity, is what has intrinsic authority, and its authority extends over all human feelings, and all human customs, traditions, and habits' (Baier 1985b: x). The prejudice derives in its modern form from the idea of Kant's banishment from the operation of reason of any heteronomous source, which included the emotions (Dolar 1995: 273).

The justification of the conjunction of reason with man and the irrational with woman has been made throughout our intellectual inheritance through a specific argument about action deriving from sexual difference. A crucial component of reason has been thought to be its association with *intended action*: we can tell that an idea, thought or belief is rational if it is the product of consciousness, reflection, choice and so then issues in intended action, rather than in unintended, natural or arbitrary action.

Traditionally women have been associated with a life in which intended action does not play an important part. Women's lives have been thought to be dictated (whether by nature or social convention) by 'natural' bodily rhythms: menstruation, pregnancy, childbearing and childrearing, the 'natural' ties of affection for family, and by extension the cyclical character of domestic work. These bodily rhythms have been constructed as issuing in unintended action in the sense of actions which follow 'naturally' from the body's 'natural' rhythms. Important conclusions concerning the dependence of the definition of reason on body and on social roles need to be drawn from this association of reason as intended action with man. The recognition of the construction of sexual difference and the dissolution of the sex/gender dichotomy in Chapter Three are thus intimately connected with the concerns of this chapter. The dependence of the *conceptual* definition of reason on the *social* evidence of men's and women's lives demonstrates just how deeply reason has been socially constructed.

Turning now to the definition of emotion, this term has been associated culturally and intellectually with a variety of discrepant (often negative) conceptions including unreason, irrationality, anti-rationality (as in fascism), hysteria, intuition, passions, nature, experience, imagination, spontaneity, and lack of control.[7] The aspect of emotion that deserves to be highlighted in a very positive sense here is the recognition (identified for instance in psychology) that emotion is associated with motion and movement, stirring and agitation. This normatively-neutral view is an extremely important feature of emotion in the context of theorizing, where reason and rationality on their own are inert. Kroon's discussion (1996) of rationality and emotion with respect to nuclear deterrence policy-making is relevant here, in detailing the way in which a wide range of conflicting points of view can all be adduced as rational. In the present book, and building on the idea of emotion as movement, one of the crucial characteristics of emotion is understood to be the element of continuity. While emotions *can* be turbulent, overwhelming and uncontrollable, they can also be steady and stable and controlled, providing a line of reasoning with continuity.

It follows from the continuity of emotion that we have an unbroken emotional life just as we can have an uninterrupted life of the mind. This continuity takes two forms. First, it is rational in that the pattern of the emotional life contains an internal rationality (even if it is characterized by overtly irrational actions and feelings). Second, the interaction between reason and emotion in the production of knowledge is not intermittent but constant. By analogy with Wittgenstein's conception of language we can say that it is as important to be emotionally literate as it is to be intellectually, linguistically or socially literate. It is worth adding that this view does not entail a taming of the power and value of the emotions.

In specifying the connections between reason and emotion in theorizing, it is important to consider the nature of emotion, and what kinds of emotion are involved. On the first question, Rorty concludes, perhaps with unwarranted pessimism, that because the history of the notion of emotion exhibits no rational logic, '[e]motions do not form a natural class' (Rorty 1980: 104). In the course of her argument, however, she describes convincingly how the history of the notion of emotion has been characterized by dichotomization, reclassification, and expansion. Thus in the first part of this history, states and activities were 'parceled out . . . to one or another side of the dichotomies' (ibid), between active and passive emotions, between emotions as either nonrational or rational/irrational, between emotions as psychological states that can either be explained by and reduced to physical processes or not, between emotions as voluntary or nonvoluntary states.

Oakley presents a view of emotions as necessarily comprising three elements, 'complex phenomena involving dynamically related elements of cognition, desire, and affectivity' (Oakley 1992: 2). While his theory of emotions contains much that is sensible, his definitions of these three elements are simplistic. He does not sufficiently recognize the consequences of realizing that while the three elements are conceptually distinct, they are in practice fused. However Oakley's method of analysing emotions does provide a way of accounting for the preponderance of different elements in different emotions, and their use in different contexts. He argues for instance that the cognitive element may be understood better in terms of 'thoughts, apprehensions, or imaginings, rather than beliefs' (ibid.: 14).

Harré makes a point about the nature of emotion which is useful here, in noting that emotions enable us to do the 'ordering, selecting and interpreting work' of our lives, but do not have ontological status in themselves. The idea that emotion words represent 'an abstract and detachable"it"' is an 'ontological illusion', and we do not have anger, love, grief or anxiety but 'angry people, upsetting scenes, sentimental episodes, grieving families'. Harré's persuasive argument, that there is no 'theory of universal emotions' and that we 'reify and abstract from that concreteness at our peril' (Harré 1986: 4), will be developed later in the chapter, in the section on social construction.

On the question of what kinds of emotion are involved in theorizing, we become involved in the contentious issue of competing classifications of emotions. Baier notes for instance that 'Aristotle, Descartes, Spinoza, Hume, all gave us lists of human passions, introducing some sort of systematicity into their lists' (Baier 1985a: 123), whereas contemporary philosophers of mind tend to analyse the constitution and features of particular emotions. However we do not need to become engaged with the question of how comprehensive or narrow a classification of emotions need be. This is not necessary in this chapter in order to establish the importance of the connections between reason and emotion in theorizing.

On this central question Stocker argues soundly that 'almost all, if not all, the emotions, are found in both the intellectual and nonintellectual spheres of our life', and that what 'distinguishes the intellectual emotion from the traditional, "active" ones is . . . In the one case their object is intellectual and in the other case their object is some traditionally-considered activity or state' (Stocker 1980: 332). But while it is clear that all emotions may impact upon intellectual work, there is also a strong case for noting that some emotions are more directly relevant to, used in, and developed in the course of intellectual work. Examples include care, curiosity, interest, criticism, interest, attention, respect, fear, hate, appetite, aversion, and also a more generalized love or purity of heart, and sympathy for intellectual problems. It is also clear that a range of other emotions may be involved in motivating or propelling intellectual work but does not have a positive role to play in its actual construction. Examples include jealousy, anger, arrogance, envy, loneliness, compassion, and frustration.

The 'modern' idea of reason and cognitive observation as providing privileged (or indeed sole) access to cogent argument and 'true' knowledge which is universal, absolute and objective, has been challenged from many different quarters. As a result, there is now a widespread consensus that a retreat from Enlightenment claims about the status of reason has been effected. Likewise the optimistic claims made about progress and change that accompanied 'true' knowledge, whether it be in political theory, the so-called social sciences, philosophy or even the natural sciences, have also been shown to be grossly inflated. Along with this retreat has gone a revision of the ideas of prejudice, tradition, faith and the notions of embodiedness and embeddedness, from which 'modern' reason claimed to be able to achieve emancipation.

In consequence, a number of recent political and social theorists have withdrawn from the larger claim about reason and rationality in favour of either an Aristotelian synthesis of reason and emotion in the form of a practical wisdom appropriate to moral and political questions, or a (not unrelated) notion of 'reasonableness', in the context of the shared nature of deliberations in a community characterized by liberal moral pluralism and perceived group differences. The Aristotelian and liberal 'reasonableness' routes are worth examining briefly in order further to clarify the link between reason and emotion that is at stake in the current work.

What might be called broadly the Aristotelian route is taken by a range of moral and political theorists. A key exponent is Nussbaum who argues directly against the view that emotions cannot contribute to rational reflection, that emotions are 'unreliable, animal, seductive' and 'lead away from the cool reflection that alone is capable of delivered a considered judgment'. She says that a 'central purpose' of her book, *Love's Knowledge*, is 'to call this view of rationality into question and to suggest, with Aristotle, that practical reasoning unaccompanied by emotion is not sufficient for practical wisdom'. She contends that Aristotle's account of practical rationality contained 'a defense of the emotions and the imagination as essential to rational choice' (Nussbaum 1990: 55). Nussbaum develops a cogent case against both the idea that 'emotions are unreliable and distracting because they have nothing to do with cognition', and the view that 'they have a great deal to do with cognition, but they embody a view of the world that is in fact false' (ibid.: 40). Part of the reason for Nussbaum's advocacy of the Aristotelian method is that she is 'committed to regarding nothing as unrevisable and above (or beneath) criticism' (ibid.: 285).

Oakley (1992) agrees with Nussbaum's demonstration that emotions have a 'cognitive dimension in their very structure', and therefore that emotions are 'intelligent parts of our ethical agency, responsive to the workings of deliberation and essential to its completion' (Nussbaum 1990: 41). He expounds a case for the important role of emotion in moral value understood in terms of the Aristotelian notion of living a humanly flourishing life, developing Aristotle's claim that 'moral virtue requires not only acting well, but also having the right emotions in the right way towards the appropriate objects and to the right degree' (Oakley 1992: 2).

Molloy's proposal for a just polity based on an indigenous New Zealand model, which 'recognizes affect and reason not as separate and separable functions, but as mutually defining aspects of justice' (Molloy 1995: 107) is also relevant here. Molloy identifies impersonal, rational, universal metaphors in the models of community suggested by feminists such as Yeatman, Young, and Gunew, and argues that it makes 'more sense to try to undermine the affect [that is, emotion]/reason duality which underlies these models than to opt, once again, for a traditional model of the nation' (ibid.). Little (1995) also identifies the role of emotion in understanding moral concepts along these lines, challenging the 'traditional compartmentalization' of reason and emotion which underpins the dispassionate stance widely thought appropriate to moral wisdom during the 'modern' period.

While the work of Nussbaum, Oakley, Molloy and Little is important and useful, it does not represent the kind of connection between reason and emotion which this chapter is seeking to establish. This chapter is concerned with the link in the mind (part of the body) that affects *all* reasoning, not just in matters of practical judgment in ethics and politics. However there is a connection which is worth specifying: the links between reason and emotion in moral and political knowledge and judgment are increasingly acknowledged. This chapter argues that these links are valid also in matters of more abstract reasoning, in theorizing which does not have an immediate situated practical object.

In contrast with the Aristotelian route there is the liberal 'reasonableness' route. However, there are at least four reasons for arguing that the current notion of 'reasonableness' represents no more than an unsatisfactory compromise. Moreover a clear case can be made for a rationality that can be sustained without its previous universalistic, absolute and objective features, without having to resort to 'reasonableness'. The first problem with reasonableness is that it emulates the basis of legal rather than political interpretation and so tends to reduce politics to law. The second problem is that it elevates the notion of judgment without providing sufficiently convincing criteria. In the third place, the notion of reasonableness threatens to underestimate the problem of power inequalities in real rather than under ideal conditions. Fourth, reasonableness suggests a kind of majoritarianism, through either a consensual or deliberative theory of rational acceptability, with all the problems that majoritarianism entails (Putnam 1981: 179).

All these four problems are found in Rawls' influential idea (1993) of reasonableness, a notion upon which he placed great weight in the move from

*A Theory of Justice* to *Political Liberalism*. A harsh but sound case can be made that the term 'reasonableness' is all but denuded of conceptual work in Rawls' theory, precisely because it fails to bridge the gap he subscribes to between culturally-specific social practices and an abstractly-specified distinction between morally relevant and irrelevant principles (Mulhall and Swift 1996: 234–8, Bellamy and Castiglione, 1997: 605). While Rawls' use of the term 'reasonable' is ambiguous, in a primary meaning he makes an unconvincing accommodation to his communitarian critics by supplementing the 'rational' basis of the earlier argument with a 'reasonableness' which sums up the impact of the context of social practices in which we live. For example, Rawls argues that '[r]easonable persons . . . are not moved by the general good as such but desire for its own sake a social world in which they, as free and equal, can cooperate with others on terms all can accept' (Rawls 1993: 50), on the grounds of reciprocity. In this, however, he is providing us with little more than the notion that we accept a compromise for the benefits of living in a social world.

Whatever the problems with Rawls' own particular definition of the reasonable, it is clear that the looser notion of reasonableness is not appropriate in the systematic use of reason in thinking and theorizing. The looser notion can be summed up in terms of the kind of practical reason that seeks to integrate abstract universal principles with a necessarily pragmatic approach to issues of difference and contestation in the context of a particular society, in courses of action consistent with reason but not based on reason. If by 'reason' the present work had meant only 'reasonable', then an interdependence with emotion would have been far less difficult to establish. But theorizing is not concerned with setting out ideas that will be found *reasonable* by the academic or some other community (although the reception of ideas and the rhetoric of texts are both valid and important concerns), but with exploring rational arguments openly to their (conditional) conclusions. Theorists work within a community, a tradition, a literature, and a set of social practices and conventions, but the aim is not simply to arrive at consensus, let alone consensual action. While an action may be rational but unreasonable, or reasonable but not rational, *thinking* as the intellectual power of reasoning following public conventions of rationality, to produce an internally-coherent and publicly-defensible train of argument, need not be simply reduced to action, as ideology, and so the criterion of reasonableness is inappropriate.

The point is brought out well through an example. Amelie Rorty, in an otherwise thoughtful article which attempts to respect the value of emotion, sees reason in the form of reasonableness as trumping emotion, when she argues that '[i]t may be not only irrational but inappropriate to be frightened of lions in a zoo, but it is not inappropriate to be frightened before one has had time to be reasonable [in the light of] . . . one's more considered reactions' (Rorty 1980: 122).

The 'modern' dichotomy between reason and emotion also maps directly on to the 'modern' scientific dichotomy between objective and subjective, forming a clear elevation of 'objective reason' over and against 'subjective emotion'. Putnam registers clearly the negative effects, with respect to reason, of dichotomies in general as well as of the objective/subjective example in particular. He says:

> once such a dichotomy as the dichotomy between 'objective' and 'subjective' has become accepted, accepted not as a mere pair of categories but as a characterization of types of views and styles of thought, thinkers begin to view the terms of the dichotomy almost as ideological labels.
>
> (Putnam 1981: ix)

The undermining of the idea that reason has an objective character (resulting in dictates to which individuals ought to conform) can be complemented by the challenge to the idea that emotions are merely irrational subjective internal physical movements. Indeed the (rational) criteria according to which both reason and emotion can generate knowledge ensure that both forms of knowledge are both objective (public and contextual) and subjective. It is on the basis of this understanding of the terms reason and emotion as interconnected but still conceptually separate that knowledge can be seen as being able to recognize both. As Nozick notes, emotion (which for him incorporates feeling, evaluation and belief) can provide a route to the desirable unity of mind and body, as well as linking our internal experience to external reality (Nozick 1989: 91).

In the objective/subjective dichotomy, the meaning of 'rational' depended as much upon what it excluded as on what it included, and here too the meaning of 'rational' depends upon its relation to emotion.[8] But it is worth stressing that while reason and emotion, as understood here, entail one other, they are not the same. What is proposed here is not a unitary concept but an area of significant overlap on a continuum between two distinct capacities. The continuum has the pure reason of formal logic near one extreme, and pure emotional expression as in hysteria near the other. However this description is qualified by the recognition that, on the one hand, even logic is affected by emotion in a limited sense (in Hobbes's terms all thinking is driven by passions, and in that a reader's perception of even a text of logic contains feelings of being drawn toward it or of aversion from it, as part of the process of judgment). On the other hand even hysteria can be understood as in a limited sense a rational response, and takes different culturally-influenced forms.

### *Reason and emotion in knowledge of emotion*

The point of this part of the chapter is to demonstrate the rationality of emotion, and to distinguish this aim from the next one, which is to explore the emotional component of rationality.

In a broad sense, whenever we try to make sense of something we are attempting to be rational. And whenever explanation 'fits the facts', we have a rational explanation. Now these two things can refer to emotions as much as to empirical evidence, the practical world, and pieces of thinking. Reflective, considered emotions are no less authentic than spontaneous ones. Indeed Nussbaum (1990: 285) notes the crucial role played by reflection in knowledge of emotion.

As De Sousa rightly notes, the emotions are neither 'irrational', nor 'arational' 'like sensations, stomachaches or involuntary twitches . . . if they were, they would not be amenable to rational evaluation' (De Sousa 1987: 5). There are at least three links between reason and emotion which can be specified here. First, we speak of particular emotions as being 'reasonable', in the sense of being normal or appropriate, or subject to argument and justification: these are 'notions central to rationality' (ibid.). Second, we use emotions as excuses and justifications, and thus 'we assume that they have intrinsic value (good or bad) and so are *motivators*' (ibid.: 6). The 'power of an emotion to motivate is independent of its own rationality. This suggests that one role of emotions is to ground assessments of rationality regardless of whether the emotions are themselves rational' (ibid.). The third link concerns the thought-dependency of emotion. De Sousa provides a useful example when he notes that, '[i]f I am grieved by bad news, my grief cannot survive the discovery that what grieves me did not, after all, take place' (ibid.). He concludes from this example that thought-dependency suggests that emotions can be rational, 'though derivatively so. Even when emotions involve physical manifestations, it is their mental causation that defines them as emotions and grounds our evaluation of them' (ibid.).

It is important to bear in mind that the rationality of emotion is different from, though often confused with, the question of moral justification; rational and moral justification can easily arrive at different conclusions. A crucial aspect of judging the rationality of emotions (see Oakley 1992: 41–8) is their appropriateness or fitness to a given context. Emotions are rational only if two conditions are satisfied: that they are likely to further one's rational self-interest (that is, one's ends or goods), and that they exhibit a fitness to the context or situation in which they are expressed. In this way the rationality of emotion depends as much upon a social value and judgment as upon an evaluation of a particular person's emotional state or action.

De Sousa confirms the rationality of emotions at length and in detail both in his book (1987) and in the chapter, 'The Rationality of Emotions' (1980). On the question of knowledge *of* emotion, his sound starting point is that in 'various ways, emotions provide us with information about ourselves and the world' (De Sousa 1987: 107). He frames the question of knowledge of emotion in terms of objective and subjective knowledge, being concerned to demonstrate (ibid.: xv) that emotions are objective, in the sense of being subject to rational assessment. By objectivity De Sousa does not mean transcending any particular perspective, in contrast with moods which are subjective (ibid.: 148), for there are strong grounds, he argues, for a view of emotions as conveying objective information about the real world. He then considers the important problem that while 'the real world is partly the world we make' (ibid.: xvii), 'there is also being right and wrong, the achievement of creation and of knowledge' (ibid.: xviii). In other words, 'even if emotions do relate to real objects, are the properties that arouse our emotions really in those objects, or are they mere shadows of the emotions themselves?' (ibid.: 107). He concludes persuasively that 'I have argued that an objectivist answer . . . can sometimes be supported: emotions tell us things about the real world. To be sure, their mode of objectivity is relative to the characteristic inclinations and responses of human and individual nature' (ibid.: 203).

To build on De Sousa's work, what is meant by emotion here is the capacity to feel (by which is *not* meant sense experience) a variety of more or less powerful value-laden cognitive responses, understood as rational responses to experience in the form of other feelings, actions, events or ideas. This presupposes that there is an underlying rationality in the way feelings operate (notwithstanding that they can and often do become dysfunctional), and that the emotional life develops in ways which can be understood (if not always initially felt) as meaningful.

Baier's exploration of a range of emotions (not especially intellectual emotions, but things like pride, distrust, trust, hope, admiration, contempt), and her well-supported view that '[p]assions [by which she means emotions] are real, with real physical effects, just as actions are' (Baier 1985a: 128), establishes the rationality of feelings with respect to other aspects of mind and mental actions such as intentionality, action, and belief. Rorty's analysis of emotions also presupposes their rationality, and she denounces 'hard-core zealot physicalists [who] have yet to give us an account of how to proceed with the reductive analysis' of intentional states to physical ones (Rorty 1980: 117). She also notes that '[n]owhere does the mind-body problem raise its ugly head with a stiffer neck than in the analysis of the thought component of the emotions' (ibid.: 116). Armon-Jones also supports this case, observing that, if 'emotions are cognition-based, then this allows that they can be subjected to rational persuasion and criticism' (Armon-Jones 1986: 44).

Scruton also endorses the notion of the rationality of emotions, which in his view is closely tied to their social construction and to practical knowledge within a particular culture. He argues strongly that 'all emotion involves both understanding and activity', and that 'it is possible to educate an emotion, to the extent that it is possible to educate the understanding and activity that are involved in it' (Scruton 1980: 524). He makes the judgment that it is 'perhaps only a vestige of Cartesianism which prevents us from seeing this, and from seeing that a man [sic] ignorant of the art of emotion is a man who is in a significant way *confused*' (ibid.). In a similar vein, Nozick underlines the role of rationality in knowledge of emotion when he says, '[r]ationality gives us greater knowledge and greater control over our own actions and emotions and over the world' (Nozick 1993: 181).

In the earlier part of her article, Jaggar (1989) makes a number of important points about emotion which are also very helpful to understanding the rationality of the emotions, in particular in cautioning against the risk of replicating the mind/body dichotomy that is contained in the widely-popular cognitivist theory of emotion. In the body of the article Jaggar discusses the importance of attending to a knowledge of emotions, and her general postpositivist 'claim that emotion is vital to systematic knowledge' (Jaggar 1989: 149), is convincing. However her argument for recognising the epistemological value of women's 'outlaw' emotions, within the heuristic of the epistemological privilege of oppressed groups (and so within the project of feminist epistemology in this sense), is flawed. For Jaggar does not fully recognize the potential conflict between the claim to epistemological status for 'outlaw' emotions, and the call for the reeducation of emotions skewed by patriarchal socialization. The problem of deriving knowledge from unmediated experience is one of those raised in the discourse of feminist epistemology.

## *The role of emotions in knowledge and theorizing*

Emotion plays an important, indeed crucial, role in areas of practical reasoning and so even in political theory as well as in art. Macmurray for instance argues that the 'field in which emotional reason expresses itself most directly is the field of art. The artist is directly concerned to express his emotional experience of the world. His [sic] success depends upon the rationality of his emotions' (Macmurray 1962: 14).

In a range of ways it is emotion that brings political and social issues from the abstract to the determinate, that bridges the gap between the general 'that' and the particular 'this'. Young for example cogently criticizes the 'dichotomy between reason and desire [by which she means emotion] . . . in modern political theory' (Young 1987: 63). She demonstrates how in the Western tradition the notion of normative reason and the virtue of impartiality, 'stands opposed to desire and affectivity' and has operated to 'expel particularity and desire', and so not to recognize heterogeneity (ibid.: 67). Mansbridge cogently discusses the 'moral emotions' necessary to effective democracy in the light of the strong gender-coding of reason and emotion and the 'restrictive elision of the dichotomies "reason/emotion" and "male/female" (Mansbridge 1993: 357–8). Another example is found in Spelman's observation that 'there is a politics of emotion: the systematic denial of anger can be seen as a mechanism of subordination, and the existence and expression of anger as an act of insubordination' (Spelman 1989: 270). It follows then, she argues, that 'in so far as dominant groups wish to place limits on the kinds of emotional responses appropriate to those subordinate to them, they are attempting to exclude those subordinate to them from the category of moral agents' (ibid.).

But emotion also plays a vital role in reason, in the very determination of lines of thinking and theorizing which have no immediate reference to the practical world (Williams and Bendelow 1996: 151). Steuernagel articulates one conception of the way in which links between reason and emotion are important in politics as well as in theorizing (Steuernagel 1979: ch. 6). Nussbaum also notes that there are contexts in which 'the pursuit of intellectual reasoning apart from emotion will actually prevent a full rational judgment' (Nussbaum 1990: 41). Thus the scope of the role of emotions in knowledge and theorizing is not concerned only with obvious areas where passion and emotion enter politics and political theory, such as in debates over nationalism, xenophobia, ethnic cleansing, ethnocentric fascism, racism, or even multiculturalism. Between that view and the rationalist myth that disembodied and disembedded reason is a higher faculty, separate and necessarily distinct from perception, reflection and deliberation upon felt experience, there is another view.

This third conception of reason, envisaged here, refers to rational reflection, that is reflection expressed in arguments that can be defended publicly with intelligible reasons. This conception of reason utilizes emotion in a variety of ways to be specified below. Theory or knowledge can be taken to mean the outcome of theorizing which involves (conditional) closure. Theory or knowledge is something which accounts for many but not necessarily all observations and reflections, and which is expressed in a reasoned manner, that is, in a way that can be discussed and justified.

Worley is certainly right to point out that there is a weak or unsupported link in the claim of some feminist epistemologists that the 'fact that we can't get outside our culture and can't have knowledge of a world that is independent of our minds' somehow on its own gives us 'reason to believe that empathy and connectedness are what's needed' (Worley 1995: 144). She correctly notes that we 'can't reject a method just on the grounds that it leads to bias and subjectivity if any other method would also lead to bias and subjectivity' (ibid.: 146). This is why the links identified and examined here are so important, perhaps especially in the arguments concerning salience and the way emotions accompany and motor reason.

In general terms emotions play a crucial role in knowledge because the production of knowledge, the discussion of ideas, and the recognition of a piece of theorizing as knowledge, all involve social activities expressed in particular social practices. As Turner demonstrates convincingly, 'the most fundamental dimensions of face-to-face interaction involve the activation of emotions . . . for mobilising energy and attention, for attunement, for sanctioning, for moral coding, for valuing/exchange, and for decision-making' (Turner 1996: 24). In other words, 'emotions have an intrinsic as well as an instrumental value . . . life without any emotion would be life without any meaning' (Jaggar 1989: 139).

When Macmurray (1962: 3) posits that '[a]ny enquiry must have a motive or it could not be carried on at all, and all motives belong to our emotional life', he might by some be interpreted as advocating the view that intellectual enquiry and the substantive direction an argument takes are motivated by things like anger or small-mindedness or revenge. That kind of influence of emotion on the development of rational theorizing would indeed be illegitimate. However, what Macmurray is acknowledging is that at several different points the emotions play a complex and vital role in providing the dynamic for intellectual enquiry.

Before going any further, it is important to address in more detail the way in which the terms 'emotion' and 'affect' are sometimes confused, which leads to a serious misconception of the relation between reason and emotion. This confusion arises from the widespread presupposition of an opposition between 'cognitive' and 'affective' capacities. Moreover it derives from the way in which the dichotomy between abstract reason and practical reason is mapped on to one between cognitive and affective capacities. The powerful effect of the dichotomies between abstract and concrete, and object and subject, forces emotion – already designated as 'other' – into the role of concrete, and so elides emotion with body, and into the status of the merely subjective.

This chapter is concerned, among other things, to consider the *relationship* between reason and emotion, rather than proceeding on the basis of opposition and hierarchy. However, there are two grave consequences which arise from the confusion between the 'cognitive' and 'affective' capacities. One is that emotion is misidentified with body through the notion of 'affects', and the second is that the full meaning of emotion gets lost in the middle of the cognitive/affective dichotomy.

'Affective' strictly speaking refers to two phenomena which focus on the body: the affective consequences on the body of cognitive or emotional activity, and the way empirical sense data impinge on the body. It is because of the biologization of emotion, and because of the implementation of the mind/body dualism, that emotion has been reduced to, and then is only recognized in terms of, bodily sensations and states. As Harré notes, it is only since the seventeenth century that the conception of the emotions developed 'as simple, non-cognitive phenomena, among the bodily perturbations' (Harré 1986: 2). Arnold notes, furthermore, that emotions fell into disrepute also because, under the scientific paradigm, they refer to experience which is unverifiable, unobservable and unrepeatable (Arnold 1968: 9). This is another reason which accounts for the reduction of emotions to sensations, affects and behaviour.

However it is very important to recognize, as Harré (1986: 3) notes that contemporary theorists are beginning to do, that emotions are part of the mind, feelings in the mind, in contrast with feelings in the body. De Sousa also confirms that emotions are part of mind not body. 'Emotions are mental phenomena', he says (De Sousa 1987: 77), although of all the elements of what 'we call the "'mind"', emotions are the most deeply embodied' (ibid.: 47). Notwithstanding the importance of Jaggar's cautionary note mentioned earlier, the cognitivist theory of the emotions (that emotions are not simply affective states, but are 'about' something) is valuable for its recognition of the mind-based status of emotions. The cognitivist theory is, as Spelman (1989: 265) observes, 'widely taken now to be an eminently defensible one'.

The negative effects of seeing only a dichotomy between cognitive and affective capacities and of misconstruing emotion as affect lead for instance to Taylor's designation of theory as equal to contemplation, and to his view that 'theoretical understanding aims at a disengaged perspective' (Taylor 1982: 89). The problem for this view is that it cannot account for the consequence that, even when one's reflections are disengaged from sense experience and its goals, the link with the self remains and the emotions accompanying knowledge acquisition also remain intact. Taylor also dramatically articulates the (misconceived) case for the superiority of pure reason over engagement which involves emotion. We must, he says, 'distinguish this disengaged perspective from our ordinary sense of engagement, and . . . one values it as offering a higher – or in some sense superior – view of reality' (ibid.). Again this view cannot account for the manner in which the exercise of pure reason, in 'disengaged' thinking, *also* involves emotion.

In contrast with Taylor's view, body theorists such as Grosz and Butler, along with some postpositivists, have demonstrated that mind, and so reason, is embodied and situated, so that a full understanding of reason must contain a contextual element. These writers have also crucially succeeded in delineating this view without reducing the understanding of embodiedness to a species of materialism. But it is also important to emphasize, and this is a major theme of the present work, that emotion is located in the mind (part of the body), and not in the senses or affects felt in the body.

There are many ways in which emotions play a role *in* knowledge, ways in which emotion enables the use of reason. Five major methods will be examined here. They concern, first, salience, or normative as well as instrumental senses in which emotions supply value to cognitions; second, the manner in which emotions accompany intellectual concentration; third, the way they underpin the development of reason; fourth; the way emotion and reason are interconnected in language; and fifth,. the intellectual virtues.

Baier's discussion of Hume's claim that reason is, and ought to be, ruled by the passions (and by passions she means emotions), demonstrates three of the ways in which emotion plays a role in knowledge. In doing so it also illustrates that these five ways are interconnected. Baier's main point is to elucidate Hume's contention that reason should be ruled by the (emotions of the) moral sentiment merged with a pure pride (Baier 1980: 417). But her discussion elicits more broadly a respect for the role of emotions in the construction of reason, and the means by which for Hume rational knowledge of the emotions is possible and emotions underpin the development of reason.

The five links specified here between emotion and reason in theorizing do not exhaust the connections which could be made. Other links could explore the way that anxiety about a deadline can increase the speed and effectiveness of intellectual work, and the manner in which the specificity of a person's emotions (for instance in patterns of emotions, perceptions and experience of them, and the particular connotations and resonances they hold), expressed in motives, intentions, projects and endeavours, all help to define the person as an individual self. Further links could also include the way emotions enable us to defend our own interests (intellectual as well as 'personal'), competencies, abilities, and confidence.

### *Salience*

The literal meaning of salience is the quality of leaping or springing up, jutting out, of prominence among a number of objects, standing out from the rest, of conspicuousness. In terms of the way in which the emotions play a role in knowledge and theorizing, salience refers first to the way the emotions identify which observations, perceptions and reflections are significant, that is valuable, noteworthy, apt, appropriate or fitting.[9] Salience refers, second, to the manner in which the emotions pick out some cognitions as having normative value. Thus when, for example Moulton (1989: 8) argues that '[t]heory changes occur because one theory is more *satisfying* than the other, because the questions it answers are considered more *important*', she is referring not just to empirical criteria in terms of evidence etc., but to the role of salience in generating normative considerations as the basis for making judgments.

The double importance of value in emotions which these two meanings of salience highlight is attested to by Nozick (1989: 92–5). The double work of salience is also implied in Grosz's description of the two processes involved in the dynamics of languages and systems of signification. The function of salience in emotion, which provides the dynamics of theorizing and knowledge, can be likened to the role of relations of *selection* (metonymy, displacement) and relations of *combination* (metaphor, condensing) interacting together to construct a system of signification (Grosz 1990b: 98). The relational rather than dichotomous connection between metonymy and metaphor is well brought out by Grosz when she says: '[i]f the metaphoric process generates the signified from the chain of signifiers, and the metonymic process ensures that each signifier has multiple connections and associations which relate it always to other signifiers and thus give it meaning', then as she says, 'it becomes clear these two processes must work hand-in-hand' (ibid.: 103). She also discerns clearly that metaphor and metonymy are 'not readily separable but could be seen as two elements of one process, since every condensation is also a displacement . . . and every displacement relies on terms generated by condensation' (ibid.).

De Sousa's work provides a sound argument for valuing the role of emotion in theorizing through the dynamic of salience. He depicts how, '[d]espite a common prejudice, reason and emotion are not natural antagonists. On the contrary . . . when the calculi of reason have become sufficiently sophisticated, they would be powerless in their own terms, except for the contribution of emotion' (De Sousa, 1987: xv). For emotions, he goes on, help to control the 'crucial factor of *salience* among what would otherwise be an unmanageable plethora of objects of attention, interpretations, and strategies of inference and conduct' (ibid.: xv–xvi).

As De Sousa argues, as well as controlling the salience of features of perception and reasoning, emotions also circumscribe our practical and cognitive options, play a role that could be played neither by belief or desire, and tip the balance between different motivational structures. All of this confirms the irreducibility of the axiological (valuing) level to either the cognitive or strategic levels. And while patterns of salience are subjective in De Sousa's sense, they are subjective without being viciously projective (ibid.: 172). For emotions act as frames for both perception and belief (ibid.: 257).

The first way in which emotions are important in theorizing, then, concerns the way emotions work to give *normative* value to cognitions, and to identify *instrumentally* which cognitions are valuable. Emotions enable us to select and sift present as well as past perceptions for a particular end, for instance in research and thinking. Nozick recognizes the importance of the way emotional capacity constitutes one portion of our value-creating powers, in the sense that emotion as well as ethics is a source of value which reason on its own requires (Nozick 1989: 95). He views emotions as 'analog representations of values' (ibid.: 93), and indeed argues that '[e]motions are to value as beliefs are to fact' (ibid.: 92). Putnam also recognizes the value which emotions carry when he notes that '[a]ny word that stands for something people in a culture *value* (or disvalue) will tend to acquire emotive force' (Putnam 1981: 209).

Returning to the general question of the value that emotions contribute to reason, close attention is merited by De Sousa's persuasive argument that '[o]ften our emotions constitute the apprehension of properties of a certain sort that I call *axiological*' (De Sousa 1987: xv). Emotions are best regarded as a form of 'perception, the objects of which are what I call axiological properties', he says (ibid.: 45). In order to highlight the role of emotions in the double process of valuing De Sousa considers what someone would be like who had no faculty of emotion at all (ibid.: 2), and considers that they would be either an angel or a mechanism. This line of hypothesis leads him to the important conclusion that, the 'faculty of emotion is actually required for the more conventional mechanisms of rationality to function' (ibid.). For the ideas of animal-machine and Kantian angel have in common a 'complete determinacy', in the first by mechanism, in the second by reason. De Sousa argues that these are 'equally mythical', in the sense of being unattainable by human beings. For even two machines or two viruses will not behave identically under all conditions, and with respect to angels 'there is no such thing as fully determinate rationality' (ibid.: 191).

De Sousa also assesses other capacities which have an important bearing on the connection between emotion and reason. He examines how emotions contribute to the rationality of beliefs, wants and behaviour. In human beings, who exhibit intentionality, pure reason – whether cognitive or strategic – will need supplementation, he argues, because we need to know when *not* to retrieve some irrelevant information from the vast store which we possess. That is, pure reason on its own cannot help us *select* from all the information ('facts') we have. But how do we know it is irrelevant unless we have already retrieved it? He argues that 'emotions spare us the paralysis potentially induced by this predicament by controlling the salience of features of perception and reasoning'. Emotions 'temporarily mimic the informational encapsulation of perception and so circumscribe our practical and cognitive options. In several ways, this idea confirms the irreducibility of the axiological level', he says. Emotions 'tip the balance between conflicting motivational structures, but they do so neither in a merely mechanical way nor merely by adding more reasons' (ibid.: 172).

Further consequences follow from De Sousa's argument. Criteria of emotional 'success' by reference to 'paradigm scenarios' suggest that emotions are objects, while the role of emotions as determinants of salience suggests that emotions are subjective. But the subjective and objective characterizations of emotion are not incompatible, he argues convincingly, since '[p]atterns of salience can be subjective in some senses, without being viciously projective' (ibid.: 194). However if this is so, we need a concept of 'individual normality, in terms of which the rationality of an emotion might be judged. Correct axiological assessment is then control of salience by a normal scenario' (ibid.). Moreover this problem of the selection of relevant information, is 'not reducible to the problem of induction . . . [which] is about what inferences are warranted' (ibid.). For 'we need to know whether a consequence will turn out to be relevant *before drawing it*'. For if it is 'relevant and we have not retrieved it, we may act irrationally. But if it is irrelevant and we have already drawn it, we have already wasted time' (ibid.).

Both cognitive and strategic reason are on their own insufficient and deficient, De Sousa continues (ibid.: 194). Logic, he contends, 'leaves gaps. So as long as we presuppose some basic or preexisting desires, the directive power of "motivation" belongs to what controls attention, salience, and inference strategies preferred' (ibid.: 197). The 'gaps' are filled by the roles of emotion, and for this reason 'emotions are often described as guiding the processes of reasoning – or distorting them, depending on the describer's assessment of their appropriateness' (ibid.).

De Sousa has developed a convincing case that 'our emotions underlie our rational processes' (ibid.: 201). Emotions function 'to take up the slack in the rational determination of judgment and desire, by adjusting salience among objects of attention, lines of inquiry, and preferred inference patterns' (ibid.: 203). It follows that in this way, 'emotions remain *sui generis*: the canons of rationality that govern them are not to be identified with those that govern judgment, or perception, or functional desire. Instead, their existence grounds the very possibility of rationality at those more conventional levels' (ibid.).

Anderson supports this role of emotion in respect of reason in science and philosophy in her notion of rationality as reflective endorsement, since both the reflective and endorsement aspects of it involve the salience feature of emotion. She maintains that, '[r]eflective endorsement is the only test for whether a consideration counts as a reason for having any attitude or engaging in any practice of inquiry' (Anderson 1995: 53). This view is based on the argument that, 'we ask, on reflecting on the ways the consideration could or does influence our attitudes and practices and the implications of its influencing us, whether we can endorse its influencing us in those ways' (ibid.). She also acknowledges the constructed and socially contextual dimension of this understanding of reason, when she notes that this 'conception of reason as reflective self-government rejects the ideal of individualistic self-sufficiency' (ibid.).

### *Accompanying and motoring*

The second way in which emotions play a role in knowledge is closely related to the role of emotions in salience, but here focuses upon the manner in which emotions accompany and drive intellectual concentration and attention. Both in identifying salience and in accompanying and motoring inert reason, emotion crucially provides the cogency of theorizing, argument, and knowledge. The point here is that reason, on its own, is static and emotion, on its own, is dynamic: emotion shows the way to get from A to B, gives direction, selects and stimulates. In this way reason and emotion are quite interdependent. As Stocker demonstrates, there 'is as much movement, as much controlled, directed, purposive, goal-directed movement, and as much desire, force, vigour, energy, drive, urge, and urgency in intellectual action as in physical action' (Stocker 1980: 328).

This function of emotion in knowledge holds true, notwithstanding the fact that we can also be carried away, overcome and buffeted by emotions. Emotions *can* be disruptive and get in the way of rational knowledge; they can be agitations that prevent one from being able to concentrate on the train of logical reasoning. Emotions can also distort rational judgment, misinterpret rational perceptions, override rational cognitions, and be based on wrong beliefs. The validity in some cases of the judgment that a subjectivist fallacy of '*argumentum ad populum*', or appeal to emotion (Kelley 1994: 132, 134, 154), has occurred is not in doubt. As De Sousa notes, emotions have 'their peculiar way of interfering, and being susceptible to interference, at every level of thought and activity' (De Sousa 1987: 48).

Despite these possibilities, the importance of the rational role of emotions as accompaniment to trains of reasoning holds true. It also holds true despite the fact that we can have false beliefs that are rational and true beliefs that are irrational. Even here, however, as Little points out, the 'view that obtuseness is caused *only* by the obscuring effect of emotion . . . operates on the faulty picture that seeing is passive' (Little 1995: 121). The view in which emotion again gets 'cast in the familiar role of contamination . . . clouding what would otherwise be clear' (ibid.), also discounts other reasons for lack of clarity.

Emotions can also be self-absorbed, subjective in the sense of purely self-engrossing. It is from this possibility that there developed 'the old view that we are in bondage to our emotions, a bondage we can escape both in action and in the pursuit of truth' (Baier 1985a: 123). However, emotions need not be self-absorbed; when they look outward, and are directed to a purpose, they can also serve reasoning. The idea that emotions are *always* self-absorbed rests upon a false dichotomization of the subjective/objective distinction. Thus notwithstanding the possibilities of self-deception, self-feigning, and self-absorption, emotion plays an important part in the richness of experience, thought and the moral life. Moreover, emotion does not have to be equated with spontaneity, as assumed by Mansbridge (1993: 358), for emotions can be long-term stable accompaniments to thinking.

A strong emotional accompaniment is necessary for theorizing, in order to sustain the development of the comprehensive implications and consequences of a piece of argument. Without a sustaining emotional force, the development of rational implications does not occur. A line of argument, in itself, is inactive, and does not get developed without emotional agency. Thus emotions enable us to motivate our projects and endeavours. While one is engaged in theorizing (exploring concepts in a spirit of openness, in the sense of not knowing the outcome in advance) one constantly monitors, supervizes, and reflects upon that thinking. Thinking entails not just rational judgment (such as 'does it follow?', 'is it consistent?'), but also emotional responses (favourable and unfavourable, comfortable and uncomfortable, positive and negative). These emotional judgments are made by sweeping the range of the memory and selecting material from it which is relevant for the thinking in hand.

It is important to distinguish emotion from judgment, and to clarify that emotion and judgment are not being conflated here. Writers such as Solomon (1976) take the cognitivist theory of emotions to the extreme of arguing that emotions are not only 'about' something but are judgments. Spelman (1989), takes the same view, equating emotion with a combination of feeling and judgment. However there is an important distinction to be made between emotion and judgment. Judgments evaluate the weight of different considerations, which are expressed in rational arguments (underpinned and motivated by perhaps conflicting emotional accompaniments). If this is the case and the range of considerations can all be taken to be equally rational, then judgment cannot be made simply on grounds of rationality; but neither is it the same as emotion. Judgment is made by weighing up and coming to a decision as to which emotional accompaniment (which takes into account wider questions of relevance, appropriateness, etc.) carries the strongest positive force.

One important reason for emphasizing that emotion and judgment are not the same is brought out by Velleman. He argues plausibly that reasons for acting are not the same as motives, and that our actions (including thinking and knowledge) are neither driven by our inclinations, nor simply determined by conformity to moral principles. As he emphasizes, there is a realm of autonomous rational activity which is distinct from both the realm of motivating inclination and the realm of moral principles. Velleman identifies this realm of autonomous rational activity as 'behaving in, and out of, a knowledge of what you're doing. And it thereby exerts a rational influence distinct from the motivational influence of the desire that it's about' (Velleman 1996: 725).

What Velleman's discussion brings out, and what is important for the present argument, is one of the ways in which reason and emotion are distinct. The arena of autonomous, conscious, deliberate and reflective activity, which is crucial to thinking and knowledge, is an arena in which reason and emotion are indeed distinct. However Velleman understates the connection between these two. He is led to overstate his case by the desire to distinguish between reason and emotion.

Several important links can still be articulated, however. First, in the example Velleman gives about acting to prevent a glass breaking, if reason and motive were opposed it would cause a conflict in the person. Second, a reason carries its own emotional charge in the salience and memory senses. And third, for a reason to be compelling, for one to *want* to act upon it, an emotional commitment to it is involved.

Hobbes understood the force of the emotions, in both their positive and negative guises. Negatively, emotions can be expressed in a rhetoric which whips up a rabble or multitude and leads to the breakdown of order and the overturn of legitimate authority. Positively, emotions drive all endeavours and purposes. They also operate uniquely in each individual, even though their general characteristics are universal. Emotions also have a third guise in Hobbes, in making us restless, with no final good to arrive at. There is a positive dimension of this aspect, in driving us to seek greater understanding and less conditional philosophical meaning. The secondary literature on Hobbes overwhelmingly highlights Hobbes's castigation of the force of negative emotions in politics and the public realm, but for the most part overlooks the positive features of his view of emotion (but see Skinner 1996).

More generally, the role of emotions in accompanying and driving our intellectual concentration and attention exemplify the way in which all our conscious life is accompanied by feelings which are not simply affects. Mainstream philosophy tends to ignore or discount any significance of this characteristic of experience. Indeed only cognitive experience, narrowly understood, tends to count for much in mainstream philosophy. This view is built upon the false dichotomization of reason and emotion. Everything we know and understand through discursive subjectivity is immanent at any particular time, although different knowledges and understandings are foregrounded at different times. What transforms this mass of knowledge and understanding into a vast filing system is the role of emotions. The immanence of any particular piece of material is captured, and we are thus reminded of it and able to draw upon it, by the *emotional resonance* or emotional charge that accompanies all consciousness. In this way the very notion of significance, the manner in which a piece of material from this mass can be deemed significant, refers first to this capacity of the emotions to pluck it out of the filing system, and second to the emotional charge it carries. Sometimes emotions are markers of a strong feeling tied to the memory of an experience or idea. Stronger emotion is evoked when the full memory is resuscitated. Sometimes emotions guide the intellect to the memory of a judgment which has been made in the past.

A useful example of the role of reason in intellectual life (the 'life of reason') can be found in the operation of memory and forgetting. With increasing age it is common for the ability to recall to deteriorate, so that one forgets for instance the details of the arguments of different books. What is always retained however is an emotional residue of how one *felt* about the work: for instance whether one liked it or not, thought it was original or not, agreed with it or not, found it distressing, compelling, distasteful, severe, persuasive, austere or not. These overall impressions, formed at the time, remain with us. Usually they are judgments of the whole, but are sometimes about one part such as the beginning or the end, or about one distinctive feature (such as Oakeshott's style of writing, Condren's use of language, Berlin's architecture of dichotomy). In this way we draw on memory in order to recapture thought. We start with feelings about it, and on this basis are enabled to retrieve the detail of the argument. The role played by the initial feeling is crucial, for it provides the entrance into one's assessment and memory of the thought, and also helps to select memories of the detail of reasoning.

These are important features of intellectual life, for the life of reason is not just about the *rational* quality of a piece of argument, important as that is. The task of resuscitating and understanding the rational quality of a piece of argument cannot be sustained without the emotional responses which accompany it. These emotional responses include those concerning the connections of a piece of the argument to the whole text and those about the emotional charge attendant in the writing. Moreover it is important to recognize that such emotional responses are elicited by a text and are particular in each reader. Emotional responses accompanying the commencement of a book, for example, are crucial. If, as one starts reading, the book is found interesting, then there is an emotional quickening of interest, and a judgment to take it seriously. At the other end of the scale there might be a sense of recoil, or of confusion, and in between these responses there is a flat sense of suspending judgment until further on.

However, it is important not to suggest that the writer presents a rational argument to which the reader has an emotional response. Emotion and reason are involved in both writer and reader, and the rhetoric of the text is important in conveying and in being a medium of transmission of an interdependence of reason and emotion. It is precisely because of the interconnection between reason and emotion in the writing and reception of a text, that the interpretive scope of a text exists. Thus emotions are involved in a complex way, in enabling us to have memories (that is summaries of experience) and to evoke memories (both general and intellectual). Moreover, emotions enable us to link up, connect, and relate different memories and perceptions and other emotions. Without emotion, our experience through time would be disjointed and discontinuous. Emotions enable us to respond, that is feel a response, both instantly and later on in reflection, to events, ideas, and pieces of reasoning. Furthermore, in describing a piece of thinking to someone else, one typically does not start with a close description of the reasoning. This would render the audience all at sea. What is required is a colourful description or some other summation of the whole, and such a characterization relies very strongly on communicating and eliciting an emotion.

Care and concern as well as interest are emotions which are crucial to the way in which emotions accompany and motor reason, although they are not always recognized as such. Oakley outlines two important ways in which this is so. First, a researcher's dispassionate interest, or a judge's disinterested impartiality, can nevertheless 'express a passionate commitment to truth or justice respectively'. And second, we can distinguish unemotional senses of care (for instance, 'day care' or 'nursing care') from the legitimately emotional sense which is present in intellectual work (Oakley 1992: 36–7).

### *Underpinning the development of reason*

The third way in which emotions play a role in theorizing is by underpinning the development of reason. Emotional development occurs in the private realm, in the family (however conventionally or unconventionally defined), in coming to understand and use love, hate, connection, dependence, autonomy, interdependence, and responsibility. This kind of emotional development is a necessary condition for the development of reason in the private realm, as well as in a public setting in work situations, with colleagues, in professional relations, in academic study, and in philosophy. The value of this crucial emotional development for reasoning, which cannot be provided in the public setting, often goes unrecognized in our Western liberal tradition.

Within the liberal tradition, built upon a crucial public/private divide mapped on to mind/body and autonomous/constrained dichotomies, it has been an article of faith that individuals make (moral) decisions through the exercise of independent rational freedom. That is, they make autonomous rational choices, and the making of such choices is seen as a cognitive faculty. The liberal tradition since Kant assumes that rational free choice so defined is a moral good in itself. Individualistic rationalistic liberalism privileges the self's freedom to act in the world over freedom within interdependence and relation. However, the logical conclusion of the idea of cognitive rational independence is unworkable, for rational choices, in themselves, are built upon and presuppose an individual with a well-nourished and continuing emotional interdependence. This emotional basis, this 'becoming oneself', requires at least two things. It requires an individual with a rich sense of situatedness. And it can only be achieved through an adequate experience of care in which trust, love and hate have been learned and expressed and taken responsibility for, and in which the multiple identities of the individual (for instance as daughter, sister, girl, dancer, friend, historian) can develop.

Support for the role of emotions in underpinning the development of reason comes from a variety of sources. Skinner, in his recent book on Hobbes (1996), implicitly gives powerful weight to the idea of the limits of reason, the conditionality of rationality, and the dependence of effective reason on a developed emotional capacity. The social mapping of 'ratio' and 'oratio' on to science and rhetoric and so on to reason and emotion is clear, as is Skinner's implicit endorsement of the general view that the terms of each pair are positively related, not oppositional. He observes that 'Hobbes's . . . contention is thus that, if the findings of civil science are to be credited, they will have to be proclaimed with eloquence, since reason cannot in itself hope to prevail' (Skinner 1996: 352–3). Skinner goes on that '[t]he conception of civil science embodied in *Leviathan* rests on the assumption that reason is of small power in the absence of eloquence' (ibid:. 376).

Tully adds weight to this viewpoint when he discusses the limits and limitations of rational agreements. Whereas conventional thinking has the capacity only to lead to rational agreement (including the agreement to disagree), a form of critical enquiry which goes beyond this has the capacity to lead to the more important goal of shared understanding. It is not reason that is the essential ingredient in any shared understanding. Rather it is trust, which is affectively (by which he means emotionally) rather than cognitively acquired. Tully says that 'once we free ourselves from the convention that we are free and rational only if we can justify the grounds of any uses we follow', then 'we can see that there is a multiplicity of ways of being rationally guided by rules of use' (Tully 1989: 183). As he puts it, '[b]etween the Charybdis of autonomous reflection and the Scylla of the dead weight of custom lies the vast, Aristotelian landscape, where our critically reflective games of freedom have their home' (ibid.).

Frank considers how emotions play a vital role in social interaction generally, in supplying 'commitment devices that help resolve . . . dilemmas' arising from a narrow view of rationality as self-interest, where rational action is that which most efficiently promotes the pursuit of the actor's interest (Frank 1988: 5). Kroon discusses the way emotions can underpin the use of reason in a policy-making context of nuclear deterrence. He argues that because of the inertness of reason and the possible multiple rational responses to a situation, 'the ineluctable role that emotion plays in our lives' is one of the 'important components of our rational make-up'. Taking the example of anger, he contends soundly that 'anger is the sort of emotion that can "make" an agent do the rational as well as the irrational' (Kroon 1996: 368). It is 'only if the agent is "overcome" by anger, and as a result is blind to rational-making features of options, that we can fairly accuse the agent of acting irrationally' (ibid.), whereas 'the situations that provoke her to act out of anger may well be ones where her actions continue to be rational but where anger is the appropriate response' (ibid.). Kroon makes a strong case that the idea of 'the angry agent as inevitably irrational . . . comes from a tradition that is now generally rejected' (ibid.).

### *Language*

The fourth way in which emotions play an important role in theorizing concerns the expression of theorizing in language. Language is never simply a neutral instrument for naming. Language is saturated with value so that we respond to language with both reason and emotion. It carries an emotional force, as well as being rhetorical in the sense that its meaning depends upon its use, which is always particular. Language is also metaphorical, generating proliferating chains of association. As Grimshaw (1996) discusses, rules attempt to reduce and control this proliferation, but the use of language can involve rule-breaking as well as being rule-governed. Metaphors are not invented by fiat; they catch cultural meanings. And a particular command of language is shared by speakers at a specific time. Philosophical theories are not exempt from these features, for they are always expressed in language, and therefore they generate responses which cannot be controlled. Thus it is also through the way in which language operates that all reason has an emotional charge which is inescapable.

In a recent article, Aronovitch makes a convincing case for the rationality of analogical reasoning and the important role of metaphor as 'fundamental to reasoning and justification in law, morality and politics' (Aronovitch 1997: 83). A strong argument can also be made that analogical reasoning and metaphor are just as important in theoretical argument. (See Prokhovnik

1991: chs 1, 2.) On the importance of the contributory role of metaphor and analogy to reason (specifically with respect to political reasoning), Aronovitch notes that the 'presence of images, not to mention more discursively presented analogies, far from being an indication of unreason is rather a manifestation of the form that reasoning typically and rightly takes in politics' (Aronovitch 1997: 86–7).

A further consequence follows from the argument that all thinking has an emotional charge which sustains it and provides it with coherence. It is this quality which is picked up in attending to the rhetoric of a text. In this way emotions not only enable us to respond in action, that is in the action of using language, propelling reason. They also enable us to express the reason and the emotion in the non-neutral vehicle of language. The role of emotions in language is well expressed in Nussbaum's *Love's Knowledge.* One of Nussbaum's major themes in that work is the preoccupation with the way in which, 'with respect to any text carefully written and fully imagined, an organic connection [exists] between its form and its content' (Nussbaum 1990: 4).

### *Intellectual virtues*

The fifth way in which emotions are important to theorizing concerns the 'intellectual virtues'. In common parlance, 'spoken from emotion rather than reason', means spoken from a motive such as anger, envy, love, hate, jealousy, which clouds the mind, obscures reason. Intellectual virtues like fair-mindedness, honesty and integrity are commonly held to be exempt from motives which cloud the mind. However, when the distinction between emotion and the intellectual virtues is considered in more detail, it becomes clear that it is a complex one, for the intellectual virtues themselves also involve emotion. They involve emotion in a positive sense, rather than in a negative, immediate, passionate, clouding sense.

Goleman's work (1995) is relevant to this discussion. He points to the importance of emotion, not only in the sense of the intelligent knowledge of emotion, but also in the sense of the impact of emotion on theoretical intelligence. Goleman argues that the conventional view of human intelligence has been far too narrow, and that emotions play a much greater role in thought, decision-making and individual success than is commonly acknowledged. 'Emotional intelligence' has been underrated, for capacities such as self-awareness, impulse control, persistence, zeal and self-motivation, empathy and social deftness, all crucially involve emotion. Goleman also claims plausibly that emotional intelligence is not fixed at birth, and that it can be nurtured and strengthened. All these points support the view that emotion influences the development of the intellectual virtues.

The intellectual virtues refer to those capacities and abilities, whose meaning is constructed and whose developed use is learned, which are virtues or 'excellences' (Stocker 1980: 334) involved in developing good habits, good patterns of intellectual theorizing, and good passions of intellectual life which 'must be mastered and developed if we are to get on intellectually' (ibid.: 325). Stocker includes under this term examples like 'directing the mind as opposed to letting it wander; . . . [learning] to recognize and keep to the point; not to stop thinking when the problem is too easy or too difficult; not to be satisfied with just any answer' (ibid.). He also includes the capacity 'not to be too concerned with detail at the expense of the general, nor the general at the expense of detail' (ibid.).

Reason and emotion are crucially interlinked in the intellectual virtues, for to establish these good intellectual habits requires what Stocker calls the 'intellectual emotions' (ibid.: 330). These include a harnessing of the emotions to intellectual ends, the nourishing and refining of certain emotions, and a requirement for attention and respect to be given to certain emotions. Stocker also includes capacities like 'caring for the subject and having care in it', which he notes 'are humanly essential to doing a certain sort of intellectual work and doing it well' (ibid.: 331).

The links between reason and emotion in the intellectual virtues are very important to the argument of this chapter. They indicate one of the ways in which philosophy – the epitome of theorizing composed of abstract reason 'untainted by emotion' – is concerned not just with conceptual relations, or with an 'articulated body of truths or statements, and . . . formal patterns of argument, evidence, and proof' (ibid.: 326) as the dominant 'modern' definition has contended. Philosophy also involves a dynamic of theorizing in which reason and emotion interact in the intellectual virtues. Intellectual activity involves having a commitment to openness and a sympathy with intellectual problems. Moreover, as Stocker depicts it, we 'investigate, try out solutions, follow leads and arguments, mull things over, form hypotheses, consider alternatives, review what has gone before, use our imagination, engage in criticism' (ibid.: 328). Philosophy crucially involves dynamic process, and this is what Stocker means when he refers to the active nature of theoretical intellect (ibid.: 325). It is emotions that provide precisely that dynamic.

Not only is the dynamic process through which philosophy is composed crucial to the achievement of, as well as the meaning of, the conceptual relations that are its output. That dynamic process is also crucial to its output being understood by others. Conceptual relations are not convincing or unconvincing simply in themselves; as Stocker demonstrates there 'is no purified intellect' (ibid.: 328). Conceptual relations are convincing or unconvincing through an engagement with actual persons (or their texts) involved in dynamic theorizing, all undertaken within a particular intellectual context. It is clear that intellectual work does not happen nor have meaning in a vacuum of purely abstract concepts. Rather, it takes place in a context of intellectual practices in which the emotions as well as the reasoning of the actors are actively engaged, in the form of the intellectual virtues.

Intellectual work is in this sense crucially socially constructed, to the extent that neither the reason involved in its composition nor the conceptual relations of its output are determined by abstract principles external to the process.

In terms of the kinds of relation between reason and emotion that are explored in this chapter, there are two capacities which are sometimes regarded as intellectual virtues which are not directly relevant to the current argument. Their specification helps to identify the kind of link that is examined here. In the current work the intellectual virtues do not refer to intellectual honesty and intellectual scrupulousness (Stocker 1980: 324) and such reciprocal intellectual vices as arrogance and closed-mindedness, plagiarism and sloppiness. While these virtues and vices are undoubtedly extremely potent and influential, the force of their moral content is beyond the scope of this inquiry. Also excluded from consideration are intellectual emotions as examined by Averill. By 'intellectual emotions', Averill has in mind 'interior emotions' of which hope is exemplary, emotions which 'tend to be primarily cognitive or intellectual in nature, with little bodily involvement' (Averill 1996: 25). Hope is too generalized and nonspecific an emotion to be included here.

It is important to recognize, as Stocker outlines, the way that the intellectual emotions can play a dysfunctional as well as functional role. He notes that one 'can be involved in intellectual error and failure because one does not have enough of the right intellectual emotion – for example, care and respect for a discipline' (Stocker 1980: 332). The converse is also true, that 'by having too much of such an emotion one can go wrong'. He gives the example that if 'one has too much care and respect for a discipline, one may do nothing but march up and down in the same place for all one's intellectual life' (ibid.).

It is also important to reaffirm that in specifying the interaction of reason and emotion in intellectual work in terms of intellectual virtues such as forms of respect, attention and care, a case is not thereby being made or established for intellectual work as thereby somehow 'subjective or nonrational' (ibid.: 333). Such a judgment would depend upon subscribing to subject/object and rational/irrational dichotomies which are deeply misplaced. As Stocker notes, some emotions, for instance, 'letting one's intellect be guided by one's hopes or fears' (ibid.), may indeed transmit subjective and nonrational features to intellectual work. But as he says of his own work, and this also holds for the treatment undertaken here, there is 'no reason to believe either that the emotions I have been considering do this or that anything I have argued suggests or depends on their doing so' (ibid.).

## The social construction of emotion

With some of the important links between reason and emotion in theorizing now identified, this section focuses upon the features of a particular understanding of the social construction of emotions. The development of the argument for the social construction of emotion takes up some of the threads discussed earlier in this chapter in the work on social construction by Rorty (1980), Armon-Jones (1986) and Scruton (1980).

A double problem is being tackled in this section. One part is that, notwithstanding the current vogue in some philosophical circles for the cognitivist theory of emotions, a foundational biological explanation of the emotions remains extremely influential more generally. The serious attention paid to Pinker's new book (1998) bears witness to the continuing but misplaced attraction of sociobiological explanations. Foundational biological explanation not only discounts a social constructionist understanding of the emotions, but is also important, more broadly, in sustaining a reason/emotion dichotomy that devalues the role of emotions in knowledge (Lutz 1996: 153–4). The other part of the problem is that the naturalized dichotomy between reason and emotion, which underpins the widespread notion of the biological causation of emotions, has itself been applied to explanation in philosophy and the social sciences. The object of this section of the chapter, then, is to argue that no mind/body or nature/culture dichotomy between reason and emotion can be sustained once the social construction of reason and emotion is recognized.

There are strong grounds for arguing that the mapping of the whole range of heavily weighted dichotomies, and in particular the mind/body and man/woman dualisms, on to reason and emotion is not required by the logic of concepts. This chapter has so far examined the interdependence of reason and emotion in theorizing. The next analytical step of the overall argument of the book will be (in Chapter Three) to show that the mapping of the mind/body dualism on to a dichotomy between man and woman can also be challenged. By showing that the operation of these important links between reason and emotion is such that they do not inherently require a gender distinction, the argument up to this point has seriously undermined the idea of the presence of a natural sex difference dictating a reason/emotion dichotomy. Indeed the argument identifying the interdependence of reason and emotion in theorizing is designed to advance the position that the *dichotomous* connection between reason and emotion breaks down, and is replaced by an open-ended range of relational connections, once it is recognized that the operation of salience, emotions accompanying and motoring reason, the intellectual virtues, and so on are not gender-specific capacities.

Before delineating the features of the social construction of the emotions, it is important to say a word about the social construction of reason. The social construction of reason has already been partially established, by some postmodern thinkers, as well as by postpositivist philosophers of science, writers within the field of philosophy of history, and feminist theorists such as Grosz (1993). The discussion earlier in this chapter of the term 'reason', and the links established between reason and emotion, also point to a social constructionist view. It is also clear that the social constructions of reason and emotion do not occur independently of each other, and that much that is said about social construction in relation to emotion applies also to reason.

However, in arguing for the social construction of reason, it is important also to note three criteria that remain constant within the framework of at least the traditional Western conception of reason. Along with the social constructionist view of reason, three things must be retained: the idea of reason as a capacity; the role of logical rules such as non-contradiction (See Lovibond 1989, Johnson 1993, 1994) (although what is meant by such rules will differ across cultures and across time); and the necessity in any particular case of actually providing a reasoned argument. Thus, the recognition that reason is socially constructed does not involve any notion of reason and its rules as arbitrary.

The history of the term 'social construction' covers a variety of meanings and usages. The idea of social construction can be used to refer to many important different matters: doing an activity in a certain way; the agent's consciousness of it and awareness in doing it; their reflection upon what is happening; its social meaning; its social value; its mediated quality. And while some practices are clearly more socially-constructed than others, even supposedly elemental activities such as breast-feeding have complex socially-constructed dimensions. For instance decisions concerning breast-feeding, especially in Western countries, are influenced by conflicting ideologies of a baby-centred 'naturalness', a male partner's primary claim on a woman's body, and an ideology promoting women as gender-neutral career individuals. But the core value of the constructionist position with respect to emotion is that, as Armon-Jones puts it, it 'goes beyond traditional theories of emotion as natural phenomena' (Armon-Jones 1986: 34). It becomes unconvincing to maintain that just because something is natural, its explanation and treatment and a positive ethical status follows from its 'naturalness' in a direct, automatic and unmediated fashion, when it is remembered that something like disease is also 'natural'.

It is crucial to differentiate clearly between two forms of social constructionism which are often confused but can readily be distinguished. The first is a social *constructionist* understanding which maintains that particular actions can only be understood as particulars, and are subject to rational appraisal. The second is a social *constitutionist* explanation which is deterministic and dependent upon causal conditions. Social – and cultural – construction refers here to the former, the idea that all human experience and understanding (of subjectivity, intersubjectivity, the social environment, the natural environment) is experienced not only through the level of language, thinking, and ideas, but also through the social meanings and social values expressed in social practices. In particular the distinction between construction and constitution refers to two very different accounts of the relation between a felt emotion and the socioculturally-prescribed system of functional significance in which it is registered. The constructionist position emphasizes the value of the first part of the relation, the felt emotion, while the constitutionist position emphasizes the second, the prescribed system. The form of social constructionism employed here regards emotions as contextual in the sense that they are, in part, necessarily socioculturally *acquired* but not socioculturally *determined* responses, neither as felt nor in their understanding.

In what follows it will also become clear that, notwithstanding the narrow anti-biological and anti-individualist strains of some social constructionist views, the characterization of social construction proposed here can be accepted as having a non-dichotomous form. It is thus not opposed to either an interactionist or a processual view of emotions, as outlined by Williams and Bendelow (1996: 146–7). The denial of the roles of nature, biology and individual agency by some social constructionist views does not in itself rule out of court a social constructionist understanding which is non-dichotomous. Furthermore, the crude social determinism of some social constructionist views does not invalidate the central social constructionist principles of non-deterministic social meanings, anti-foundationalism, and interpretation. These three principles hold that all our knowledge and experience is mediated through social and cultural practices, and through a linguistically and discursively formed set of meanings. The principles also hold that there is no attainable bedrock of reality, experience or nature underneath our mutable experience to which to appeal, and that all actions, responses, events and experience require interpretation since there is no automatically accepted, naturally 'given' meaning which necessarily trumps other meanings. Moreover as Jones puts it, '[o]ur project is neither to impose abstract categories onto a presumptively passive social reality nor to assume that social experiences produce concepts in an unmediated, automatic way' (Jones, K. 1990: 781).

Jaggar (1989) provides an important summary of six of the ways in which emotions are socially constructed. The first is found in the way that 'children are taught deliberately what their culture defines as appropriate responses to certain situations', and the second is that on a 'less conscious level, children also learn what their culture defines as the appropriate ways to express the emotions that it recognises.' Third, on an 'even deeper level, cultures construct divergent understandings of what emotions are'.[10] Fourth, the cognitive character of emotions means that they 'require concepts, which may be seen as socially constructed ways of organising and making sense of the world.' The fifth way in which emotions are socially constructed is that emotions are 'simultaneously . . . made possible and limited by the conceptual and linguistic resources of a society.' Jaggar adds that this 'philosophical claim is borne out by empirical observation of the cultural variability of emotion . . . Even apparently universal emotions, such as anger or love, may vary crossculturally.' Sixth, the 'emotions that we experience reflect prevailing forms of social life' (Jaggar 1989: 135).

There are three main features which establish the argument for a social construction, as against a biological 'naturalness' of emotions. These are the sense in which emotions are contextual, the role of individual agency and reflection, and emotions as dynamic process.

### *Emotions as contextual*

Support for the contextual feature of the social construction of emotions comes from a wide variety of writers. For instance, Scruton takes as his starting point the notion that the 'feelings, like the will, are capable of education' (Scruton 1980: 522). Because 'all emotion involves both understanding and activity', he argues that it 'follows that it is possible to educate an emotion, to the extent that it is possible to educate the understanding and activity that are involved in it' (ibid.: 524). Indeed Scruton maintains that it is 'perhaps only a vestige of Cartesianism which prevents us from seeing this, and from seeing that a man [sic] ignorant of the art of emotion is a man who is in a significant way *confused*' (ibid.).

Baier acknowledges the importance of social context in the construction of emotions when she describes how '[o]ur words for feelings, words like jealousy, respect, envy, pride, love, trust, fear, hope, suspicion, anger, despair, are, as Aristotle knew, words for the feelings possible to *social* animals, and social categories often enter into their definition' (Baier 1985a: 123). Nussbaum adds to this argument when she provides a contextualist reminder that emotions must not be taken as foundational. While it follows in general terms from their social construction that emotions could not be regarded as foundational, Nussbaum notes in particular that emotions 'are not self-certifying sources of ethical truth' (Nussbaum 1990: 42).

Waltraud Ernst convincingly details an interesting example of the social construction of reason and emotion, through the investigation of a specific historical case-study. Her study concerns madness among the colonial population in nineteenth-century India. Against those who assert a decisive correlation between gender and madness, she argues for a 'relational model of gender' (Ernst 1996: 357) in which the role of gender in madness is contextualized. She shows how the understanding of madness in this case depends upon gender being recognized as a factor which is not necessarily as important as 'other factors, such as social class, ethnicity and assumptions of colonial prestige and racial superiority' (ibid.: 381).

Harré identifies four important aspects of the contextual nature of emotions as socially constructed. The first is that, as he puts it, it is an 'ontological illusion' that 'there is something *there*, the emotion, of which the emotion word is a mere representation', an 'abstract and detachable "it"' (Harré 1986: 4). The second aspect is that because emotions are culturally specific it follows there can be no meaningful theory of universal emotions, and the third aspect is that we can seek to abstract, reify, and universalize from concrete episodes, scenes, and people, only 'at our peril' (ibid.). The fourth aspect of the contextual nature of emotion as socially constructed concerns the way in which emotions are 'strategic', in that they crucially 'play roles in forms of action', where 'actions occur in situations' (ibid.: 12). In consequence, Harré underlines, 'the investigation of an emotion must be widened to include the social contexts in which their display and even their being felt (for those cultures that recognize emotional feelings) is proper' (ibid.).

The argument for emotions as contextual is designed to make a major point, namely that it is not necessary to the social constructionist case to exclude, in a dichotomous manner, the role of other factors. Social construction can be defined in several ways, one of which is that social construction (of some aspects) is posited against the natural biological basis (of other aspects), in a manner which thus retains a naturalized base for the distinction between the two. Grosz, in *Volatile Bodies*, rightly objects to social constructionist theory on this ground, and goes on to develop an alternative theory based on difference (Grosz 1994: 16–17). But given that the form of social construction which depends upon a naturalized basis of distinction is untenable, her view is not incompatible with the relational constructionism put forward here. Furthermore it is not at all clear how 'difference' is to be perceived and recognized, if not through socially constructed practices which realize it.

In coming down on the social constructionist side in the debate on theories of the source of emotions, it is not necessary to take a narrowly constructionist view, which would see social construction as the only factor at work. The present work acknowledges the role of other factors, but sees social construction as the crucial, dynamic force at work in explanation. De Sousa is therefore surely correct when he sums up that the contextualist view is crucial (De Sousa 1987: 45), for 'physiology generates no theory of how emotions can have objects, or any kind of meaning' (ibid.: 48), while contextualism does not deny the important insights offered by other theories. For example, he observes that '[f]rom the feeling theory, we must retain the importance of felt quality' (ibid.: 46). From 'behaviourism, we must remember that most emotions are intrinsically tied to the organization of our capacities for action, interaction, and reaction' (ibid.), and the 'cognitive theory draws our attention to the constitutive role of information' (ibid.). But 'the evolutionary perspective suggests that those capacities have roots far older than our birth, even when they are most specific to particular individuals' (ibid.).

Both of the intransigently polarized naturalist and constitutionist extremes can be refuted in favour of a relational constructionist position. For instance Ben-Ze'ev and Oatley (1996) provide a sound argument for resisting a naturalist classification in terms of 'basic' emotions such as those associated with biological evolution and survival, and 'non-basic' emotions such as those associated with a social and intentional sphere.

A complex example of the importance of recognizing that emotion is not simply biologically given emerges from Lutz's study of how emotion is *conceived* as gendered in contemporary American society, a perception not borne out by her findings. Perceptions of emotional patterns and their meaning can, *because* they are constructed, be inaccurate as well as accurate. As Lutz says, because it is *constructed* that emotion is 'relatively chaotic, irrational, and antisocial, its existence vindicates authority and legitimates the need for control. By association with the female, it vindicates the distinction between the hierarchy of men and women' (Lutz 1996: 166). Moreover, Lutz notes, 'the cultural logic connecting women and emotion corresponds to and shores up the walls between' a public/private dichotomy, between 'the spheres of private, intimate (and emotional) relations in the (ideologically) female domain of the family and public, formal (and rational) relations in the primarily male domain of the marketplace' (ibid.).

The constitutionist extreme is represented by Harré's assertion that '[w]e can do only what our linguistic resources and repertoire of social practices permit or enable us to do' (Harré 1986: 4). Armon-Jones provides a strong argument against the social constitutionist position that all emotion is 'an irreducibly sociocultural product' (Armon-Jones 1986: 37–40).

Between these two extremes, the relational contextualist constructionist position understands as integrated *three* elements. First are 'natural' emotional predispositions, though even these are only understood through a cultural interpretation (see the section on memory and history below). Second are socioculturally-prescribed rules of emotional meaning, function and expectation. The experience of shame, for instance, involves cultural knowledge and differs cross-culturally. The third is the role of individual agency in experiencing and potentially understanding an emotion as a particular and unique event.

Neither the naturalist nor the constitutionist positions can take into account each other's source of explanation, let alone this third element, because both positions are tied to (opposite) causal, determinist explanations of emotions. The relational constructionist view does not integrate the three elements by holding that some emotions are natural while others are sociocultural products. (The problems involved in such a thesis are prodigious.) Rather, it argues that emotions are dynamically built up through experience and through sociocultural learning upon predispositions, forming patterns which are reinforced, but are also subject to the possibility of reflection and change and understanding over time.

The relational constructionist view also avoids the inadequate and dichotomous choice presented by the naturalist and constitutionist positions, as they map on to the body/mind dichotomy through views of emotion as either biological (about bodily affects) or sociocultural (about mental states). Not only are the either/or choices posed here inadequate in describing emotion; they also misrepresent the two things they describe. As Jaggar cogently sums up, 'mature human emotions are neither instinctive nor biologically determined, although they may have developed out of presocial, instinctive responses' (Jaggar 1989: 143). Like 'everything else that is human, emotions in part are socially constructed; like all social constructs, they are historical products, bearing the marks of the society that constructed them' (ibid.).

A further important aspect of the contextual nature of emotion is the notion of emotion not as a fixed entity but as a *process* (logical, dynamic, in time) in which each of its dimensions (the behavioural, social context, agency) plays a part. When emotion is recognized as occurring as an integrated process, it cannot any longer be regarded as either an uncontrolled response or a cold colourless appraisal. Emotions are cognitive, social, individual, interactional, linguistic and physiological, and draw on the human body, human consciousness and the world around the person. They are embodied experience but cannot be reduced to body.

Thus, social construction need not be seen as one side of a culture/nature dichotomy, with a natural or biological explanation on the other side, but can recognize the interdependency and interconnection between nature and culture. This is, incidentally, one of the most important insights found in Gilligan's work (1993) on moral development. To reiterate, the conception of social construction employed here entails that on the one side nature is understood as socially constructed, in the sense that we cannot apprehend 'nature' directly, free from the mediation of individually and culturally-constructed understandings. On the other side, culture is not independent of nature. It follows that the culture/nature opposition is not itself simply natural, because it does not have to be accepted as a given. In its present form it is a construction of 'modern' science and philosophy, closely related to other dichotomies such as objective/subjective and mind/body.

'Modern' science and philosophy have depended upon these dichotomies appearing to be natural and neutral. Hartsock notes for example how, in the construction of the dichotomous 'other', sociologically-particular judgments, of women as emotional and colonized peoples as primitive and non-rational, were transformed. 'What is actually a sociological point', she says, 'becomes labeled as being biological, or preferably, metaphysical' (Hartsock 1990: 162).

The challenge to the human/nature dualism could therefore be extended much farther than Plumwood (1995) undertakes. Her effort is focused upon refuting the devaluation of nature, one side of the dichotomy, but in doing so she leaves intact the terms of the dichotomous relation itself, and the 'givenness' of the dichotomy. Plumwood argues that according to the human/nature dualism, what 'is taken to be authentically and characteristically human, defining of the human, as well as the ideal for which humans should strive' is what is thought to separate and distinguish the human and the animal, 'especially reason and its offshoots', rather than being 'found in what is shared with the natural and animal (e.g. the body, sexuality, reproduction, emotionality, the sense, agency)' (Plumwood 1995: 156).

What is proposed here is a form of social construction that is not set against nature or natural construction. As Grosz (1994: 12) rightly emphasizes, bodies are cultural weavings of biology; understood in this way there is no dualism between the things represented by essence and social construction.

Another major theme of the argument for emotions as contextual is that a social constructionist position does not have to identify completely with the cognitivist theory of the emotions. The development of contemporary social constructionist theories of emotion has coincided with the emergence of the view of the cognitive character of emotions (Harré 1986: 3), but there is a dangerous trap which follows from fusing the two. Constructionism holds a theory of mind in which emotions are cognition-based, that is in which the dynamic part of emotions is held to be located in the mind and not in accompanying bodily affects. Emotions are 'about' something, are related to judgment, are subject to appraisal, and are engaged in intellectual knowledge (Armon-Jones 1986: 36). But when fused with the cognitivist theory, constructionism is led into the trap of identifying two differently-valued components, in mind and body. As Jaggar rightly notes, this separation perpetuates the dichotomy between reason and emotion (Jaggar 1989: 134). It follows from the point made already in this section – the possibility and clear value of accepting the value of other aspects of emotion – that the social constructionist view advanced in the current work avoids this trap.

Ortony develops an interesting connection between cognition and construction, setting out the view that 'cognition is the result of mental *construction*.' He argues that '[k]nowledge of reality, whether it is occasioned by perception, language, memory, or anything else, is a result of going beyond the information given' (Ortony 1979: 1). Knowledge of reality, he reasons, 'arises through the interaction of that information with the context in which it is presented, and with the knower's preexisting knowledge'. In this way, 'language, perception, and knowledge are inextricably interdependent' (ibid.).

Furthermore Ortony makes a persuasive case that the relativism that might be implied by this viewpoint need not represent a problem. Such relativism is only vicious if one has the expectation of being able to gain a 'truly veridical epistemological access to reality' (ibid.). 'Modern' science held out the promise of such an access and so fed that expectation. Latterly the claims of science have become more modest. It also follows from this view that in the philosophy of science (which has, in our society, been taken as a test case for all knowledge), language and knowledge are radically metaphorical. As Ortony notes, 'the necessity of metaphor lies in its role in establishing links between the language of science and the world that it purports to describe and explain' (ibid.: 15). The problem posed by this perspective, that all language becomes metaphorical, so that a meaningful distinction between literal and metaphorical language breaks down, is also only apparent. For if it is acknowledged that the meaning of language depends upon its use in particular contexts, then it is clear that the ascription of literal and metaphorical language depends upon the specific context in which it is used.

### *The role of individual agency and reflection*

De Sousa is rightly adamant that social construction does not have to preclude a vital role for individual agency. Emotions 'are not social creations in the same sense as chess moves or even language.' For a 'discrepancy between the socially prescribed scenarios and those that evoke an individual's feelings is not necessarily settled in favour of the public dialect' (De Sousa 1987: 236). Moreover, 'the relation between the individual and social norms is partly a political one' (ibid.).

Jaggar deals with the same issue when she observes that within 'the very language of emotion, in our basic definitions and explanations of what it is to feel pride or embarrassment, resentment or contempt, cultural norms and expectations are embedded' (Jaggar 1989: 143). At the same time however it is clear, she comments, that 'the hegemony that our society exercises over people's emotional constitution is not total' (ibid.: 144).

Craib also makes a sound case that a social constructionist view of emotions need not eliminate a role for individual agency, nor trap us in cultural particularity, nor lead either to a reductive determinism or to biological essentialism (Craib 1995: 151–3). We are constructed but not constituted. Our experience and understanding is not simply a trap which is constituted of conceptualizations deriving from shared language, cultural beliefs and social rules. Self-reflection is another aspect of the way in which the elaboration and modification of emotions takes place in individuals. At the same time the kind of individual agency posited by the theory of social construction promoted in this work is intersubjective in two important ways. Appraisal and reappraisal take place in the social realm of engagement with others. And the process of constructing emotions, although done by individuals acting in and on their world, can only be accomplished through interaction with others.

The work of Crawford, Kippax, Onyx, Gault and Benton on the social construction of emotion is framed by a more general theory of the development of identity. These authors underline and develop in important ways the complex connection between agency, intersubjectivity, and the social world. Emotions play a crucial role in this complex connection, for '[e]motions are the markers of agency' (Crawford *et al.* 1992: 126). Their work is particularly useful because it explores a well-developed social constructionist view of emotions, but one which allows a strong sense of reflective agency (ibid.: 195). One of the most important aspects of their work concerns the acquisition of emotion. They make it clear that emotions are not acquired in 'a straightforward learning process. Emotions are socially constructed . . . human consciousness is produced and organized in [dynamic, interactive] participation in socio-cultural practices' (ibid.: 114). Thus 'although reflection is an individual process, the capacity of human beings for reflection is premised on intersubjectivity' (ibid.: 117).

Crawford *et al.* recognize that the construction of emotion occurs intersubjectively (ibid.: 189), and that through constructing our emotions we construct ourselves (ibid.: 190). Individuals 'reflect in order to resolve contradiction and to produce intelligibility as they construct their identities' (ibid.: 126). Crawford *et al.* also identify the way in which '[c]onsciousness does not precede interaction, it arises in it' (ibid.: 115), and they make a good case for arguing that it is in deliberation and reflection that we construct ourselves as agents (ibid.: 122). The intersubjective nature of emotion is also recognized by Harré. He points out that 'many emotions can exist only in the reciprocal exchanges of a social encounter' (Harré 1986: 5).

At the same time Crawford *et al.* recognize that '[r]eflection is itself essentially social' (Crawford *et al.* 1992: 114), and that emotions are socially *prescribed*: their presence demonstrates the person's commitment to the cultural values exemplified in particular situations and episodes. As they point out, emotions are 'cultural products'. Emotional development 'involves the acquisition of the social norms and rules that provide the component responses of the emotional syndrome with their coordination and meaning' (ibid.). However emotions 'are not . . . culturally *imposed*. They are appropriated from the social and cultural realm of interaction' (ibid.: 123; emphasis added).

Two important insights follow from the recognition that, in the context of agency, emotions are socially prescribed but not culturally imposed. Individuals 'reproduce the social structure [precisely] because they have freedom of action' (ibid.: 126). In addition, 'as members of collectivities . . . [individuals] have the chance to transform the social structures' (ibid.: 126).

The cognitivist theory of emotion plays an important part in supporting the role of agency in a constructionist theory of emotion. It overcomes the problem associated with previous organismic theories, which defined emotion as fundamentally an involuntary biological process. Notwithstanding its drawbacks the cognitivist theory recognizes that emotion, properly understood, does not come into being without reflection. Thus in linking emotion to motive, the cognitivist theory considers physiological responses associated with emotion as ancillary, and recognizes that reflection involves a conception of a self-conscious individual.

The theory of the social construction of emotion which recognizes the role of agency and reflection can thus also take account of the nature of the connection with biology. But as De Sousa soundly cautions, 'emotions need a place of their own in the theory of the person and are not reducible to more primitive faculties or functions' (De Sousa 1987: xvi). The version of social constructionism proposed here takes up a position against the view posited by William James in the nineteenth century, that emotions are affects – the apprehensions of bodily conditions – and agrees with Crawford *et al.* that, '[w]ithout denying the possible innate beginnings of emotion, emotions finally are the product of an evaluative process' (Crawford *et al.* 1992: 114).

### *Emotion as dynamic process*

The social constructionist view of emotion suggested here also recognizes the importance of memory – the historical dimension of emotions – to the capacity for appraisal and to the meaning of a situation. Memory, in the social construction of emotion, reinforces the crucial role played by individual agency, and leads to the realization that social construction is an on-going and dynamic process. Thus the social construction of emotion does not only involve an initial construction in an individual within a social context; it also involves the way in which each later activation of that emotion is influenced by the accretion of memories and meanings built up in personal memory, as well as in the social memory of language, cultural practices, etc. In this way social construction theory is both social and individual. Craib (1995: 153) reinforces a dynamic and historical view of emotions when he argues that it is most reasonable to suppose that there is a 'two-way process' between cognition and emotion.

Many of the accounts of emotion by both philosophers and psychologists suffer from seeing emotion in a static, time-slice way. They attempt to assess the nature and value of emotions by reference only to single, static, frozen instances with fixed, once-and-for-all meanings. The very great importance of writers such as Crawford *et al.* lies in the extra dimension that is gained from understanding the nature of emotion as dynamic, on-going in time, working upon patterns, allowing for the interplay of 'natural' predispositions, sociocultural learning and individual reflection.

Thus the memory element of the character of emotion reminds us that emotions occur in time; they are not given once and for all but are modified and elaborated over time. Moreover, some emotions are constructed in self-reflection, in secondary and tertiary reflections on events. In this sense emotions can involve deliberate as well as intuitive reflection to make sense of episodes, rather than just finding and appropriating a common meaning. Memory and history are also important in that emotional life does not only consist of situations attached to emotions. (This concrete social grounding of emotions is another meaning of social construction.) It consists also in further present reflection upon those past episodes, constructing interpretations, making sense of or resolving contradictions or conflicts in those episodes, all of which can generate other emotions. The importance of memory and history also resides in the way in which we construct what are characteristically distinct emotional *patterns* (of which we may or may not be aware) which we reinforce, contest, and articulate in particular episodes. Such patterns guide but do not necessarily determine further emotion situations. Even instincts or the 'basic' or 'elementary' or 'pure' emotions discussed by some writers are perceived, constructed and felt in concrete situations and take their meanings from that interdependence. In this way an emotional life is developed in time.

Rorty also acknowledges the element of dynamic process in the social construction of emotions (though curiously she leaves out the role of agency in emotions) when she identifies three 'closely interwoven strands' (Rorty 1980: 105). The first strand refers to 'the formative events in a person's psychological past, the development of patterns of intentional focusing and salience, habits of thought and response' (ibid.). The second strand is concerned with 'the socially and culturally determined range of emotions and their characteristic behavioural and linguistic expression' (ibid.). The third strand relates to 'a person's constitutional inheritance, the set of genetically fixed threshold sensitivities and patterns of response' (ibid.). Rorty also usefully highlights the integrated character of mental life. She says, 'an account of the etiology of the intentional component of emotional dispositions is nestled within a general psychological theory: it is inseparable from theories of perception and theories of motivation' (ibid.: 122). Rorty concludes that the 'holistic character of mental life makes piecemeal philosophical psychology suspect' (ibid.).

## Conclusion

This chapter has proposed an expanded conception of reason which acknowledges its dimensions of emotion, and in which emotion enables the use of reason. To this end the chapter has examined the interrelatedness of reason and emotion in the process of theorizing, and has considered in detail five specific ways in which this interdependence occurs in the production of knowledge. The value of the role of emotion in theorizing is strengthened by distinguishing clearly between a rational knowledge of emotion, and the knowledge gained through theorizing, that is, a knowledge generated by the interaction of reason and emotion.

The second half of the chapter developed a social constructionist theory of emotion to support these conceptions of reason, theorizing, and knowledge. The relational theory between the determinist naturalist and constitutionist poles sees emotion as dynamically integrating three elements: culturally-interpreted natural emotional predispositions, socioculturally-prescribed rules of emotional meaning, function and expectation, and the role of individual agency.

The following chapter examines another area in which the naturalization of exclusionary barriers, in both theory and social practices, has occurred, and proposes a relational alternative. A cluster of dichotomies around sex, gender, sexuality, and the sex/gender distinction is explored, to show that, in the term 'rational woman', not only is 'rational' dynamically interdependent with 'emotion', but also that the inherited category 'woman' rests upon a highly contestable man/woman construction.

# 3

# SEX AND GENDER

## Beyond the sex/gender dichotomy to corporeal subjectivity

This book is concerned with the two major dualisms contained in the term 'rational woman'. We come now to consider the nature of and relationship between the terms sex and gender, which is fundamental to the second implied contrast, between woman and man. Haraway notes that, '"[g]ender" was developed as a category to explore what counts as a "woman", to problematize the previously taken-for-granted' (Haraway 1991). However one of the major effects of the sex/gender distinction was to reinforce the dichotomization of sexual difference. The argument of this chapter builds on the work of influential writers such as Grosz, Gatens, and Butler, who challenged two linked dichotomies generated by the dichotomization of sexual difference. These are the bipolar male/female dichotomy (based on anatomy), and the bipolar heterosexual/homosexual dichotomy (based on sexual orientation). This chapter significantly develops the argument to show that, as a result of the dichotomization of sexual difference, which underpins the specific dichotomies of man/woman and heterosexual/homosexual, the sex/gender distinction also operates dichotomously.

Another important advance the chapter presents, again building upon the insights of many feminist theorists, is to exhibit how these *three* dichotomies (male/female, heterosexual/homosexual, sex/gender) operate as a cluster, that is, how they are interrelated and reinforce each other. The sex/gender distinction, as well as being designed to distinguish (mistakenly) between the natural and constructed aspects of identity, operates socially to map on to the binary pair between anatomical sexes, and on to the mind/body split. In this way, man equals gender, which is associated with mind and choice, freedom from body, autonomy, and with the public realm; while woman equals sex, associated with the body, reproduction, 'natural' rhythms and the private realm. Thus the sex/gender distinction, instead of giving women their promised liberation through gender role choice, actually functions to reinforce their association with body, sex, and involuntary 'natural' ryhthms. Therefore the sex/gender distinction has acted to consolidate the man/woman dichotomy. The consequences of the privileging and prioritizing of 'man' over 'woman' in social value, and so in status and in a range of social practices radiating out into all aspects of life, has been well documented by feminists (see Brown 1987, Fraser 1987, Pateman 1988, Tapper 1986), though often without the core of the theoretical problem being fully recognized.

The third major development that the chapter contributes to the sex/gender debate rests in the thesis that the *logic* of exposing the social construction of sex as well as gender makes it essential to extend the aims of the debate. It is imperative that the debate (at least as a goal) go beyond being caught within the cluster of dichotomies built upon the significance given to sexual difference, to a notion of corporeal subjectivity. Once the basis of the dichotomous force of the sex/gender distinction (biology/social construction) is exposed as false, then it can be seen that there is only one (multiple) thing at issue here, and that its character and features need to be re-theorized. On this basis the problems of essentialism, and the equality/difference dilemma, that have plagued second wave feminism, can be shown to rest on a misplaced mind/body dichotomy.

The argument of the chapter is constructed in the following way. First the reconceptualization of the sex/gender distinction begins by recovering the logic of its recent history. The purpose of this part of the chapter is not only to clarify the meanings of the terms through investigating their history, which is seen to be composed of six stages. The underlying aim of recovering this historical evidence is to demonstrate the extent to which it has been problematic because it has operated on the basis of values which belong to a positivist social science. Valuable work on this question has been done, for instance by Barrett and Phillips (1992: 1–9), and Gatens (1996a: 3–20).

This section also outlines further consequences for the sex/gender argument of the use of a social science founded on dualistic self/other principles and a determinism (whether biological or social) which disallows the impact of agency and reflection. Specifically, the aim is to demonstrate that an alternative methodology, based on the understanding of the specific form of social construction utilized here, can provide greater insights into the sex/gender conundrum. These arguments deserve to be presented explicitly again, in the light of the continuing hold of the positivist view of social science, which rests on a form of social determinism in the notion of socialization as well as importing a reverence for biological determinism.

The chapter then delineates and develops further the critique of the sex/gender distinction, in particular with respect to the heterosexual/ist norm. This leads to the argument that the *whole* distinction between sex and gender collapses, once the value of a relational social constructionist viewpoint is recognized.

In the final section of the chapter the notion of corporeal subjectivity is examined, building upon the excellent work on corporeality set out in particular by Grosz (1993, 1994) and Gatens (1996).[1] The idea of corporeal subjectivity can express the sense of going beyond not only both 'sex' and 'gender', but also beyond the conventional but bankrupt sex/gender distinction. However corporeal subjectivity can only be realized as the second stage of a two-stage process. For without the prior establishment as a short-term goal of the crucial recognition of gender visibility, the conceptualization of corporeal subjectivity would only dissolve into the familiar and unsatisfactory male-defined notion of gender neutrality.

In this way the chapter explores three levels of attention elicited by the sex/gender distinction: the body, social relations, and subjectivity. The chapter thus addresses issues which straddle the mind/body dichotomy. Moreover the chapter argues that in tracing these three levels of attention we follow the logic of the dichotomy, in that a mutually exclusive definition of man and woman is mapped on to sexual preference and practices, on to social, professional and work relations, and on to subjectivity. The chapter argues that these three levels of attention are vitally interdependent, and seeks to develop an understanding based upon a comprehensive relational conception of the body, social relations, and subjectivity across the mind/body dichotomy.

The three major points that this chapter seeks to establish are, first, that there is only one (multiple) thing, not a plausible sex/gender distinction. The second point concerns the work that the 1960s sex/gender distinction was designed to do. That distinction was primarily concerned with identity, and it attempted to identify separately, but also to relate, a constructed identity and a 'natural' one. This chapter holds that in the complex multiplicity of identity, a 'natural' identity cannot plausibly be isolated from constructed elements.

To take up just one aspect of this point, we only know 'natural' elements of ourselves through actions and behaviour which occur in a constructed world of social practices and their multiple and contested meanings, and thus have no access to any separately 'natural' base (Moore 1988 ch. 2, Ortner and Whitehead 1981). For instance, while eating is a biological imperative, the full meaning of eating is derived only from understandings of culturally-variant conventions (about mealtimes, the dining table etc.) and social practices (concerning family life, sociability, communication, intimacy) in which this activity occurs (McMillan 1982: 14), as well as from resistances to it, for example in anorexia. Eating has a meaning for us we cannot construct from hunger alone. The meaning of the biological imperative of childbirth is likewise not absolute and 'given', but is constructed differently in different cultures as well as in different women's experience. In a third example, Henrietta Moore (1988: 25–30) draws upon extensive anthropological research to demonstrate how the meaning of motherhood is socially constructed.

The third major point is to take seriously the challenge to the dominant heterosexual/ist norm that comes from lesbian, gay, and queer theory. The impact on the discussion of this challenge is very important, and is as yet under-recognized. Its importance does not reside only in posing sexual identities no longer seen as 'other', or in enabling a monolithic heterosexuality to be reconceptualized relationally. The importance of this challenge is that it is also, and especially, very effective in undermining the dichotomous basis of the fixed heterosexual/ist norm, in favour of a notion of a partially contextually-influenced and partially agency-affected continuum of stable bisexuality or intersexuality.

Therefore this chapter seeks to go beyond 'sex and gender'. It goes 'beyond sex' because it identifies some of the extended implications of the idea that biology is not neutral, and shows how the dichotomy between sex and gender on this basis is flawed. There have always been and always will be men and women, but the categories 'man' and 'woman' have been constructed differently (and not always dichotomously) at different times. The chapter does not advocate that there be no men or women. It envisages that, in a nonhegemonic and a nondichotomous relational mode of theory and practices, the man–woman distinction would cease to operate as the key which genders reason, work practices and social practices in an exclusionary manner.

The chapter also goes 'beyond gender', by showing that once the social construction of sex as well as gender has been demonstrated, it follows that the ground is cut from under the uniquely 'social' definition of gender. The sex/gender distinction referred precisely to an untenable natural/constructed contrast. As radical feminists have been pointing out to liberal feminists throughout the second wave, the social construction of the *social*, in socialization, is no more easy to affect or change than the social and cultural meaning of biological imperatives like eating and childbirth. The form of social constructionism employed here contends very strongly that, as far as understanding the sex/gender conundrum is concerned, there is a shared conceptualization of what is involved in change in the social construction of both social meanings and biological imperatives. Writers who have convincingly argued for the social construction of sex have not followed the logic of the argument far enough. The *theoretical* distinctiveness of gender from sex is untenable once it has been shown to share with sex a basis which is in crucial respects constructed.

The chapter also goes 'beyond sex and gender', by contending that it has not been sufficiently recognized, in mainstream political and social theory and in philosophy, that the significance of having bodies extends far beyond their anatomical sex. The sex and sexuality of bodies, as understood in biology and medicine, has colonized and transfixed the whole recent discussion of bodies. Bodies *are* sexed but perhaps even more importantly bodies are used to express a range of other things. For instance bodies are the tangible location of personal narrative and social identity, and centres of compassion and caring, as well as of pain and suffering. Furthermore the particularity of bodies enables them to be identified in terms of family resemblance, and so located in a family history and social genealogy. They can also be identified as ethnically coded, and dressed and inscribed to manifest chosen and unchosen social, class, cultural and generational values.

Bordo soundly elaborates on the diverse constructions of the body: as a 'medium of culture', a 'powerful symbolic form', a 'metaphor for culture', and a 'practical, direct locus of social control' (Bordo 1989: 13). Grosz (1993: 202) makes another extremely important point about bodies when she notes that they are both 'inscribed' and 'lived', simultaneously and interdependently. That is, bodies can be understood as inscribed, coded in socially-constructed and externally-judged meanings, and they can also be understood as lived, dynamic and containing unique subjectively-judged meaning. As Grosz crucially reminds us, avoiding a falsely dichotomous objective-as-true/subjective-as-opinion view of knowledge, the 'inscribed surface is not neutral' (ibid.: 202).

Thus that we have bodies, as *both* lived and as constructed, is an insight which contains a whole range of theoretically significant dimensions. Within this range, the 'fact' of biological difference cannot be taken as foundational. Bodies do have an inescapable biological materiality but the way they are lived and experienced in culture is not reducible to biological explanation. In other words, the understanding of bodies as lived and as constructed is richer than, and goes beyond, biology, and cannot be reduced to a deterministic, causal and foundational biological explanation. Conversely, biological difference between bodies cannot in itself disclose the meaning of bodies as lived. A society (such as ours which constructs a match or fit between biological difference and constructed social roles can demonstrate an explanatory link between biology and constructed bodies only tautologically (Kaplan and Rogers 1990: 206) and only by excluding much that is important.

As Whitbeck cogently notes, '[n]ot only are our bodies ourselves (rather than being something that we, as minds, possess), but the bodies, intellects, emotions, souls, characters, and configurations of relationships that we are can be adequately understood only in relation to one another' (Whitbeck 1989: 63). However our culture still clings to the privileging of the biological definition of bodies, with its profound investment in biological reductionism and biological determinism. The mind/body and culture/nature dichotomies are powerfully at work in our culture's view of bodies, and still prevent us from recognizing how radically mind, body and emotions are interdependent.

The quotation from Whitbeck also points to the way in which the emphasis on intersubjectivity, so crucially highlighted by some exponents of the ethics of care, is not simply a dimension of the individual self which can be attached or detached at will. In Western societies the individualist view remains the presupposition of the dominant mainstream liberal political theory, which is highly suspicious of ties of attachment. Whitbeck's argument reinforces the case for holding that relationship is a non-negotiable part of what it means to be an individual self, even though particular kinds of relationship may be negotiable.

Whitbeck characterizes the body as an integral part of ourselves rather than as something owned by the mind. It follows that the thinking and theorizing of the mind is expressed not only in spoken and written language but also in body language and gesture, and in action. Moreover the uniqueness of bodies holds open the possibility of valuing their diversity and difference. This offers a way to rectify the historical view of persons which has often operated to effect exclusion through the classification of their bodies into dichotomously-valued paired groups (male/female, white/black, able-bodied/disabled, young/old), a view aggravated by the abstract and universalized characterization of the 'gender-neutral' person in liberal theory. It is for these reasons that the retention of the sexed body as the most important aspect of the meaning of bodies, remains a problem with feminists such as Irigaray. Later in the chapter the discussion will show that even though Irigaray's aim is the laudable one of seeking a way of valorizing women's bodies, this does not prevent the proliferation of severe problems (Jones, A. 1981), despite the work of writers trying to rescue this aspect of Irigaray's project (Ping Xu 1995).

The view of bodies put forward here implies a profoundly different attitude from that which is thought generally in our society to follow from the social construction of bodies. Drawing on the work of Grosz (1994), Gatens (1996a), Butler (1990b) and Lloyd (1989) in particular, this approach does two things. If the dominance of the explanatory equation of body and anatomical sexed body is removed, it opens up the theoretical space in which a range of different kinds of body can be recognized, with a plurality of uses and expressiveness and meanings beyond the sexual. It also recognizes how the body can be seen to interact dynamically with other aspects of identity, particularly with respect to the 'mind' dimension of body and the 'emotion' part of mind. The exclusionary effects of the finite two options (male and female anatomy) offered by the sex/gender distinction can then be replaced by the possibility of a properly-grounded recognition of difference. The promise of a multiplicity of gender roles made by the sex/gender distinction is illusory and unreachable while it remains underpinned by mind/body and culture/nature dichotomies which undermine relational modes of understanding.

This extension of the theoretical argument 'beyond sex and gender' thereby attempts to explode two deeply-ingrained values in our culture. It supplants the presupposition in our culture that the fundamental thing about men's and women's bodies is their anatomical sex. However, in the second place this presupposition is trumped in our culture by another one, about the neutrality of (men's) bodies in the public sphere. This second, underlying presupposition has had the effect of endowing women (identified with the private sphere) with the burden of the bodies of all and so confounding the reception of women into the public sphere. Thus this extension of the theoretical argument also discloses how the sex/gender distinction operates as a dichotomy, and how it is at heart about the man/woman dichotomy because it is about body, about corporeal being.

Before moving into the substance of the chapter, it is very important and instructive to specify how the sex/gender distinction is a false dichotomy in a different way from the manner in which reason and emotion is a false distinction. There are both historical and analytical arguments about the difference between reason/emotion and sex/gender. The historical argument, discussed in more detail later in relation to the term 'sex', points to the historical and cultural specificity of the sex/gender distinction, which cuts the ground from under its claim to universality.

According to the analytical argument, it is important that reason and emotion (and body) be retained as categories which, while they should be understood as implicated and invested in each other, nevertheless describe things which can be distinguished. Reason and emotion are capacities of the person, which interact, and our lives are lived for the most part in this interacting and interdependent area. Problems occur when a balance between reason and emotion is not struck. At the same time it is still possible to distinguish logically between pure reason at one end of a continuum and pure emotion at the other end.

On the other hand, keeping sex and gender as identified by the sex/gender dichotomy as separate categories is confusing and exclusionary for two reasons. First, there are many more than two things at work here, and second, the definition of gender is dependent upon a definition of sex. The sex/gender distinction, when unpacked, carries a variety of activities and capacities within it, but the 1960s meanings of the terms 'sex' and 'gender' are misdefined points of corporeality. Corporeality contains a number of points and there is no 'pure' sex or 'pure' gender.

In the chapter on dichotomy it was contended that while the dominance of the dichotomous mode of thinking needs to be corrected, dichotomous argument sometimes has a useful part to play in validly highlighting differences. That contention can be utilized here to clarify the difference between the reason/emotion and the sex/gender dichotomies. While most of our lives are lived in the middle relational area of the reason-emotion continuum, the two categories can logically be distinguished. With respect to sex and gender, however, this chapter aims to show that the relational mode is the appropriate mode of theorizing, and entirely supplants the false dichotomization of corporeality.

## The (recent) history of sex and gender

There are six stages in this schematic history of the *logic* of the argument concerning sex and gender. The starting point and first stage, presented by second wave feminism, is the sex/gender distinction developed in the 1960s. This began with a critique built upon the observation that historically there has been the idea that a person's anatomical sex defines and determines their (intimate, personal, family, social, economic, political, cultural, religious) roles in society. This idea underlay the prioritizing of 'man' over 'woman'. The critique questioned the necessary link between anatomy and social position.

The second stage is represented by those feminists who drew on the work of De Beauvoir (1952) to reject some of the implications of the determinist link between anatomical sex and intellectual and social roles in the public and private spheres. They distanced themselves also from the values associated with that link. It was claimed that women too could be rational, could recognize and live by the force of abstract justice and individual rights; that these things were truly universals, and that it was only historically contingent that women had been excluded from them. This claim on behalf of women, for what had been held almost exclusively by men, remains a powerful argument for some feminists, including some feminist followers of Arendt. For instance Elshtain assumes that sex is a biological given. She says (1987: 148), the 'sex distinction is ineliminable and important'. The androgyny line of argument, seeking to abolish the social effects of anatomical sex difference between men and women, also developed from this perspective.

These two lines of argument sought from opposite starting points to liberate women from their traditional sex-defined roles. In other words, in this second stage feminists commandeered the male logic of the public realm, and presented emancipation to women by the prioritizing of mind over body. While De Beauvoir does analyze structures of subordination, her principal line of argument emphasized the universality of minds. The androgyny line of argument (which crucially fails to look at why stereotyping occurs) sought to impose universality through eliminating the importance of bodies and body differences.

It is no surpise that from this point on, the problem of essentialism has plagued second wave feminism. The paradox of promising women, defined as a group by inherent anatomical sex difference, emancipation into the world of universal and neutral mind, rests upon the retention and indeed the elevation of the value of a mind/body dichotomy. The problem of essentialism arises as a direct result of the mind/body dichotomy into which second wave feminists understandably but mistakenly bought. However this chapter shows that essentialism can now be recognized as no more than a red herring, the product of underpinning the meaning of 'gender' with the notion of a given 'natural' sex difference. When mind and body are conceptualized as interdependent rather than as separate and hierarchically arranged, and sex as well as gender is recognized as constructed, then the problem of essentialism for feminism in both its theoretical and political dimensions loses its force. Women are no longer forced to embrace the false paradox of claiming 'mind' for a group defined by 'body'.

Three things now become clear about the essentialism question. First, the essentialist question cannot be answered, because the terms in which it is framed are not subject to definitive proof. Biology can prove nothing about social position because there is a logical gap between biological capacity and social value that can only be bridged by one of a diversity of socially-constructed understandings. Second, the essentialist question does not ultimately matter, since it is social, political or moral values which provide arguments that ground choices and that trump spuriously biological arguments (such as those proposing social policy on the basis of supposed racial superiority), *whatever* the answer to the essentialist question. Thus, third, an essentialist answer could not be used to *ground* other issues anyway. A good example of these three points concerns the mid-1990s debate over whether there should be stronger affirmative action policies to encourage more women into parliament. It follows from these three points that there is a strong case for such policies, *whether or not* it can be proved that there is an essentialist nature of women. In dealing with social and political matters, recourse to a reductive essentialist answer and explanation does not help or solve the social dilemma. In sum, whatever answer is given to the essentialist question, the imperative for our society in this context is to recognize social diversity in general and differences between women in particular, and to recognize the value of different women's choices.

The third stage of the logic of the history of the sex and gender debate built upon and extended the use of Robert Stoller's psychological analsysis of transsexualism. Stoller (1968) employed a notion of 'gender identity', in which a definition of sex specifically in terms of biology was contrasted with an idea of gender in terms of role theory. His distinction quickly became paradigmatic among feminists such as Millett and Greer, who then argued that masculine and feminine social roles are a product of socialization rather than of biology. The separation of culture from nature seemed to offer women both liberation from biology and entrance to a realm of social choice equal to men.

Gayle Rubin's identification of a 'sex/gender system' within a Marxist framework as a system of social relations oppressive of women was also extremely influential. It pointed to the way in which gender can be used as an analytic category to identify one of the methods through which the vital relationships of power are exercised. In 'The Traffic in Women' (Rubin 1975), she argued that a sex/gender system operated to legitimize the appropriation of women as the property of men. Women's sexuality is exchanged by men, she said, through structures of kinship and marriage. These early proponents of a sex/gender distinction seemed to offer – and feminists were keen to take up – a social-scientific causal explanation of the oppression of women. This causal explanation (through socialization or through the theorizing of power relationship) seemed to provide a comforting certainty and validation of the claims by women for redress against discriminatory practices.

In a fourth stage of the logic of the argument, the sex/gender distinction that had been established led to two interpretations within the social sciences, in political theory and in the study of politics. Both drew on the idea which the distinction seemed to promise that gender is about social relationships and that women could choose their social identity (in all its aspects according to 1960s notions of liberal freedom and choice). Their identity was no longer determined by their (still) 'natural' sex. This thinking, however, presupposed a positivist account of empirically-identified sexed bodies, which remains active in contemporary sociology and political science, an understanding of there being two 'natural' genders (Hawkesworth 1997: 650).

One of the most important expressions of this fourth definition of sex and gender concerned the effects of the contraceptive pill on women's perceptions of work and career opportunities. This argument was particularly attractive to middle-class women, the beneficiaries of broadening educational opportunities. Broadly, the predominant interpretation was that women can combine a minimized female role (incorporating planned reproduction into a busy life, and utilizing extensive paid child care) with a career and an active role in the public sphere along with men. The subordinate interpretation was that women are no longer at the mercy of the 'sex' imperative, but can choose to indulge it, stay at home with children and cultivate a vocation of motherhood through the 'female' virtues and values. However one of the problems with this vision of gender, held over from the third stage and not adequately addressed, was the disjunction between gender as choice, overcoming social norms, and gender as given by socialization.

The fifth stage of the argument has come about through the work of feminist biologists and theorists, demonstrating that 'sex' as well as 'gender' is socially constructed. It is also characterized by the articulation of a contradiction in the use of the term 'gender'. For 'gender' has been both embraced by feminists, and seen as a primary weapon of critique against discriminatory 'gendered' social practices. Dissatisfaction with role theory, with the Marxist structural account, and with the causal explanation of the earlier social scientific basis of the sex/gender distinction, has also been a marked feature of 1980s critique (Barrett and Phillips 1992, Gatens 1996). Lloyd in particular (1989: 13-18) raises some penetrating questions about the relations between sex and gender. (See also Morgan 1996, Moore 1994.) However for these writers, and even in Lloyd's subtle treatment, two things – sex and gender – remain.

At the same time feminists in the 1980s challenged the essentialism and ethnocentrism presupposed in the notion of woman presented by the sex/gender distinction, and explored the implications of the social construction of gender. In order to pursue these aims, the critique introduced the notion of 'difference' to contest the seemingly 'given', universal and a-historical identity of the category 'woman'. It emphasized differences between women, and therefore also fragmented the tendency to impose a monolithic identity on feminism (Diprose 1994, ch. 4). 'Gender difference' now referred to differences between women (especially race and class) rather than between men and women (Spelman 1990). The 1980s critique also utilized the notion of difference to argue that recognition of the cultural diversity of women is important for effective feminist political action (for instance in black feminism, lesbianism, Young's 'group difference') and for the political participation of other marginalized groups. At the same time feminists like Bordo (1990) expressed well-founded doubts about the development of gender scepticism.

The sixth stage of the history of the sex/gender distinction will be represented by the proposal developed later in this chapter.

This brief history has been designed to demonstrate how a number of methodological and disciplinary presuppositions have become enmeshed in the sex/gender debate, and so to disclose some of the tacit assumptions that make the debate extremely complex to analyze. It has also been intended to exhibit how the sixth stage proposal follows *logically* from the combination of the insights articulated by the 1980s critque, together with the criticisms of the earlier sex/gender definition. Thus this sixth stage builds upon two developments which destabilized the balance that the sex/gender distinction sought to establish. Gatens and others revealed that the significance of anatomical *sex* is not a given, but is constructed. Hawkesworth and others showed on the other hand how *gender*, while being 'a category specifically devised to avoid biological determinism, covertly invokes the very biological ground it set out to repudiate' (Hawkesworth 1997: 662). Notwithstanding its brilliance, even Grosz's *Volatile Bodies* (1994: 13–19) does not ultimately take this next step of going beyond sex and gender. Thus the sixth stage proposes that the previous distinction between sex and gender is no longer viable. It is a false distinction and needs to be replaced by an understanding of a single, but variegated (or containing 'diversity' rather than 'multiplicity', in Mullin's (Mullin 1995) characterization), porous, permeable notion of corporeal subjectivity.

## The critique of sex and gender

This chapter, in criticizing and going beyond the sex/gender distinction, discloses a cluster of at least three interrelated meanings of this distinction operating in disciplines in, or relevant to, the social sciences. The reason for specifying them here is to support the case that the confusion surrounding these terms is not only attributable to the deep ambiguity in the way they are understood in Anglo-American liberal culture generally. It is also owing to the different uses made of them in different academic disciplines and practices.

For instance, in politics and political theory the impact of anatomical sex on gender is now largely thought to be non-causal. An important part of the argument of this chapter is that this non-causal connection rests, however, upon an unacknowledged underlying causal connection. Thus it is precisely because anatomical sex has been (covertly) taken as foundational, that the relationship between sex and gender can only be envisaged as operating in one direction, from sex to gender.

The second relevant discipline in which the sex/gender distinction is very important is sociology. Here, notwithstanding the areas of sociology which study the role of chosen social identities, (the two) genders are covertly defined causally on the basis of anatomical sex.

In a third disciplinary background, one which has had a major impact on feminist writers, authors such as Irigaray criticize the oppressive effects of the sex/gender distinction. It is her thesis that '[w]omen's exploitation is based upon sexual difference; its solution will come only through sexual difference' (Irigaray 1993: 12). In this argument Irigaray is utilizing a conceptualization based on the significance of a grammatically-defined gender, which she takes as an ontologically-grounded given. Thus the sex/gender distinction in this formulation directly describes a body/language or material/discursive distinction, and so maps on to a body/mind dichotomy which resonates strongly in the tradition of French philosophy. This perspective contains a sophisticated causal view of the relationship between sex and gender, grounded in the manner in which, in the French language, the masculine plural trumps the feminine plural, in definite and indefinite articles, nouns, and pronouns, and in the way that valued objects are more likely to be represented by masculine nouns. The English language operates differently since, although where gendered language does occur it is likely to discriminate against women, nouns, articles and pronouns in English are not systematically gendered. In the English-speaking world the ontological status of language is also differently constructed. This point discloses the cultural specificity and so the, at most, theoretical conditionality of Irigaray's theory.

The rich field of ambiguities that the sex/gender distinction evokes is made even more complex by the practice according to which 'sex' and 'gender' are often used interchangeably, designating the same thing, as when liberal theorists like Rawls are accused of 'sex-blindness' or 'gender-blindness'. Sometimes, furthermore, 'sex' is used simply as the noun with 'gender' as the corresponding adjective. On other occasions 'gender' is used as a euphemism for biological 'sex'. The net result of these ambiguities is that one cannot explain the sex/gender distinction in terms of 'sex' describing male and female while 'gender' describes masculine and feminine. Any such explanation simply raises a whole set of problematic points and does not adequately explain anything.

In order to explore the range of problems with the sex/gender distinction it is worth elucidating in more detail what is currently understood by the term 'sex/gender distinction' and by the terms 'sex' and 'gender' in the social sciences. To establish the ground for the argument for corporeal subjectivity later in the chapter, it is important to make some more detailed observations about these terms, and about 'the heterosexual/ist norm'. The resistance to the latter, especially by lesbian and queer theorists, has led to the most comprehensive (though not untroubled) problematization of gender so far. Moreover, while many second wave feminists have seen (mistakenly) the term gender as emancipatory, lesbian and queer theorists have extensively explored the homogenizing and oppressive dimensions of the gender 'woman'.

It is also worth stressing that the purpose of disclosing the ambiguities of meaning and the multiplicity of usages of the terms sex and gender is not to identify a single meaning and a single usage as correct and to banish others. The goal is rather to survey the rich complexity of cultural meaning and social usage that is involved in this subject. One of the aims of this chapter is to signal the untenability of the sex/gender distinction, by pointing to the problematic mind/body dichotomy that underpins many of these ambiguous meanings.

## *Sex*

Within the scope of the sex/gender distinction, 'sex' can refer to or stand for at least ten different things: Freud's view of sex as the mainspring of psychological makeup; reproductive capacity in terms of anatomy, sometimes referring to external genitalia but sometimes including internal organs, and sometimes referring to the body pre- as well as post-puberty; reproductive capacity in terms of a broader notion of biology – that is, anatomy plus genetic chromosomes plus hormones – leading to reproduction and childbearing; (male and female undifferentiated) sexual libido or desire or appetite or drive; sexual preference or orientation, across a range, heterosexual, bisexual, transsexual, and homosexual (gay, lesbian); the activity of sexual acts and practices and pleasure; sex as love and intimacy and the surrender of the self; sex as a means of expressing power (Haste 1993: 170–1); sex as identity, leading to sexually-differentiated gender; sex as representing the body in general, notably in the way that women have been given the burden of body for all persons (Grosz 1994: 22) following from the liberal positing of the public sphere as 'gender-neutral'.

The rich ambiguity between these overlapping meanings of the term sex in the sex/gender debate renders it extremely difficult to plot a critical course. Nevertheless a strong case can be made that the integrity of the anatomical sex part of the sex/gender dichotomy has effectively been undermined by three things. First is the recent case made for the social construction of sex. Second is the acknowledgment that biology does not provide us with *givens* in this area after all, and does not after all carry the kind of epistemic weight attributed to it. This means that biology plays a role, but not a determining one. The third factor is lesbianism and the development of queer theory. Second wave feminist lesbianism and queer theory represent the most effective of the explicit challenges to the heterosexist basis of patriarchy, since the existence of gay men has increasingly become tolerated over the past thirty years. Such tolerance can even work to reinforce patriarchy where gay men 'pass' as straight and where gay men are unsympathetic to issues outside the ambit of the male gay world.

Another notable problem with the use of the term 'sex' in the sex/gender distinction has been the slide in its use from designating a distinction in terms of anatomy, to designating sexual preference, including assumptions about sexual performance. Bisexuality and intersexuality (understood not as representing a descent into chaos or indeterminacy, but as positive orientations in which sexuality is neither undecided nor unstable) are also relevant here. They demonstrate even more clearly than do male homosexuality and lesbianism the falsity of making assumptions about gender roles on the basis of anatomical sex, of attributing specific preference and performance from anatomy.

While queer theory is discussed in detail later on, it is worth emphasizing one of the ways in which queer theory has effectively sought to unsettle and destabilize the sexual norm. This arises from the recognition that the expression of sex as sexuality is not immutable. The expression of sexuality can and does change, for instance from heterosexuality to homosexuality or in bisexuality or intersexuality, and so is not necessarily fixed and immune to context. It is one of the assumptions of heterosexism that anatomical sex automatically and immutably discloses 'normal' sexuality, whereas as Wilson (1995: 126) argues cogently, the 'connection between what we call sex and the (physically identifiable) sexual or reproductive organs is contingent not conceptual'. It follows that anatomy tells us nothing conclusively significant about identifying a person's sex (that is the scope of the references of the term 'sex'), and that choice, context, agency, mind, and emotion also affect the material element.

Freud's theory of sexual difference remains extremely influential in defining the term 'sex' in anatomical or physiological terms. Despite his belief that sexual identity is fundamentally a matter of the psyche and not biology, he is influentially taken to have theorized the link between the threshold of adulthood, the recognition of adult identity, and the emergence of biological sexual identity.

In considering Freud's legacy, it is also important to note the contextual conjunction of several factors. Freud's theory occurred at a time when social science promised causal explanation, when compulsory heterosexuality had become entrenched, and when gay, lesbian and other sexual identities were assessed not only as deviant, abnormal and morally wrong, but also as diseases. Thus it is no accident that we have inherited a view in which sexual difference and adult identity are strictly about male/female and the tension between them (between fathers and daughters, and mothers and sons). However a strong case can be made for allowing a broader vision and for seeing the construction of the *whole of identity*, of all the dimensions of identity, as what happens at the brink of adulthood. In this way it is possible to reinstate Freud's understanding of the links between body and mind, rather than to focus on the either/or dualism of Freud's legacy. It is thus possible to recognize a diversity of sexual identities, to redress the balance in the corporeal dimension of subjectivity, to emphasize how body interacts with mind and emotion, and to move away from the obsession with male/female anatomical sex.

Strong arguments come from a wide variety of sources against the dichotomy of man/woman defined by anatomical sex and its consequences whereby 'woman' is 'an enforced cultural option which has disguised itself as natural truth' (Butler 1987: 142). Gatens argues soundly that '[s]ex is itself both produced by, and productive of, a complex of sociohistorical norms' (Gatens 1996b: 163; see also Butler 1987: 135, Hubbard 1983, Vance 1992, McMillan 1982 ch. 4, Haste 1993: 22, Segal 1994: 217–22). Gatens follows Foucault in observing how the 'biological body . . . allows the assignment of a "true sex", necessary for an individual to occupy her or his "proper place" in society by performing the appropriate functions, according to biological norms which are interleaved with social norms and moral judgments' (Gatens 1996b: 163). What she calls 'the "truth" of the sex of a body', that is the social definition of bodies as male or female, 'acts to condition differentially the *force* of the norms which define one's social, economic and civil status' (ibid.).

Hood-Williams also advances a historical and analytical argument for the thesis that sex is socially constructed. He denies that 'the differences between the sexes are naturally given in the dimorphic facts of human biology' (Hood-Williams 1996: 3), and challenges effectively the 'alleged constancy of sex' in the established contrast between sex as immutable and gender as mutable (ibid.: 5). Nussbaum also recognizes that sex as well as gender is socially constructed. She observes that the manner in which 'the difference in external genetalia figures in social life . . . is interpreted by human cultures; thus we are never dealing simply with facts given at birth, but always with what has been made of them' (Nussbaum 1995a: 62). Thus it follows, she argues, even the 'common distinction between "gender", a cultural concept, and "sex", the allegedly pure biological concept, is inadequate to capture the depth of cultural interpretation in presenting even the biological "facts" to human beings, from the very start of a child's life' (ibid.).

The social construction of sex involves a number of elements: the material dimension, social norms, and agency (based upon reflection, self-consciousness, and the power of ideas). The argument for the social construction of sex does not advance a case for social constitution in the sense of social determinism, and it does not see the material dimension as foundational in the sense of biological determinism. Both of these arguments fail to take account of the mediation of social understandings, reflection and agency. It holds that a strong version of the argument for discursive constitution is not necessary in order to demonstrate a link between individuals and social practices. Neither does it overestimate the role of agency, in the culpable way maintained in some readings of Butler's work, nor trade on that argument to form an explanation.

The argument for the social construction of sex outlined here is designed to counter two uses of 'natural' in the notion of 'natural sex difference' (Thiele 1986: 36–7). There is of course the substantive 'natural difference' which refers to a particular understanding of biology, anatomy and the physical. But this meaning also trades upon an underlying process of 'naturalization', whereby whatever is 'natural' is what is sustained by common sense and taken-for-granted assumptions (Grosz 1990a: 334–5). The force of such naturalization is very powerful for, as Haste notes, '[a]ppeals to "naturalness" are justifications of the status quo' (Haste 1993: 61).

'Social construction' moreover, despite the tortuous and labyrithine lengths of Butler's recent discussion (Butler 1993: 4–12), can be taken reasonably straightforwardly as describing our partial social construction. It is partial not because a natural base mitigates against full social construction, but because agency and reflection mitigate against such a deterministic formulation. 'Construction' in this sense refers to the way in which there is no discrete material foundation upon which construction might be founded: there would be no subject without that construction. This notion of social construction supersedes the presupposed nature/culture dichotomy. There is no discrete foundational sex upon which gender is constructed, because what matters is the *signficance* that is attached to gender definitions, or rather through which gender is constituted. The physiological dimension of sex is not isolable from the network of social conventions and practices which influence the meaning of sex.

The social construction thesis could be used to support diametrically-opposed views about agency. On the one hand, it could be used to argue that, because there is no 'I' outside socially-constructed identity, individuals therefore have little or no personal agency. It could equally be used to claim that because social and cultural norms are socially-constructed and not 'natural', individuals have through their performativity great scope to *re*construct the world. In this chapter social construction refers to a middle course between these two views, in which partial social construction does not prevent us having, at least collectively, agency to engage in the political contestation of practices.

Hood-Williams draws on an extensive literature that documents how, for many centuries of our history, in contrast with our modern two-fold division, a one-sex model prevailed whereby women were regarded as imperfect men. Before the nineteenth century although there were plenty of derogatory theories concerning women's sex (Zemon Davis 1994), there was no strict dualism of the sexes, they being regarded as having a common origin (Hood-Williams 1996: 6–7; see also Okin 1996: 33). Sex in the sense of reproductive organs as the 'foundations of incommensurable difference' was only 'invented' in the eighteenth century (Hood-Williams 1996: 12). Thus the notion of bipolar sex difference which our contemporary culture largely takes to be 'natural' and so outside of history, has a pedigree of only two hundred years.

Further, Kaplan and Rogers document the way in which the notions of the normal and of normality, instigating the 'myth of biological norms', were only introduced in the nineteenth century (Kaplan and Rogers 1990: 218–20), and they identify a range of problems inherent in the use of these terms (ibid.: 223). In addition it is clear that prior to the entrenchment of the notion of bipolar sex difference, a whole range of performances and preferences was at different times accepted as normal (for instance, homosexuality in ancient Greece) or at least tolerated (for example, lesbianism in the Victorian period).

In putting forward a social constructionist view of sex, the argument of this chapter is *not* that sex difference should be abolished. This chapter regards it as uncontentious that, historically, versions of a male–female sex distinction are likely to have been regarded as important in all cultures, in the light of the importance of reproduction to a society's continuing existence. But even a little historical research discloses very different constructions, in different times and places, of the *context* of sexualities in which a male-female sex distinction has been understood. The exclusive and dominant heterosexual/ism that has characterized the recent history of Western liberal society, in which a 'natural' sex difference is mapped on to every other element contained in the terms 'sex' and 'gender', does not have to be accepted as a given.

Peter Winch expresses the still resonant view that a world without a mutually exclusive and bipolar sexual distinction would be a confused and muddled place, on the grounds that 'masculinity or femininity are not just *components* of life, they are its *mode*' (Winch 1970: 110). The view that Winch articulates is a legacy of the nineteenth-century development of a strict dichotomy between the sexes, which emerged as the culmination of a period of 'profound anxiety . . . the fear of confusing the sexes' (Fraisse 1994: 193). Fraisse accounts for this fear of 'confusion of sexual identities' (see also Gatens 1991: 9–10) as a response to the claims made by women to citizenship rights in the debates which followed the French Revolution (Fraisse 1994: 193–6). She shows how women, excluded from political membership, were subject to a 'distancing . . . already present at the origin of democracy', and she notes that '[w]omen were relegated to the state of nature at the very moment that men were becoming emancipated from it' (ibid.: 196). Winch's view also acts as a sobering reminder to those like Mann (1997) who consider that a positive meaning of the current destabilization of gender relations can be posited in an easy and uncontroversial fashion.

The bipolar definition of sex was consolidated only in the twentieth century with the entrenchment of a biological notion of a natural sex difference based on the presence of X and Y chromosomes, which was taken as providing explanatory force. However, recent biological evidence presents such a complex picture of sex difference that a simple bipolar definition on the basis of genetic chromosomal and hormonal criteria cannot be maintained. In addition the extent of cases of deviance from the norm calls into question the utility of those criteria. It is now clear that biologists rely upon assumptions about sex difference which go beyond the scope of their scientific method and evidence, and that this undermines the scientific claims made by them (Hood-Williams 1996: 9–11; see also Rosner and Johnson 1995). Furthermore there is as yet no decisive specification of the criteria for the biological basis of sex determination: should it rely upon observable genitalia, reproductive capacity, genetic chromosome formation, hormonal makeup, all of these or some of these? Different practical answers for sex determination follow from each criterion, and it has been by no means clear in the debate which of these criteria should be pursued and on what grounds they should be preferred.

Another problem arises from the wider social logic of the biological, essentialist definition of sex. This definition contains three crucial parts. First, anatomical sex is regarded as an *essential* distinction to retain, a fixed and foundational definition of people into the mutually exclusive classes of men and women. Second, sex is defined in terms of reproductive capacity. And third, this definition is maintained even though perhaps only half of all women are actually fertile at any time, due to physiological problems, malnourishment, or simply because women are fertile only between the ages of approximately 15 and 45 and only at certain times of the menstrual cycle (Hood-Williams 1996: 5).

It follows from this definition that the social claim that is actually being made for a foundational sex difference is that potential for childbirth (together with an ambivalence about a 'natural' link to childrearing) is the *most* important fact to establish in distinguishing people in our society. In other words, if this one specific aspect of reproduction – childbirth – is seen as *the* fundamental way of dividing people into groups, so that the significance of sex-as-reproductive-capacity overrides any other feature of their corporeality, then important consequences follow from this claim that radically conflict with our culture's self-definition. For not only does a foundational sex difference elevate childbirth to be the most important aspect of human beings' bodies; it also underpins, through the mind/body opposition, the basis on which rationality is seen as the most important aspect of their minds. Interestingly then, the historical identification of rationality with men and irrationality with women can be seen to depend upon, but to be a *secondary* consequence of, a prior identification of bodies. This conclusion is important because it radically conflicts with the predominantly liberal character of Western culture, which downgrades the significance of a foundational sex difference and emphasizes the significance of rational freedom and autonomy.

It follows that the mind/body split which is complexly active here (Bordo 1993: 5), as well as discounting the role of emotions, elevates mind but covertly ties the definition of mind to a foundational body. This mind/body split is accentuated by the divergence which is seen to exist between the values and significance of childbirth and rationality. Hood-Williams maintains that the constructed sex/gender definition 'is wrong to award such significance to the fact that humans reproduce sexually'. He argues convincingly that there 'are simply no necessary social consequences to this fact any more than there are necessary social consequences to the fact that humans may have black skins or green eyes' (Hood-Williams 1996: 13). He accounts for this attribution of false significance by noting the fundamental assumption in sociology (and one may note throughout the social sciences) that 'what is called culture is variable and what is called nature is obdurate' (ibid.). However, it is clear that 'sex cannot operate as a sort of material base to the superstructure of gender. Gender is always already implicated within the attempts to define sex – whether as difference or similarity' (ibid.).

An interesting example of this point is found in the way that gender stereotypes of feminine passivity and masculine assertiveness are imported into biology. (See also Moore [1988: 35] on their importation into anthropology.) Despite the conclusive evidence of research that 'the extreme fragility of the sperm, which swim "blindly" in circles and mill around, unless "captured" and "held fast" by the adhesive molecules on the surface of the egg' (Segal 1994: 220), the stereotyped images persist. As Segal documents, the 'ovum is variously depicted in contemporary medical texts as "floating", "drifting" . . . and contrasted with the "masculinity" of the "streamlined", "strong" sperm: "lashing their tails" as they make their "perilous journey" through the "hostile environment" of the vagina to "penetrate"' the egg (ibid.: 219).

When Pateman (1988) drew attention to the 'sexual contract' underlying the social contract in liberal political theory, one of the things she highlighted was the way in which women in effect promised to reproduce, that is, to use their bodies, only with their husbands. Current liberal theory attempts to make women equal to men (rather than men equal to women), but this attempt only overlays and masks, but does not abolish or overcome, the underlying equation of women with reproduction and bodies. It is clear that there is a real sense in which many men still distrust women in the public realm, in case they bring their bodies with them: disrupting the workplace with maternity leave, with claims for sick leave for pre-menstrual tension, claims for leave for their bodies by extension to care for sick children, claims of sexual harassment, and by introducing sexual temptation into the 'sexually neutral' workplace. Pateman was right that this liberation is self-contradictory, and that the underlying dichotomy remains.

An argument developed elsewhere on citizenship (Prokhovnik 1998) is designed precisely to contest the liberal view which rests upon the opposition in which it is mind that is active in the public sphere and body active in the private sphere. This view implies that access to the world of agency can only be gained through transition to the public sphere. The alternative notion of citizenship that was developed was grounded in the sense that free and autonomous (including relationally connected), rational (including embodied and emotion-bearing) individuals can be active in *both* spheres.

Kaplan and Rogers also challenge the attribution of a 'natural' sex difference which underlies the sex/gender distinction, accentuating the way in which 'biology is not "value-free"' (Kaplan and Rogers 1990: 205). Rogers's essay (1988), also challenges examples of biological determinism, criticizing the way in which such theories employ reductionism, uni-causality and division into dichotomous categories. Like Hood-Williams, Kaplan and Rogers provide a wealth of well-documented evidence which undermines the methods and findings by which biologists (for instance through cranology, metabolism or hormones) purported to substantiate a range of natural bipolar sex differences. It also counters sociobiologists who continue to attempt to provide reductive behavioural explanations by locating a natural sex difference in genetic makeup (see for instance Diamond 1997). Kaplan and Rogers also highlight the way in which a medical model of human sexuality, in terms of anatomy and disease, is used to reinforce the belief in natural bipolar sex difference and its heterosexual/ist consequences (Kaplan and Rogers 1990: 223). They note for instance the importance of environmental factors such as nutrition and stress, whose influence has conventionally been denied, in modifying the chromosomal identification of sex difference, and in hormonal changes (ibid.: 212–4). They conclude that in the light of the complexity and variations found in the biological evidence, the 'rigid either/or assignment of the sexes is only a convenient social construct, not a biological reality' (ibid.: 214).

Recent research on the social construction of sex has also emphasized that biology does not determine personality or disposition, and so cannot serve as a cause of social identity and roles. This is the sound starting-point of the argument that led to the false conclusion concerning gender. As a result of this evidence, and following from Grosz's argument (1994), it must be recognized that embodiment need not be defined narrowly by anatomical sex or sex difference, but by an increased status of the body in general, its capacities and its dynamic interrelations with mind, emotions, environment and context.

Specifically Grosz articulates the socially constructed sense of sexual drive when she highlights the significance of meaning as dynamic and malleable, in contrast to the fiction of a given or natural inert material truth. She notes succinctly that 'we desire objects not to gratify our needs, but because they mean something, they have value or significance' (Grosz 1990b: 4). As with the examples of eating and childbirth given at the beginning of the chapter, motherhood is a drive but is also socially constructed in the sense that its meaning occurs within socially-meaningful practices.

One of the insights developed within the discourse of the ethic of care is that caring is constructed, in at least three senses. Drive or instinct alone would not result in an adequate notion of care in any particular culture and society. Second, care is mind-affected: that is, seeing, hearing, and noticing the needs of others are sentient activities which are previously unrecognized parts of care (Deveaux 1995, see also Walzer 1996). Third, care involves commitments which are developed over time and which are powerful because they are freely given, not coerced (Sevenhuijsen 1995). In the same way, sexuality is a drive but is at the same time socially constructed. How the drive is expressed is mediated by social construction, in conforming to or in transgressing social practices. What the drive means is socially constructed, in that its meaning occurs in a framework of social meaning and contestation. And what is accepted and unacceptable is socially constructed.

## *Gender*

The meaning of the term 'gender' is both very clear and very confused, and by exploring this ambiguity some important conclusions can be drawn. As Haste notes, '[w]e inhabit an engendered world. Gender is the primary category of our social relationships' (Haste 1993: 60), and yet the discussion that has already been rehearsed in this chapter has shown that the term 'gender' is deeply ambiguous.

Butler captures well 'the ambiguous nature of gender identity', when she asks how gender can 'be both a matter of choice and cultural construction?' (Butler 1987: 128). This ambiguity is replicated in the academic study of the sex/gender distinction, in which 'gender' refers to at least three things. The first is the social construction of masculinity and femininity, in social roles. This is the sense in which for instance Moore considers 'the cultural construction of gender' (Moore 1988: 13–16). The second is behaviour (social and personal and intimate), and third is an individual's identity recognized from the outside on the basis of a 'natural' sex difference.[2] The use of the term 'gender' in the feminist literature also has multiple aims: to describe the social normative frame through which discrimination occurs, as a critical tool for feminists to use to overcome women's oppression; and as the means through which feminists can assert a distinctive identity which consists neither of being non-men nor of being absorbed into (male-defined) society.

Two pertinent examples can be used to illustrate the ambiguity of the term 'gender'. First, as Hawkesworth notes, we need to attend to a whole range of meanings of gender. 'Gender' can stand for 'crucial distinctions such as sexed embodiedness, sexuality, sexual identity, gender identity, gendered divisions of labour, gendered social relations, and gender symbolism, rather than collapsing such diverse notions into the single term "gender"' (Hawkesworth 1997: 682). In the second example of ambiguity, gender refers to (only) two kinds of *social* persons and social behaviours, for instance in the study of gender inequalities, but it also refers to (multiple) choice in the idea of gender performance.

This second example maps in complex fashion on to different usages in sociology and political theory. In Stoller's definition, which is still influential in some areas of sociology, where 'gender roles' are seen to derive directly from 'socialization', gender is non-malleable. Gender is here thus defined directly by a strictly dichotomous anatomical sex distinction. The term 'gender' makes sense here in the context of studying, for example, 'the story of the creation of a gendered workforce' in the nineteenth century (Scott 1988: 46), or the importance of considering the impact of gender divisions in the study of areas of social change (Charles 1993). Lutz is working within this bipolar notion of gender, even when she relates evidence which contradicts the stereotype of systematic differences in emotional response patterns between men and women (Lutz 1996: 152).

In contrast, in mainstream liberal political theory 'gender' is essentially a term defining choice, agency, and freedom from a sexed body. In areas of sociology which embrace a social constructionist viewpoint, gender is again about choice. Note for instance Mara Miller's persuasive evidence that in traditional Japanese knowledge and culture, in which gender is understood as culturally constructed, '[w]hat is "feminine" is acknowledged to be a social construct, achievable by persons of either sex, regardless of the sexual body' (Miller 1993: 484). In knowledge, though not in social role, she notes, 'one's utilization of a "masculine" or "feminine" style or way . . . is not a simple function of one's biological sex, but is a function of one's choices, intentions and purposes' (ibid.).

This social constructionist view of gender is not free from internal contradictions, however. The social constructionist definition of gender employed in this chapter can be used to illustrate these contradictions. It takes from the 'gender' side a problem identified from the 'sex' side in the previous section. In one of the dominant current social scientific discourses, 'gender' concerns the social roles that people take on – typically in activities like employment, in the workplace, in voting, in media consumption, in the distribution of household and childcare and family tasks, shopping, driving behaviour, patterns of social life – covering a multiplicity of social, political, economic and family life behaviours. According to this view, in our society a range of gender performances can be linked to either sex. In our liberal society dominated by middle-class values, there is thought to be only a weak link between the essentialist claim of the body (in anatomical sex) and the world in which gender is thought to operate. In this world body is (thought to be) in general not nearly as significant as other factors; it is a world of communication largely through the mind and language and agency. At the same time, however, we are besieged by visual representations of bodies. The power of the desire for conformity to certain body images, in particular to the portrayal of absurdly thin women's bodies, is seen for instance in the development of the phenomenon of anorexia (Bordo 1988, Lloyd, M. 1996).

The internal contradiction for 'gender', between the predominant liberal elevation of mind and the power in Western liberal societies of particular body images, is clear. Thus one of the dominant views in the contemporary social sciences is that the sex/gender distinction provides potentially all persons with access to the world of agency in a positive, emancipatory way, through a liberal egalitarianism which generously downplays the importance of the body. However, the neat separation upon which this perspective rests, of *body* active in the private realm and passive in the public realm, and of *mind* operative in the public realm, is subject to enormous complications in practice. Many issues continue to problematize this dominant viewpoint and its attempted disregard of the body in the public realm, including maternity leave; the ambiguous or lower status of jobs which involve the body, for example those of models or building site labourers or even factory workers; power dressing at work; and now the formalization of sexual harassment procedures in the workplace, which acknowledges (though unsatisfactorily) the existence of this public/private transgression. Despite these problems liberal theory and practice still cling to the fiction that a neat separation holds.

However the conceptual problems at stake here are more serious than has been generally recognized. For the *norm* establishing the way in which 'men' and 'women' are identified in gender roles continues to be defined deterministically in terms of their anatomical sex. The result is that the opportunity offered to agency in the public world of gender is always being evaluated according to values which come from the identification of women with body and the 'natural' and the naturalized freedom of men from body (Brown 1987). In this way the liberal theory of autonomous individualism, especially in its extension to include women, is persistently undermined by the unacknowledged tie to a biological sexed body.

For instance, when sociologists and other social scientists study patterns of 'gender inequality' in the workplace or in political participation, or when employers consider ensuring a 'gender balance' on an interview panel, there are four unacknowledged problems. First, rather than a variety of possible gender performances following from 'natural' sex difference in a non-causal manner, as described above, the study of 'gender inequality' etc. already assumes a determinist relation between sex and gender. Thus the gender of persons is identified directly on the basis of their sex, in a purely essentialist fashion. This usage of the term gender, which depends upon an essentialist view, is sometimes found in self-defined feminists who would want to promote a non-essentialist theory of difference. The outcome is that the determinist and non-determinist definitions of gender coexist in a wholly unsatisfactory fashion in some areas of social science.

Second, and as a result of this confused situation, because of the asymmetry between male and female in the definition of 'sex' (men are sexed in the private sphere but male norms define the 'neutral' person in the public sphere), it follows that women are free to take on a variety of 'gender' roles only by transgressing their sex. Third, there is a resulting confusion in the literature between 'gender roles'. In one sense the term refers to traditional occupations and behaviours of men and women (in which there are only two possible genders), whereby men's roles map on to occupations in the public sphere and women's to the private sphere. In the other, 'gender roles' refers to the alleged diversity of choices (in which there are theoretically a multiplicity of possible genders) for women as well as men in the public sphere.

The fourth problem arises from there being no agreed standard by which to judge what counts as gender equality, and to measure what degree of inequality is acceptable. There is the statistical 50 per cent view, which is underlying or assumed, though very uneasily, in many studies (for example, 'until we have 50 per cent of women MPs in parliament, 50 per cent of the workforce' etc.). There is the critical mass theory, which argues that reaching a threshold, defined at around 30 per cent, brings about a change. There is a third statistically-based view, which considers that a three per cent measure of difference between men and women counts as a gender gap. And there is the view that gender gaps should be measured differently according to the functional practice being studied. This view could be expressed in the notion that the meaning of gender equality is situational and needs to be cashed out in terms of gender equity. The absence of a comprehensive and theoretically-grounded discussion of the meaning of gender equality seriously limits the value of research undertaken by empirical social scientists in this area.

## *Sex and gender*

The view that the sex/gender distinction means that there is an essential difference between men and women, determined by the reproductive capacities of their bodies, is still so widely held as to remain dominant. Hawkesworth for instance documents how recent works on gender continue to 'replicate rather than undermine the natural attitude' (Hawkesworth 1997: 654), seeing gender as having ontological status and causal force (ibid.: 680). Or, more accurately, women *as a group* continue to be seen as having reproductive bodies, whereas men do not. Hawkesworth argues that there are strong grounds for recognizing that sexual dimorphism is not given in nature. Three unacknowledged consequences follow from this view.

First, there is an asymmetry between the essentialist definition of women and the non-essentialist, gender-neutral definition of men. This asymmetry accounts for instance for the unresolved tension inherent in the gender-neutral requirements of equal opportunities legislation. Thus while it is now not lawful to ask a women at a job interview if she is planning to have children, or how she intends to manage the care of her children when at work, the gender-neutral definition of 'person' carries with it the *assumption* that men are free to escape from their bodies into autonomy, freedom, rationality and productive work. Men are assumed to make this transition in direct form, while women are assumed to make it only indirectly, through the cumbersome process of equal opportunities requirements trumping the underlying and persistently sexed bodies of women.

Second, because it is women as a group who are thought to have this reproductive capacity, this sets up a norm from which specific women who cannot have children become regarded as abnormal or deviant. And third, because it is women as a group who are seen to have reproductive capacity, it is women as a group who take on the burden of the body defined according to this one narrow and specific capacity.

Once the biologization of 'sex' is recognized, along with the limited nature of the liberal definition of gender as a critical tool, two things become clear. First, the *significance* of all the meanings of 'sex' and 'gender' is socially constructed. It is socially constructed not in the liberal sense that simply (but incoherently) prioritizes mind over body, but in a sense that involves and takes into account the integral roles played by the three components of a material element, social norms, and agency. Second, the commonalities between 'sex' and 'gender' are more important than are the differences that the attempted distinction between sex and gender is designed to show. As Lloyd concludes, 'our bodies, as they figure in our self-consciousness, are always already socially constructed' (Lloyd 1989: 20). The biologization of 'sex' creates a false distinction between a 'natural' component as given, and a constructed gender component as given but malleable. While at the anatomy and biology end of the continuum we are closer to a material element, this is not to posit that materiality as reality or foundation, for the meaning of materiality is also socially mediated.

The arguments rehearsed in this chapter so far show the theoretical untenability of both a foundational 'natural' sex difference and the liberal definition of gender. It follows that 'sex and gender' is a false distinction, the product of a 1970s mistake. The history of the sex/gender distinction so far, and the examination of the two terms, lead to the conclusion that either the terms sex and gender are both inert or the notion of gender choice is too thin. Two of the three options put forward by the sex/gender distinction see both sex and gender as non-volatile in an important sense. For as long as gender only trades on a foundational 'natural' sex difference (which undermines an effective difference between the two terms), then all the elements of the sex/gender distinction are determined, either biologically or socially or both. The third option is equally unsatisfactory because it cannot adequately redeem the reductive, determinist basis of the first two options. Even though sex is seen here as biologically given and gender as socially constructed and therefore reconstructable, this liberal view has only a thin notion of choice derived from a mind/body dichotomy.

Hood-Williams sums up a persuasive challenge when he argues that the 'integrity of the concept of gender' deserves critical inquiry (Hood-Williams 1996: 14). He provides a range of valuable evidence for the view that the sex/gender problematic is 'wrong in its apparent assumption that a straightforward distinction may be made between these two terms' (Hood-Williams 1996: 13).

This argument shows that there is not just one simple distinction at stake. In the sex/gender distinction there are a whole range of things going on, some of them overlapping, covering a whole range of practices, all involving mediated understandings. The term 'sex' has a range of meanings : sex as psychological mainspring, as reproductive capacity defined either by anatomy or by biology more broadly, as a drive, as sexual orientation, as sexual activity, as love and intimacy, as power, as identity, and sex as representing body. 'Gender' similiarly has a wide taxonomy: gender as sexed embodiedness, sexuality, sexual identity, gender identity, gendered divisions of labour or social relations, and gender symbolism. It is vital to note that all of these have been mapped on to a man/woman dichotomy that has been read through, and interpreted in terms of, an underlying mind/body disjunction.

### *The heterosexual/ist norm*

One of the consequences of the reductionist biological explanation on which the sex/gender distinction rests has been the idea of strict bipolar sex assignment, and the 'natural' attraction to the 'opposite' sex (Kaplan and Rogers 1990: 217). Gay, lesbian, and queer theories challenge this naturalized explanation very effectively. Kaplan and Rogers's work raises an important criticism of simplistic biological models of sexuality, a criticism which has a significant bearing on the strict bipolar definition and the rigid boundaries it sets up, which are crossed, ruptured, and transgressed by gay, lesbian and queer theorists. They point to the disjunction between the theory that genitalia are the major determinant of sex assignment, and the way in which sexual attraction is usually based on something other than primary sexual characteristics. It is ordinarily based on 'clothing [and] secondary sexual characteristics . . . which can lie anywhere along a continuum on which the categories of male and female overlap . . . [and on] behaviour', as well as on a 'range of much less sexually specific characteristics (eyes, voice, ears, body size, smile, smell, laughter, personality, etc.)' (ibid.: 224).

Patriarchal culture, prioritizing as it does values associated with men and regarding women as 'other', contains two dimensions, and the second is designed to reinforce the first. Thus patriarchy is not only about men as a group dominating women as a group (and now also about the exclusion and marginalization of non-dominant masculinities). Patriarchy is also about the imposition of a heterosexual/ist norm. The first dimension relies on a notion of gender determined reductively by a conception of 'natural' sex difference, and the second dimension depends upon a notion of sexuality which is also based on a conception of the natural complementarity of a given biological foundation. Hoagland underlines the crucial dichotomous characteristic of heterosexualism when she defines it as 'a way of living that normalizes the dominance of one person and the subordination of another' (Hoagland, quoted in Lee-Lampshire 1995: 34). And as Butler notes, '[f]or Wittig, when we name sexual difference, we create it; we restrict our understanding of relevant sexual parts to those that aid in the process of reproduction, and thereby render heterosexuality an ontological necessity' (Butler 1987: 135). Butler comments, in respect of the way the two dimensions of the heterosexual/ist norm have a common basis, that here 'Wittig contests the social practice of valorizing certain anatomical features as being definitive not only of anatomical sex but of sexual identity' (ibid.).

The heterosexual/ist norm is part of what feminists identify as patriarchal culture, because its primary aim is to enforce heterosexuality on women for the benefit of the dominant (heterosexual) masculinity. According to some feminists, patriarchal effects such as male violence and domestic labour are not only sustained by a cultural identification of persons as masculine and feminine, and the valuing of the former and alienation of the latter. They are also maintained by the force inherent in the active/passive norms of heterosexual sexual relations, such that '[h]eterosexual desire is eroticized power difference' (Jeffreys 1994: 62). That norm is compulsory, in that to venture beyond it and announce that one is outside the norm, is to be judged to be marginal, 'other', lacking legitimate existence and purpose in society. Some categories of women (for instance single mothers in Britain, and even more so prostitutes) are sometimes derided and regarded with contempt, as 'other' to dominant men, but they are nevertheless included in heterosexual/ist society. However, lesbians and some gay men (especially transexuals and transvestites) and bisexual and intersexual persons are 'other' to the economy of the whole heterosexual/ist dualism that helps to define society. Some gay men are accommodated, if they 'pass' as heterosexual men and seem to subscribe to male dominance over women.

Butler highlights the dichotomous perspective which informs the heterosexual/ist norm. She argues that 'the heterosexual imperative enables certain sexed identifications and forecloses and/or disavows other identifications'. As she continues, this 'exclusionary matrix by which subjects are formed thus requires the simultaneous production of a domain of abject beings, those who are not yet "subjects"', but who form the constitutive outside to the domain of the subject' (Butler 1993: 3). Subjectivity is so crucial here because only a subject can have autonomy and a self-determining life. In the same way citizenship is crucial because only citizens (in constrast, ironically, to subjects) can be recognized by and in the political community as having a fully participative and fulfilling life.

The heterosexual/ist norm makes three important assumptions. It assumes the complementarity of the (two) sexes. In consequence, the conventional idea of 'sexual preference' (which can only mean between men and women) is coeval with sex difference, and with gender difference. As Smart notes, the 'presumption that most people make . . . [is] that all people are heterosexual unless they declare otherwise' (Smart 1996: 233). The second assumption concerns a *norm* of heterosexual behaviour and performance, which results not only in homophobia based on what is regarded as aberrant, deviant and unnatural, but also in a heterosexual norm which is hegemonic.

Heterosexuality can, however, refer to a diversity of expressions and performances outside its monolithic and hegemonic meaning. Smart, for instance, calls for the deconstruction of the single and unified meaning of heterosexual identity for women, 'to heterosexualit*ies* at the very least' (Smart 1996: 234). Segal makes a good case for the view that heterosexuality has at least two facets. First, it has been a compulsory norm, which leaves the question now of how to 'struggle against phallic hegemony in defining sex and gender, to affirm more enabling constructions of the female body?' Heterosexuality is also internally problematic. She argues that '[s]exual relations are perhaps the most fraught and troubling of all social relations precisely because, especially when heterosexual, they so often *threaten* rather than confirm gender polarity' (Segal 1994: 254–5). 'Every time women enjoy sex with men, confident in the knowledge that this, just *this*, is what *we* want, and how *we* want it', Segal continues, 'we are already confounding the cultural and political meanings given to heterosexuality in dominant sexual discourses. There "sex" is something "done" by active men to passive women, not something *women do*' (ibid.: 266). Segal concludes with the important comment, '[s]traight sex . . . can be no less "perverse" than its "queer" alternatives. Ridiculing hierarchies of sexuality and gender, it too can serve as a body-blow to the old male order of things' (ibid.: 318).

The third assumption, then, is the definition of any lived identity or preference or performance outside this double norm as deviant. Butler notes the 'persistence of *dis*identification' that women and gay people suffer, and remarks that 'it may be precisely through practices which underscore disidentification with those regulatory norms by which sexual difference is materialized that both feminist and queer politics are mobilized' (Butler 1993: 4).

A long list could be constructed of preferences and performances, designed to demonstrate the point (also important to queer theory, as discussed below) that the male/female and hetero/homo sex dichotomies belie the diversity and mutability of sex. Such a list also raises the issue of what the notion of 'performance' is taken to entail. Butler argues that 'in no sense can it be concluded that the part of gender that is performed is therefore the "truth" of gender' (Butler 1997: 20). For gender 'is neither a purely psychic truth, conceived as "internal" and "hidden", nor is it reducible to a surface appearance; on the contrary, its undecideability is to be traced as the play *between* psyche and appearance'. Further, she says, 'this will be a "play" regulated by heterosexist constraints though not, for that reason, fully reducible to them' (ibid.: 19).

Butler's point also provides an answer to the problem that a list of preferences and performances describes all subject positions, self-chosen identities, whereas sexuality is also subject to dynamic power relations, in two senses. One is the sense of the attraction of power, whoever may hold it, whatever their identity; the other is the sense that the meanings of all the options in a list occur within a society of patriarchal power relations. On this second point O'Driscoll's argument is pertinent, that 'the practice of particular sexual acts did not constitute an identity-forming category before the invention of the terms "homosexual" and "lesbian" in the late nineteenth century'. From this perspective, she argues, 'it would not make sense to speak of an eighteenth-century lesbian' (O'Driscoll 1996: 42). Her highlighting of an asymmetry between sex and gender is also relevant here. Whereas according to the classic sex/gender distinction, 'gender and sexuality are seen as connected' (ibid.: 35), nonconformism in gender does not necessarily imply nonconformism in sexual practice. For example cross-dressing may be involved in a variety of different sexual practices.

The development of queer theory has important repurcussions for feminism (Butler 1990b, 1993, Sedgwick 1990), not least because it 'return[s] . . . feminist theorizing to sexuality' (Clough 1994: 144).[3] Queer theory focuses on issues of sexuality, raised first by feminism only in relation to women in patriarchal culture, then by lesbians (and gay men) in relation to (heterosexist) feminism. It also aspires to go beyond feminism, in the same manner that black women challenged the white bias of second wave feminism. Queer theory, generated partly from radical feminism and the lesbian separatism to which the logic of Wittig's argument (1992) leads, can be seen as one of the most important positive responses to the institutionalization of second wave feminism, a reaction against feminism's losing of its radical way, because it represents the most significant attempt to reinvest those radical aims *vis-à-vis* patriarchal culture.[3]

The problem for feminism here is put succinctly by Calhoun, who cautions that so long as there is a central commitment in feminism to the emancipation of *women*, 'gender may continue operating as a lesbian closet' (Calhoun 1995: 30). More broadly queer theory's greatest achievement to date is to have challenged the oppressive dichotomy contained in the bipolar choice of male or female gender. As Haraway notes, the 'refusal to become or to remain a "gendered" man or a ["gendered"] woman . . . is an eminently political insistence' (Haraway 1991: 148).

Queer theory also advances the cause of one of the postmodern notions of difference, in which the advocacy of and expression of difference represents a celebration of multiplicity and heterogeneity, a resistance to the totalizing tendency of all identities, a refusal to conform to unity. Queer theorists would endorse Trihn Minh-ha's statement that '[d]ifference is that which undermines the very idea of identity' (Minh-ha 1989: 96). It also advances further the transgressive challenge made by lesbian and gay theory to the dominance of heterosexual relations, providing a rallying point for an affiliation to antihomophobic politics among heterosexuals, homesexuals and bisexuals.

Queer theory is trying, among other things, to establish that there is no necessary determining connection between 'natural' biological sex and gender in the sense of sexuality expressed in a world of social and cultural practices and norms. The ideas of 'transgression' and 'trespass' (and in some senses of 'disruption' and 'contestation') are designed to highlight the possibility both of deliberately flouting norms and of critically examining and perhaps reconfiguring (less radically) or undoing (more radically) those norms. But it is vital to recognize that the idea of transgressing a nature/culture link is inadequate if it retains that dichotomization (Butler 1993: 4–12), for flouting norms can amount ultimately to no more than another form of recognizing their enduring power.

The idea of homosexuality challenged Rubin's (1975) derivation of gender from sex, but only to a limited extent. Now queer theory wants to cut the connection altogether, and is adamant that a multiplicity of gender performances (including parodies of norms and conventions) in sexual practice (widely understood) cannot be read off from, and bears no relation to, an underlying anatomical sex. Butler (1990b) criticizes the (heterosexual/ist bias of the) notion of gender as a social construction of a naturalized, given, sexuality–anatomy, and argues against a formulation of the distinction which discounts the importance of fantasy, the psyche and unconscious desire in sexuality.

Queer theory has three ambitious aims, which take it in three different directions. Moreover its three aims are sometimes contradictory. It aims first to challenge the fixed, settled meanings of lesbian and gay sexual relations, and it does so as part of an impulse to critique the essentialism of all identity politics; in this sense queer is non-reformist. As Walters expresses it, '"queer" is really radically gay, moving "against both assimilationist politics and separatist identity definitions"' (Walters 1996: 834, including quote from Sedgwick 1993: 28). Relatedly, taking its lead from Butler's influential work, queer theory also focuses on an exploration of practices of disciplinary knowledge, and so shifts away from lesbian theory's focus on an epistemology of experience (Clough 1994: 145).

Second, queer theory seeks to provide an inclusive umbrella term for the variety of transgressions of the boundaries established by the heterosexual/ist norm, an umbrella term for all 'sexual minorities'. And third, queer theory wants to identify a substantive queer identity as one constituted by (a self-consciousness of) subversive bodily acts, rather than by a subject-identity derived from gender or 'reality'. In this sense the queer perspective is characterized by an openness to difference (although in much queer theorizing, the notion of 'difference', perhaps a useful critical tool here, is not prominent), one without pre-existing assumptions about sexuality based just on anatomy or gender. Sexuality is neither determined nor chosen but negotiated (Butler 1997: 22). This third aim of queer theory is found for instance in Phelan, who describes 'queer' as 'a particular inflection of nonstraight identity, "queer"...includes lesbians, gays, bisexuals, transgendered people, and other "gender outlaws"' (Phelan 1997: 7), a definition which does not exclude heterosexual men and women with a 'queer' perspective. This aim explodes the very idea of sexual minorities and majorities and so, as another result, breaks down the shared ground of gay and lesbian theory and politics. The first and third aims explicitly seek to go beyond the heterosexual/ist binary of normal/deviant, while the second aim seeks to emancipate the oppressive quality of the not-A position in the dichotomous pair.

In sum, the objectives of queer theory are to 'reject any radical disjuncture between heterosexuality and homosexuality' (Clough 1994: 145); to demonstrate the interdependence of the homo/hetero sex opposition, and the interdependence of the heterosexual/ist norm and whatever is posited as outside it; *and* to challenge and transgress those binary pairs. It is also clear that the third objective contains a paradox, for 'queer' represents a dynamic 'resistance to regimes of the normal' (Warner 1993) which loses its force once it becomes a subject position with which one could identify in its own right, and settles into a 'political interest-representation' (ibid.: xxvi).

Butler's work is crucial in this discourse. As Clough puts it, Butler 'suggests that sex does not precede gender. Instead a regulatory fiction ["the heterosexual matrix of desire"] functions to converge sex, gender, and desire' (Clough 1994: 149). The outcome, says Butler, is that the 'cultural matrix through which gender identity has become intelligible requires that certain kinds of identities cannot "exist"'. She has in mind 'those in which gender does not follow from sex and those in which the practices of desire do not "follow" from either sex or gender' (Butler 1990b: 17). According to Butler, sexuality must take account of what comes from inside, from desire. Sexuality does not arise from the supposed naturalness of a given body, nor from bodily parts. Butler may, in the end, be overstating the argument for the significance of the underlying power of the internal, of the psychological drive of desire. Nevertheless it is certainly the case that Western liberal culture is predisposed to discount the power of the internal, in favour of a view of knowledge as scientific, coming from the external, the 'real', the tangible, the empirically observable, verifiable and definable.

In addition to its three primary aims and objectives, queer theory has also developed a notion of 'outlaw theorizing' which investigates 'the ways in which the breaking of sexual taboos can call identity categories into question without necessarily constituting an identity' (O'Driscoll 1996: 36). Thus for instance lesbian theory and gay theory focus on 'sexual practice as identity marker' (ibid.), whereas 'transgender "straight" sexuality breaks some of the most taboo barriers' (ibid.: 37). Outlaw theorizing seeks to go beyond the straight/gay distinction.

Walters articulates a series of serious problems raised by the development of queer theory, including the sense of unease induced by the 'postmodern cool' of queer theory (Walters 1996: 830), and the manner in which 'queer' has already become subject to the way the mainstream commodifies, 'recodes and cannibalizes these new images, icons, activisms' (Walters 1996: 831). She is also concerned about the vulnerability of queer theory to the inclusion of paedophiles and incest perpetrators under the umbrella of queer practices (ibid.: 838), and with the way the popularity of 'queer' 'erases lesbian specificity' and 'evacuates the importance of feminism' (ibid.: 843). She notes the naivety, 'in a culture in which male is the default gender' of seeing 'queer as somehow gender *neutral*' (ibid.: 845), and cautions against the 'implicit referent' in queer discourse to a gay male subject (ibid.: 846) and the consequent devaluing of women's sexuality all over again (ibid.: 847–8). In addition Walters expresses the timely reminder that queer theory is not occurring in a postpatriarchal world (ibid.: 850), and importantly she warns against the prospect of 'the construction of the queer hegemony' (ibid.: 837), in which feminism (and other things) disappear. While Butler, in an essay published in 1997, does recognize that if '"queer" politics postures independently of these other modalities of power [i.e. racist and misogynist discursive regimes], it will lose its democratizing force' (Butler 1997: 15), Walters' final complaint does point up a valid problem about the way queer theory is more generally discussed.

Walters' conclusions are well-made. On the positive side she argues that 'we should embrace [queer theory's] recognition that much slips out of the rigid distinctions of hetero/homo, man/woman and that our theoretical and political engagements need to reckon creatively with the excess that dares not speak its name'. She also commends the 'queer attempt to understand that sexuality and sexual desire is not reducible to gender' (Walters 1996: 963). Nevertheless she is sceptical that destabilizing gender can 'top the power of gender – a power that still sends too many women to the hospital, shelter, rape crisis center, despair' (ibid.: 866). She observes, 'we cannot afford to lose sight of the materiality of oppression and its operation in structural and institutional spaces', and she suspects that queer theory fails to understand that '[d]estabilizing gender (or rendering its surface apparent) is not the same as overthrowing it' (ibid.).

Likewise Segal rightly maintains that 'the first point for sex and gender saboteurs is to acknowledge the real constraints of women's limited social power and submissive or compliant cultural legacies', and the second point 'is to acknowledge that the codes linking sexuality to hierarchal polarities of gender, though always present, are never fixed and immutable. On the contrary, they are chronically unstable and actually very easy to subvert and parody' (Segal 1994: 242).

It is vital for queer theory to address three further problems, in addition to those implicit in the divergence between its three aims, and to those contained in Walters' comments. The first is that the terms of the argument used by queer theory are still tied to the faulty 1970s sex/gender distinction. There are real dangers in remaining committed to so flawed a distinction, particularly in such a literal way. Queer theory *plays* with the sex/gender distinction, but is tied to it in calling for the recognition of a multiplicity of genders. In its very 'transgressiveness', its very 'subversiveness', queer is announcing its own limitations. 'Queer' is in danger of meaning nothing more than supplying the exception that proves the rule. In this guise queer gains its force from the attraction of the illicit. It depends upon the continuing efficacy of the rule of the norm, the normal and the compulsory, and in doing so therefore reinforces that rule.

The danger here is that the 'difference' that queer theory wishes to implement, 'to sustain a sexual field of multiple, debinarized, fluid, ever-shifting differences' (Fraser 1997a: 24), may only make sense in the context of the persistence of a dichotomous mode of thinking. The dichotomous heterosexual/ist view naturalizes the idea that the world really is made up, naturally, of men and women, nature and culture, black and white. In so far as queer is about transgression, it remains at the point of resistance and critique, and cannot get beyond that to reconstitute the mind/body dichotomy into a relational connection. Ultimately queer transgression is only a form of trespass against convention, defying an injunction, but staying within the rules established by the law. The relational view challenges the fundamental ontological assumption of the dichotomous view, and so goes beyond the limits of queer in this form.

The second problem follows on from the first, in that it is not at all clear what might happen to 'queer' in a postpatriarchal, post-heterosexual/ist culture. It is possible that queer would simply disappear, if its transgressiveness became redundant. Alternatively it could continue to have some purchase, standing for the unsettling of conventions or for the need for critical reflection upon particular differences.

The third problem is that although Butler is careful not to employ a shallow reading of the notion of gender performance, the danger of doing so is very prevalent, and immanent, in queer theory in general. Hale expresses this problem when he notes that 'simply engaging in gender play, sexually or in public acts of self-presentation, is not as subversive as some contemporary queer politics and theory would have it' (Hale 1996: 117). The cautionary note that Diana Coole sounds in a recent article about feminism applies just as well to queer theory. She highlights the importance of not rendering gender 'merely discursive', and warns against severing gender 'from persons to become merely a cultural code of representation'. She is critical of a view of transgression whereby 'choosing one's gender and subject position begins to seem . . . like any other rational choice' (Coole 1994: 133). The continuing meaningfulness of sexual taboos of different kinds demonstrates that there are still psychological depths and social limits which frame queer theory's concept of transgression. For instance, sex between children and adults is considered to be wrong *not only* because of the unequal power relationship involved; the ethic of care cannot completely displace the power of the Oedipus metaphor. To cite another taboo, offering to mop up a speaker's overturned glass of water at a conference with the sanitary towel in one's bag rather than with tissues would still shock.

The reflections by Coole that were noted earlier also prompt her to examine in a useful manner the way that the ongoing conundrum of the relation between sex and gender has been 'an enduring problem for feminism', in attempting to work out 'how to combine cultural and structural analysis.' As she observes, '[n]o satisfactory way of bringing together ideological and material factors of women's oppression was ever agreed among Marxist feminists', or resolved by the cultural explanations of liberal and radical feminists. Moreover, she notes cogently, 'postmodernism represents a victory for cultural approaches', but 'its deconstructions are deeply problematic when it comes to material questions of the body' (Coole 1994: 133). The underlying problem here, to which Coole's observation points, and which is often unrecognized in feminist discussions, is that all these formulations are hampered by a continuing subscription to the mind/body dichotomy. It is at this point that the idea of a non-dichotomous view of the relation between sex and gender, between material and cultural elements, and between body and mind as aspects of the self, can make an important contribution.

The argument put forward here, then, is that once one part, this crucial foundational part (that is, sex as biological) is shown to be very different from how it was formerly conceptualized, it throws the whole distinction out of joint. In this sense one can sympathize with queer theory's deconstruction of the opposition between the natural and the social, with regard to the body in sexuality. As Gatens (1996b) demonstrates in pressing matters further than Coole, the dichotomization of sex as materialist and gender as idealist implies an insupportable dualism. It follows that the sex/gender distinction is redundant.

Another aspect of this third problem concerns the overwhelming promise of 'queer' to liberate and empower choice, self-expression, and voluntarist agency. This raises the issue of political viability discussed by Walters. For just as feminist opponents of androgyny pointed out that 'Androgyny!' hardly has the same emancipatory ring about it as does the call for 'Equality!', so the same can be said of the limited political potential of 'Queer!' as a rallying cry.

A further consequence is that, where identity or subjectivity was thought to come from the gender part of the distinction, it is now clear (Grosz 1994, Gatens 1996b) that in discussing identity both 'sex' and 'gender', or rather the range of things they stood for, are involved and are deeply implicated. Indeed once the dualism is shown to have no supportable foundation, all the implications of sex and gender are involved in subjectivity. Thus there is only one thing, but it is neither sex nor gender. It is important, instead, to rethink how the aspects that were described by sex and gender are parts of identity.

Joan Scott's work highlights the weakness and strength of queer theory. This book urges that overcoming gender inequality requires two steps: gender visibility and corporeal subjectivity. Likewise Scott proposes a similar process in suggesting that the 'difference dilemma' involves '*two* moves. The first is the systematic criticism of the operations of categorial difference, the exposure of the kinds of exclusions and inclusions – the hierarchies – it constructs' (Scott 1988: 48). The second is the affirmation of an equality that implies not sameness or identity but 'an equality that rests on differences – differences that confound, disrupt, and render ambiguous the meaning of any fixed binary opposition' (ibid.). Scott's argument, and the argument developed here for a two-step process to overcome exclusion, are important in assessing queery theory because it remains a central problem with queer theory that it holds that only one step is required.

However the strength of the queer theory position, also brought out by reference to Scott's article, is the recognition of multiplicity. Scott notes that the dualism created by the male/female opposition 'draws one line of difference, invests it with biological explanations, and then treats each side of the opposition as a unitary phenomenon' (ibid.: 46). As a result, everything 'in each category (male/female) is assumed to be the same; hence, differences within either category are suppressed.' This is owing to the way in which 'sameness constructed on each side of the binary opposition hides the multiple play of differences and maintains their irrelevance and invisibility' (ibid.). In contrast, Scott maintains, the goal 'is to see not only differences between the sexes but also the way these work to repress differences within gender groups' (ibid.).

## Towards 'corporeal subjectivity'

The sex/gender distinction has proved an illusory source of liberation for women, and so needs to be rethought. Whatever the intentions of feminists in investing the term 'gender' with emancipatory potential, the most important *social and intellectual effect* of the sex/gender distinction has been the mapping on to social and other activities and practices of the idea of a 'natural' sex difference. Segal sums up the conclusions of many theorists when she comments that 'the sex/gender distinction is now seen by many as a misleading distinction' (Segal 1994: 226). Supporting the idea of the extensive process of 'mapping', Helen Haste makes an important point when she argues that 'the metaphor which sustains our present conceptions of gender is *dualism*: we have a deep predilection for defining the world in terms of affirmation and negation, thesis and antithesis, and we map gender on to this' (Haste 1993: 287).

One way forward from this situation would be to advocate the fragmentation of femininities and masculinities, of the bipolar and single definitions of masculine/feminine. This solution is advocated by queer theorists, postmodernists, black feminists and some gender politics theorists, amongst others, but it has at least two significant drawbacks. First, it retains the basic gendered dichotomy with its exclusionary force. Second, the balance that the sex/gender distinction was designed to instigate has been not only destabilized but also rendered unviable, by the disclosure of the social construction of sex and the dependence of the notion of gender on a 'natural' and given biological foundation.

Another way forward is to suggest a conception of corporeal subjectivity which contains within it a recognition of the complex and diverse identities of those many things that have clustered under the sex/gender rubric. This is the proposal put forward here. This chapter has so far sought to lay the groundwork for the idea of corporeal subjectivity as a conception which goes beyond sex (in recognizing the implications of the statement that biology is not neutral, especially in so far as the dichotomy between sex and gender is therefore flawed), beyond gender (for the ground is cut from a uniquely social definition of gender, and the theoretical distinctiveness of gender from sex is untenable), and beyond sex and gender (for the wider significance of bodies is more important than their anatomical sex). The next step is to develop the sixth stage referred to earlier in the chapter. It involves a reconceptualization of the body as the locus of identities, in order to delineate the conception of corporeal subjectivity.

First, three of the major features of the proposal for corporeal subjectivity, developed by Grosz, Gatens and Butler, will be outlined, then two significant characteristics additional to those in their important work (but following logically from it) will be identified.

The three crucial features of the notion of corporeal subjectivity are that it is concerned with corporeality and not materiality, that it is relational, and that it is a locus of identity, of subjectivity as lived, and as gendered. The first additional characteristic concerns the logical and historical condition which requires that corporeal subjectivity occur as the second step in a two-step process, the first step of which can be called 'gender visibility'. These two steps can be conceptualized as feminism's short-term and long-term aims. The second additional characteristic concerns the manner in which corporeal subjectivity replaces the whole cluster of things that are comprehended so ambiguously under the sex/gender distinction.

### *Corporeality is not materiality*

Grosz, particularly in *Volatile Bodies* but also in her earlier work, develops a theory of corporeal subjectivity which must be the starting point of the discussion. Her conception of corporeality centres upon how the category of 'body' fits into the sex/gender debate, and she analyses how bodies are about sex but also about gender. In examining the character of the body, Grosz argues, we can break down the mind/body dualism in its exterior/interior guise, as yet another nature/culture dichotomy in which mind has been privileged in our understanding and knowledge.

An important feature of Grosz's conception of corporeality in *Volatile Bodies* in particular is that it succeeds in yielding an understanding which does not reduce body to materialism. A materialist interpretation of mind and body, reason and emotion, sex and gender, would grossly diminish her careful construction, which goes beyond a dichotomous view in articulating a truly relational understanding of some aspects of mind and body.

Grosz directly addresses the mind/body split in *Volatile Bodies*. She argues convincingly that the body is no longer the passive vehicle for the mind but is 'the very "stuff" of subjectivity'. The subject, she says, 'can no longer readily succumb to the neutralization and neutering of its specificity' (Grosz 1994: ix). She pinpoints explicitly how dualism 'is responsible for the modern forms of elevation of consciousness . . . above corporeality', and how Cartesian dualism in particular 'establishes an unbridgeable gulf between mind and matter, a gulf most easily disavowed, however problematically, by reductionism' (ibid.: 7). It follows that the 'primacy of a psychical interiority' presupposed by the mind/body dichotomy, in which the body is understood through metaphors of 'embodiment' or 'containment' can be effectively challenged by 'demonstrating its necessary dependence on a corporeal exteriority' (ibid.: xii) in a relational manner. Such an understanding supersedes the 'impasse posed by dichotomous accounts of the person which divide the subject into the mutually exclusive categories of mind and body' (ibid.: 21).

One of the great strengths of Grosz's *Volatile Bodies* is that it provides a very positive notion of corporeality which avoids the sterile alternatives in the mainstream discourse represented by Roger Penrose, Francis Crick, Oliver Sacks and others. That discourse takes one of two forms. Either it continues to advocate understanding through a mind/body dualism, or it advocates a materialism designed to overcome that dualism which (for instance in Daniel Dennett's hands) then reduces all phenomena, including human agency, to molecular, mechanistic explanation.

Butler's notion of corporeality also crucially distinguishes it from materiality. Her treatment of corporeality is designed to break down the opposition between the exterior-material and the interior-intangible. She articulates the theory that the 'disciplinary production of gender effects a false stabilization of gender in the interests of the heterosexual construction and regulation of sexuality' (Butler 1990a: 335), such that 'sex conditions gender, and gender determines sexuality and desire' (ibid.: 336). But, she notes, this 'construction of coherence conceals the gender discontinuities that run rampant within heterosexual, bisexual, and gay and lesbian contexts in which gender does not necessarily follow from sex, and desire, or sexuality generally, does not seem to follow from gender'. Indeed, in these discontinuities 'none of these dimensions of significant corporeality "express" or reflect one another' (ibid.).

For Butler the felt inner coherence of identity is an achievement, based upon external dressing and other coded signals of performance, not the other way around as the conventional conception of heterosexual coherence would have it. For her, identity is dynamic; it is not just given, but is only achieved by performing and reinforcing it and so stabilizing its felt meaning. Butler observes tellingly that it is 'crucial to resist the myth of interior origins' and to argue that gender coherence is a regulatory fiction, to criticize the myth of 'the interior fixity of our identities', the 'presumed cultural invariance' of the fixity of gender identification (ibid.: 339).

According to Butler's subtle, wide-ranging and easily misunderstood argument, there are 'three separate dimensions of significant corporeality: anatomical sex, gender identity and gender performance' (ibid.: 337–8).[4] Drag and cross-dressing become paradigmatic examples of her conception of corporeality. She argues that in 'imitating gender, drag implicitly reveals the imitative structure of gender itself – as well as its contingency'. In consequence, '[i]n the place of the law of heterosexual coherence, we see sex and gender denaturalized by means of a performance which avows their distinctness and dramatizes the cultural mechanism of their fabricated unity' (ibid.: 338). However her three-fold conception of corporeality raises two serious problems. It is tied to a conventional sex/gender distinction, since her paradigmatic cases of drag and cross-dressing do not go further than disruption and contestation. In this way Butler deconstructs and revalues both sex and gender, through accenting the illicit, but does not address the distinction between them. Second, she takes the term 'gender' to refer specificially to sexuality, and so its utility in the wider discussion of gender as social roles in sociology and political science is not clear.

The central point which Grosz and Butler establish is that the notion of 'materiality' occurs within a dichotomous understanding of mind and body, whereas 'corporeality' does not. Important consequences follow from this vital difference. One is that the proposal, for instance, of an 'embodied' subjectivity of materiality would privilege body and suppress emotion, while 'corporeal' subjectivity can recognize body *and* emotion as integral and interdependent elements. Another is that in the conception of corporeality, the material, the fleshly, the physical is not opposed to spirituality and the psyche. Grosz (1994:22) refers to the 'psychical corporeality' of 'embodied subjectivity', and the conception of corporeality envisaged here acknowledges that sense of 'psychical corporeality'.

It is very important, in developing the idea of corporeal subjectivity, to supplant the sex/gender divide comprehensively, and so to ensure that 'body' does not become a metaphor, a symbolic economy, or a level of discourse through which to discuss everything else. This point can be highlighted through an analogy. Postmodern theorists who elevate language and discourse to an ontological status tend to overplay its value. Such a view makes it difficult to form connections with other things (material life, politics, and power relationships in the 'real' world of social practices rather than only as the male appropriation of meaning in language). It also creates problems such as taking the grammatically-sexed character of particular languages as foundational. The present work is careful not to attempt a similar strategy with respect to 'body', and the use of the term 'corporeality' rather than 'materiality' helps to ensure that such a pitfall is avoided.

The aim is to suggest a way forward in the sex/gender debate which goes beyond the dualism without just inverting it (as Irigaray can be taken to be doing). In this it is important to acknowledge Bordo's caution against theorizing that 'depends upon so abstract, disembodied, and ahistorical a conception of how cultural change occurs as to be worthy of inclusion in the most sterile philosophy text' (Bordo 1993: 41). She points to the continuing importance of attending to the 'ongoing production, reproduction, and transformation of culture', and notes that '[d]ualism thus cannot be deconstructed in culture the way it can be on paper' (ibid.). The predisposition given by 'modern' Western philosophy and science to regard materiality as 'real' and perhaps to regard the notion of corporeality as 'only theoretical' is a powerful one. This book builds upon the work of Grosz, Butler and Gatens in successfully challenging that outlook. The conception of corporeal subjectivity developed here recognizes the reciprocal influence of theory and social and cultural practices, and is underlined by the commitment of theory to addressing the concrete existence of social hierarchy and exclusion as political issues.

The interplay of theory and practice in the conception of corporeal subjectivity is also important in two other respects, because subjectivity contains a set of identities. In discussing the identities of the subject it is important to recognize, as Gatens argues, that we have inherited an inflated view of the agency of the subject, an agency which needs to be seen rather in the context of social practices and power relations (Gatens 1996b: 164). Nevertheless it remains true that we are also reflective creatures. We cannot change the world by reflection alone, but the capacity we have to reflect on the practices through which we gain the expression of our consciousness is important. Thus the second way in which there is an interplay of theory and practice in this conception of subjectivity refers to politics. For having a voice in the political arena depends upon a clear sense of identity or identities, whether narrowly or broadly defined.

## *Corporeality as relational*

Grosz's notion of the corporeality of bodies in *Volatile Bodies* rests on a perspective which invites a relational approach in two important and valuable respects. First, her theory points beyond the bankrupt sex/gender distinction, by disclosing the importance of the suppressed 'body' in the mind/body dualism, and showing that interconnectedness is crucial to both. It establishes convincingly that the opposition and hierarchy of the dichotomy, according to which body is inferior to mind, is theoretically untenable. Second, Grosz explores the relations between the interior and the exterior of a subject. Part of her purpose is to demonstrate the necessary dependence of 'psychical interiority' upon a 'corporeal exteriority'.

In contrast to the relational approach advanced by Grosz, the dominant materialist view of bodies invokes a dichotomous understanding of mind and body in the form of a polarized hierarchy between 'thought' and 'material'. Butler's work is also important in explicating this comparison. She argues that in view of our inherited dominant dichotomous mode of thinking, and specifically in the light of the mind/body dichotomy which has been mapped or patterned on to our understanding of identity, sex, gender, body, and emotion, as currently constituted 'there can be no subject without an Other' (Butler 1990a: 326). While the dichotomous view of the subject remains predominant, the only option which is socially sanctioned in a heterosexual/ist 'binary disjunction' (ibid.: 333) is attraction between opposites biologically defined. Haste's work (1993: 15) is also useful, in describing how the dichotomous view of relations between the sexes has operated in terms of hierarchy and functional complementarity.

The conception of corporeal subjectivity is distinctively non-dichotomous. It has the potential to recognize a range of sexual differences along with other forms of difference. Furthermore, the conception of corporeal subjectivity advanced here presupposes a relational basis such that the nature of the relation is to be discovered and not assumed. This part of the chapter will take up and develop the suggestion of recent feminist writers that reform of the predominantly dichotomous inheritance is possible through a relational view of subjectivity which comprehends diversity.

Once the exclusionary effects of the bipolar notion of male/female anatomy and of the heterosexual/ist norm are identified, it is possible to recognize the profound consequences that the mind/body split has had in undervaluing the body and its relation to mind and emotion. It is necessary first to evaluate the process which leads to the naturalization of exclusionary barriers both in theory and in social practices (leaving aside the question of the status in deep psychology of deep-seated sexual taboos), before addressing a reconceptualization which revalues the body and reorients its relation to mind and emotion. As a result of a relational rather than dichotomous approach, 'body' can be seen to interact dynamically and positively with the 'mind' part of body and with the 'emotion' part of mind, allowing them to be understood as conceptions which '*necessarily* suffer or act in concert' (Gatens 1996b: 166).

Butler's insight captures the relational character of the reconceptualized notion of body when she reflects that 'the thought of materiality invariably moved me into other domains'. For '[n]ot only did bodies tend to indicate a world beyond themselves, but this movement beyond their own boundaries, a movement of boundary itself, appeared to be quite central to what bodies "are"' (Butler 1993: ix).

Gatens' argument for an 'ethological' approach to the body reinforces in important ways the support for a relational perspective. According to her an ethological approach 'does not disavow the *organs* but rather selects out the transcendental *organization* of the body's organs in favour of a principle of composition or a harmonics of bodies and their exchanges' (Gatens 1996b: 168).[5] For her ethology, whose understanding is open-ended and inclusive, and which 'does not claim to know, in advance, what a body is capable of doing or becoming', is in stark contrast to biology, whose explanations are dichotomous and exclusionary, which 'lays down rules and norms of behaviour and action' (ibid.: 169).

Butler's theory also contains a crucially relational dimension. For her the logic of the thoroughly social constructionist argument requires that 'there will be no way to understand "gender" as a cultural construct which is imposed [or chosen] upon the surface of matter' (Butler 1993: 3). The social constructionist view leads to an integrated perspective, for 'once "sex" itself is understood in its normativity, the materiality of the body will not be thinkable apart from the materialization of that regulatory norm' (ibid.).[6]

Earlier the sixth stage of the sex/gender distinction was characterized in the proposal that the distinction between sex and gender is no longer viable, and needs to be replaced by a single, but multiple, porous, permeable whole. This conception can now be specified further. First it is crucial to recognize that this 'whole' is characterized by *integrity* rather than *unity*, by relation not holism. Furthermore we need to do more than rethink the body and reconstruct the relationship between sex and gender in non-binary terms. The proposal for a relational corporeal subjectivity is directed to the same end that led Gatens to consider the possibility of 'a genuinely polymorphous socio-political body' (Gatens 1991: 139). What Gatens had in mind was a socio-political body whose recognition of a whole range of differences is rooted in each individual's grounded, embodied self-identity. Thus, both individuals and the political body are 'capable of discriminating and respecting differences among its members', with the 'ability to hear and respond to polyvocality and polyvalency', forming a political body whose 'communication with itself would be polylogical' (ibid.).

The relational character of the proposal for corporeal subjectivity here also bears a resemblance to Cornell and Thurschwell's relational account which goes beyond the sex/gender dichotomy. They seek a general perspective which is explicitly relational as a remedy for the effects of dichotomous thinking. They argue that in Lacan and equally in Kristeva, 'the constitution of the subject in and through gender categories is flawed by their failure to recognize the Other within the categories masculine/feminine themselves' (Cornell and Thurschwell 1987: 144). They utilize Adorno's thinking to criticize a reading in which 'gender is fate' (ibid.: 161), and to seek 'the truth of nonidentity' (ibid.: 160). They look to 'Adorno's insight into the failure of identitarian thinking, the mode of thought that would credit the category with a total account of its object'. They argue that both 'masculinity' and 'femininity' 'secretly harbor a "more than this" that permits an understanding of difference as relational to its core, and yet does not just replicate the traditional gender hierarchy' (ibid.: 144). The value of the notion of difference which they develop is that they explicate that it 'turns on the idea that genuine difference is inseparable from a notion of relationality' ibid.: 161).

The ethic of care can represent another significant example of relational thinking which goes beyond the destructive effects that have followed from dichotomizing gender or sexual difference. This is especially the case in the work of Tronto (1993) on the political and strategic potential of the ethic of care, in Hekman's further specification of a 'nonoppositional understanding of justice and care' (Hekman 1995: 10), and in some of the contributions to the *Hypatia* symposium on care and justice (Symposium 1995). It is clear that all individuals flourish with a foundation of care and a continuing sense of connection and interdependence, as well as with a grounded autonomy, a sense of independence, and a sense of justice in terms of fair treatment within a community as a dimension of connectedness with that community.

Another aspect of the strength of the relational notion of corporeal subjectivity is that it is grounded in the importance of *relationship*, of the formation of identity in particular contexts of dynamic, reciprocal and inter-subjective recognition. Cavarero (1996) makes an important point in highlighting the unrealized potential of the notion of identity as '*ipso*', becoming oneself as unique and irreplaceable, when identity is formed in relationship through recognition by another as an ethical subject. She counterposes this notion to the monolithic and self-mastering subject that has dominated the discussion of identity in Western philosophy from Plato to Descartes. In the latter conception, identity is '*idem*', sameness in the sense of becoming an instance of a universal, in which sovereign independence and autonomy are an achievement which is identified with becoming adult, achieving moral maturity, success in becoming man.

Several further strengths of the relational character of the conception of corporeal subjectivity can be mentioned briefly. It responds positively to the lesbian-gay-queer challenge, the challenge from the 'other' to be brought in, included, and the challenge that sexuality is not fixed and given. Furthermore, in Grosz's terms, this conception avoids the inside/outside, biology/psychology split, and avoids the reduction of mind to brain.

### *Corporeality as the locus of lived and gendered subjectivity*

This feature of corporeal subjectivity emphasizes three important aspects of it: its integrated (rather than unified) character, its lived character, and the significance attached to recognizing gender visibility as a morally relevant element of identity.

It follows that an *integrated* view of subjectivity proceeds from the recognition of the interdependence of the three dimensions of subjectivity (mind, body, emotion) which are under consideration in this book. These three dimensions *can* still be described as separate dimensions, but can no longer be regarded as constitutively independent of each other. Grosz underlines this integrated sense of subjectivity when she comments that bodies are 'materialities that are uncontainable in physicalist terms alone'. For 'they are also centres of perspective, insight, reflection, desire and agency'. Bodies 'are not inert. They function interactively and productively. They act and react' (Grosz 1994: xi).

In developing the corporeal conception of subjectivity, Grosz's theory in *Volatile Bodies* builds upon the crucial recognition that body as well as mind is something we *live* in and through. There is a strong sense of the dynamic agency of subjectivity in her work, which rejects any notion of body as insignificant to the operation of autonomy, or as passive vehicle for mind. A further important and related presupposition of Grosz's theoretical perspective reflects the consequences of recognizing that in our dominant intellectual inheritance the body has been colonized by the natural sciences. In medicine and biology in particular, assumptions are made about the body's naturalness, its pre-cultural status, in which the body is a brute given, passive, ahistorical, 'real'. Grosz, in contrast, argues that cultural inscriptions and representations literally constitute bodies. The body is the very 'stuff' of subjectivity; it is not neutral.

In the context of the sex/gender debate, a crucial aspect of our personal and social identity emerges from the preceding discussion. Despite Plumwood's hope that the sex/gender distinction 'may still be useful and viable if treated in non-dualistic ways' (Plumwood 1993: 457), so that a morally-neutral meaning of gender could provide emancipatory potential for women, the preceding debate has shown that our subjectivity is not neutral, not 'genderless', not morally irrelevant.

In a series of important essays, Gatens addresses this question by reinstating the importance of bodies as embodied and embedded subjects rather than abstract, neutral individual minds (Gatens 1996b: 7–10). She notes that 'social values are embedded in bodies, not simply "minds"' (ibid.: 65), and that 'sexual difference' is about how culture marks bodies, not about biological 'facts' (ibid.: 71). She argues for a reconceptualization of bodies that recognizes that it is not that the anatomical body is overlaid by culture (as happens in the sex/gender distinction), but that the anatomical body is itself a theoretical object for the discourse of anatomy whic is produced by human beings in culture. It is a particular culture which chooses to represent bodies anatomically, for the 'human body is always a signified body, and as such cannot be understood as a "neutral object" upon which science constructs "true" discourses' (ibid.: 70). It follows that gender is 'not the effect of ideology or cultural values, but the way power takes hold of and constructs bodies in particular ways' (ibid.). And the sexed body is no longer an unproblematic biological fact, but is itself 'constructed by discourses and practices which take the body as their target and their vehicle of expression' (ibid.). The idea of 'biological disadvantage' can then be seen in perspective, as taking its meaning from a specific cultural context. For instance, in a political community geared primarily towards *women's* capacities, men's inability to breastfeed could be taken to be a natural or biological disadvantage (ibid.: 71).

The idea of corporeal subjectivity embraces individuals' recognition of their subjectivity as not only embodied but gendered, as a undetachable part of subjectivity. It thereby resolves the problem which feminism has highlighted in liberalism posed by a neutral 'personhood' (Lloyd 1989: 13). As Butler notes, 'gender is part of what decides the subject' (Butler 1993: x). At the same time, the conception of corporeal subjectivity entails an awareness of gender which is free of gender discrimation, gender hierarchy and gender dichotomy. The meaning of corporeal subjectivity is thus very different both from Rawls' gender blindness (1973, 1993) and from the 'gender-free society' proposed by Okin (1996: 31).

Rawls's liberal difference blindness has the effect of being a denial, a difference exclusion rather than a simple difference neutrality. Sex is a morally irrelevant characteristic for Rawls. Gender is a morally relevant characteristic in a society structured by along gender lines, for Okin (1989b: 102). Her proposal for a gender-free society is subject to criticism by feminists for being negative (gender-*free*) and disembodied. But according to the conception of corporeal subjectivity, gender (or rather all the things the term represents) is also morally relevant in a society *not* structured by gender, in the sense that subjectivity does not just belong to the mind. It is also in the body, as a live force, not as passive materiality, *and* in emotional life, *and* in the claims of body and emotions and mind on each other. Wendy Brown (1987) and Terrell Carver (1966) are two important writers who, in contrast with Okin, have a strong sense that what is needed is to recognize the *diversity* of what is captured only inadequately under the term 'gender', rather than to aspire to be gender-free or gender-blind.

Nussbaum unfortunately follows up her sound understanding of the social construction of both sex and gender with a suggestion, similar to Okin's, that we focus upon *human* functioning and *human* being, concentrating 'on what all human beings share, rather than on the privileges and achievements of a dominant group, and on needs and basic functions, rather than power or status' (Nussbaum 1995a: 61–2). While her line of argument reflects her overall commitment to an *Aristotelian* conception of 'human flourishing', nevertheless her notion exhibits four classic misconceptions of *liberal* philosophy.

First, it imports the problems associated with Rawls's attempt to construct the terms of a liberal society which is gender-blind, particularly in underestimating the extent to which power relationships are entrenched and active. Second, despite her disclaimer (ibid.: 74), it imports a biologistic judgment of 'needs and basic functions' (ibid.: 76–80). Third, her proposal is framed within the old dichotomous pairing of universalism and relativism, which feminist theory has very effectively overcome (Benhabib 1992a,

1992b, 1995; Fraser 1989, Grosz 1994, Gatens 1996a). Fourth, as Nussbaum proclaims, the 'proposal is frankly universalist and "essentialist"' (Nussbaum 1995a: 63). It imposes from on high a preconceived notion of needs, rather than allowing them to be either self-defined or felt, and as such is a form of liberal imperialism. Nussbaum's proposal is basically to extend (male-defined) universal 'capacities' to women, without recognizing that the outcome would be for women to experience in another form 'the principle of equality as an effect of exclusion and homologization' (Cavarero 1992: 44). Nussbaum's proposal fails to take into account the vital point that women's equality and difference cannot be 'accommodated by adjusting and integrating it into the existing model of society and politics, but demands a radical rethinking of the basic logic of the model' (ibid.: 45).

## *Short-term and long-term goals: from gender visibility to corporeal subjectivity*

Bordo's criticism (1990) of gender-scepticism is well-placed, and it also helps to identify the way in which the notion of corporeal subjectivity has a role within feminism as part of feminism's *long-term* rather than short-term aims and knowledges.

The short-term objective is gender visibility (see Thiele 1986), that is, the relational replacement of liberal gender 'neutrality' in the public realm by two elements. First is the recognition of a diversity of gender positions. Second is the recognition of the covert manner in which, inspired by the mind/body split, women continue to bear body and sex, seen as originating in the private realm. Judith Grant's argument contains the insight that the 'visibility of gender as an oppressive structure has only become possible with the redescription of gender from the feminist perspective' (Grant 1993: 178). In other words it is only through feminist practice that the visibility of gender oppression can be reached; it 'does not come from women's experiences; rather, it is what we use to give new meaning to human experiences' (ibid.: 179).

The long-term aim envisages a more egalitarian society, corporeal subjectivity, and a political situation in which the hierarchically-valued significance of 'men' and 'women' is dissipated. Gatens's (1996b) use of Spinoza, and of Deleuze's reading of Spinoza, is helpful in suggesting one way forward for a philosophically-sound grounding for the long-term aim. However there is also a strong case that Gatens's argument, in pursuing the long-term perspective, could be developed further in deconstructing the sex/gender distinction.

The idea of making a clear distinction between feminism's short-term and long-term goals is important. Over the past two decades confusions between the two aims have generated conflicts between different feminists, so the distinction is valuable because it demonstrates the compatibility of the aims and their theoretical warrant of a diversity of different feminisms.[7] The short-term perspective extrapolates from how things are, and the long-term theory describes how things could be. Short-term aims arise directly within the context of patriarchal society. In this context the sex/gender and woman/man dualisms continue to exert an important influence over social values and practices. Politics is an area in which to contest exclusionary practices arising from those dualisms, and political action is required in order to reach an aim.

The short-term and long-term aims are not, of course, entirely separable. The logic of the short-term aim gives rise to the long-term perspective and theoretical possibilities. This perspective of how things could be then becomes an important factor in the perception of the present. The short-term aim is the political fight for the recognition of the value of women's gender visibility, because this is a fight against a current, still predominantly patriarchal identification. The long-term aim is for women to be free from discrimination. Women want their *different* perspectives, capacities, work patterns and viewpoints integrated into the way things are done and understood. Whether women's perceptions come from a viewpoint created through oppression (forced to be co-operative and passive, to take on domestic and caring roles etc.) or from an essentialist difference, *does not* affect the *value* of those perceptions. It is not necessary to identify their origins. If they are valuable, and reasoned argument can support them, they deserve to be taken seriously.

The notion of supplanting the sex/gender distinction with a single term such as 'corporeal subjectivity' is necessary in order to get beyond an assertion like Yeatman's. Her proposal rests on a notion of 'men' and 'women' that feeds straight back into the idea of a 'natural' sex difference. She registers that once the gendered division of labour (and other social practices) is recognized as 'historically and culturally variable. It is a socio-cultural construction of biological sex difference which accordingly varies', then the 'condition of being a woman can be grasped now as a social condition . . . women, no less than men, are social beings' (Yeatman 1986: 158). The sex/gender distinction is inadequate to develop the idea of women as social beings. Gender visibility on its own is not enough; only when it leads to corporeal subjectivity can it fulfill the potential of equality and difference amongst men and women.

The benefits and strenths of the idea of 'corporeal subjectivity', developed particularly from Grosz, Gatens, and Butler, are many. The long-term aim takes into account the multiple, diverse and overlapping aspects of what is covered by sex and gender. It thus avoids the essentialist trap of 'gendered' subjectivity, which carried the resonance of narrow alternatives of 'masculine or feminine' gender. 'Gendered' subjectivity also wrongly suggested that identity could be made, rationally constructed by an effort of the will, that it could ignore or override the insidiousness of inherited social practices and values. Thus the idea of corporeal subjectivity rejects, as Grosz puts it, a norm for the body, putting forward instead a 'field of body types'. It is dynamic, active, fluid, responsive, recognizing that the body is a threshold or borderline concept between the pairs of binary concepts (Grosz 1994: 22, 93–4). The conception of corporeal subjectivity takes into account that it is not enough to demonstrate the poverty of the dualism; we cannot simply dissolve oppositions and ignore them, but must construct something on the basis of them.

It is also important to recognize fully that the short-term aim of gender visibility is a prerequisite for the viability of the long-term aim. An attempt to undertake the second step out of sequence would result in disguising or masking to some extent the basis for the feminist claim for emancipation, for it is not immediately apparent that corporeal subjectivity, on its own, contains a claim for the recognition of women's perspectives. It has been commonly recognized over the past few decades that those calling for a 'gendered' perspective were predominantly women. The feminist claim for the visibility of their gender as perceived in the patriarchal gaze, and recompense for their discrimination, properly belongs to the first step. Once gender visibility is recognized and implemented in our social practices, *then* what feminists want is corporeal subjectivity which recognizes the full significance of the body for all, including but not over-emphasizing the complexity and context-dependence of personal sexuality.

### *Beyond the sex/gender distinction to corporeal subjectivity*

Moore introduces seemingly-similar notions of 'embodied subjectivity and corpor(e)al femininity'. She discusses them to bridge a 'gap' she identifies, in that 'the sexed subject and the gendered individual are not one and the same' (Moore 1994: 92). But while problematizing this 'gap', Moore retains a sex/gender distinction. The notion of corporeal subjectivity envisaged here is by contrast specifically designed to overcome the problems inherent in trying to paste together sex and gender.

To keep sex and gender as different concepts in any form, even non-binarily, is to keep the idea of 'universal man' and a universal (fundamentally male) knowledge of these matters, because in this context the term 'sex' automatically triggers a prioritization of men, and the term 'gender' feeds off 'sex'. In contrast this chapter argues that the complexity and sophistication of this multiple term, such that the interaction of variables is very complex, means that knowledge of the subject cannot be assimilated to one objective universal knowledge. Therefore an element of surprise is always to be expected; the character of a person's corporeal subjectivity (and assumptions made about them) cannot be read off from their anatomical features.

The notion of corporeal subjectivity put forward here, while it owes an enormous amount to the work of Grosz, Gatens and Butler, attempts to overcome the problem in their work that arises from keeping the sex/gender distinction. That distinction is both exhausted and inadequate. It is bankrupt or anachronistic (Butler 1987: 129) and so needs to be replaced as a matter of urgency. But it is also inadequate in the sense that it does not adequately capture either the diversity of our corporeality (as evidenced in the lists of the things that 'sex' represents and that 'gender' expresses), or the importance of our knowledge of our corporeal subjectivity. Moreover the distinction is inadequate because it cannot foster the understanding of body, mind and emotion as significantly interrelated in corporeality. In contrast to the sex/gender distinction, the notion of corporeal subjectivity contains the sense of dynamic interdependence constituted by and constituting all the elements of our lived, inscribed, felt and reflective identity. In suggesting the notion of corporeal subjectivity to replace the sex/gender distinction, the argument is not that sex and gender are unimportant. The (many) things they express are *too* important for it to be acceptable for them to be misunderstood constantly through an inherently dichotomous formulation. They *can* however be captured through the conception of corporeal subjectivity.

Grosz retains a sex/gender distinction and so is not fully systematic in pursuing the logic she sets in train. She maintains the concepts of sex and gender (Grosz 1994: 17–19) alongside the notion of corporeal subjectivity. In the case of Gatens, the argument acknowledges 'the normative operations of sex and gender without prioritizing either', using Spinoza especially through a reading by Deleuze to 'think beyond' the 'metaphysical opposition' of 'a biologism inherited from dualism and a voluntarism inherited from idealism'. This is important and has evident merit. Nevertheless she retains the categories of sex and gender, however non-dichotomously. She concludes that the 'categories of sex and gender may . . . be thought as unstable but enduring strata of organizations of molecular relations and dynamic affects' (Gatens 1996b: 171). However in the light of the diversity of things that 'sex' and 'gender' stand for, and the one-way causality between them that remains even in a non-dualistic (ibid.: 170) scenario, this conclusion cannot be allowed to stand.

Butler can also be seen as retaining the sex/gender distinction. Moore describes a widespread feeling that the particular understanding of social construction in Butler's work creates a danger, if not of seeing the body as only an effect of discourse, then at least of 'positing the body as a blank surface on which the social becomes inscribed, thus suggesting in some sense that the body is pre-social' (Moore 1994: 86). 'Gender' for Butler refers to sexuality, which twists the sex/gender distinction but does not overcome it. She examines that aspect of the sex/gender distinction concerned with sexuality, sexual orientation, sexual performance, how sexual practices are constituted as settled figures and loaded and surrounded by normative constraints, and the role of agency in this connection, seen through drag and cross-dressing. She calls this 'gender' because it involves mind and emotion. Thus Butler is not concerned with gender in the more social sense (in which her concern would be called sex rather than gender) of a gendered workforce or gendered food choices (for example, that women as a group apparently prefer chicken and fish, while men as a group prefer steak). However there is a serious sense in which she is still tied to 'natural' sex difference, because she builds a notion of gender as sex in the context of social partially-constituted practices of sex. As a result her work contains an awareness of 'natural' sexed bodies, even or indeed especially if transgressing their conventional normative consequences. This is however expressed differently in her different writings. In 'Variations on Sex and Gender' (1987), Butler tends to leave the sex side of the sex/gender distinction intact. In her 'gender trouble' work (1990a, 1990b) she is concerned mainly with problematizing the gender part of the sex/gender distinction, by means of 'gender parody'.

In the proposal to extend the use of the notion of corporeal subjectivity to replace the false and exclusionary sex/gender distinction, it is clear that the terms 'sex' and 'gender' do not disappear. They retain (limited) meanings in our language. What changes is the chain of significance that runs through the meanings of sex and into the meanings of gender, through being read in terms of a socially-understood significance.

Within an understanding of corporeal subjectivity, 'sex' and 'gender' remain, but they are deprived of their primary status for defining bodies, in another sense as well. While (a diversity of) heterosexual relations are likely to remain characteristic of the majority of the population, it follows from the relational approach that such relations would represent non-hegemonic, non-exclusivist, non-dominant sexuality (or sexualities). Such an understanding of heterosexuality would therefore occur within a context of sexualities that comprehends, rather than merely tolerating, homosexuality, lesbianism, bisexuality, transexuality, and intersexuality.

Moreover, while the drive to reproduce would still occupy a crucial place in our social construction, this drive would be recognized as expressed in a particular social construction. It would no longer be naturalized and mapped on to all the elements of the terms 'sex' and 'gender', but would be recognized as only one expression of sexuality. The either/or of the heterosexual/ist norm would therefore be replaced by a both–and context of diverse sexualities that retains but reconfigures (a diversity of) heterosexuality.

The developments of queer theory, lesbian theory, gay theory, and masculinities theory all demonstrate that a diversity of sexualities is now being expressed in social practices. Social values conceptualizing those practices still have to catch up with the developments 'on the ground'. In our liberal political culture, these developments have become tolerated without being fully comprehended and *recognized.* Among its objectives, the notion of 'corporeal subjectivity' aims to represent one attempt to reconceptualize the diversity of sexuality in positive and politically inclusive terms.

# 4

# CONCLUSION

## The third wave: the future of feminism

The previous chapters have attempted to demonstrate the potential for feminist theorizing of developing a relational mode of non-dichotomous thinking. Chapter Two advanced the case for recognizing that rationality involves crucial links between reason and emotion, for detaching the association of reason with man and of irrationalism and emotion with women, and thereby providing an alternative to both the gendering of reason and the degendering of reason. Chapter Three was concerned with theorizing beyond sex and gender to a conception of corporeal subjectivity. This chapter reflects upon the prospects for feminism more broadly, in the light of the significance which dichotomous thinking has had for it and on it. The chapter argues that a coherent third wave of feminism could emerge, based on a non-dichotomous and relational theory and practice.

The conventional history of feminism presents us with two waves, three major strands and several subsidiary strands. However, for a whole set of reasons concerned with the internal dynamics of feminism and the external dynamics of backlash, this orthodox narrative no longer explains and accounts for where feminism is now. The argument which follows makes a case for recognizing that the energy that characterized the second wave of feminism has in some important respects become dispersed. The end of the second wave is marked not by a backlash which represents the end of the story, nor yet by postfeminism, but by the possibility of the emergence of a third wave.

Crucially this chapter maintains that the theorizing of second-wave feminism operated within the context of the mind/body split that continues to frame mainstream thinking. Attempts were made by feminists to challenge that split, but largely from within the terms of the internal feminist discourse, without acknowledgement from the mainstream. The idea of difference, one of the major achievements of second-wave feminist theorizing, was always unsatisfactory when still tied to the mind/body dichotomy, because that dualism could not take body (nor subjectivity as gendered, nor emotion) seriously. There are clear signs that a sea-change in feminist thinking is now under way. The designation of 'third-wave feminism' is warranted in recognition of the fundamental nature of this change.

In a society still characterized by gender inequalities, many issues raised by feminists still need to addressed further, in non-dichotomous terms, in order to cement the step from gender-blindness to gender visibility. Only then can corporeal subjectivity become a viable widespread social understanding. Such issues include the recognition of the way in which the ethics of care underpins the ethic of justice; the revaluation of the 'other' of motherhood; gender-visible citizenship; and the reconceptualization of heterosexuality on a non-dichotomous basis capable of recognizing diverse 'masculinities' and 'femininities'. Signs of such a sea-change are already apparent in the growing coherence exhibited in feminist debates on topics such as the body, reason and emotion, and sex and gender. Further indications are found in the increase in feminist analyses of the significance of specific dichotomies, especially the splits between mind and body, and nature and culture, as well as in the awareness of the force which dichotomous thinking has exercised more generally.

This final chapter seeks to establish a case for a third wave of feminism along these lines, placing this development in the context of the history of feminism. An important side-effect of such reflections is that they provide a historical perspective through which the diversity of practical aims and theoretical endeavours of the different strands within second wave feminism, which seemed so distinct at the time, gain coherence.

## The end of the second wave

### *Internal dynamics*

The thesis that we are now embarking upon a third wave of feminism rests in part on three arguments, all of which concern development through the internal dynamics of feminism. The three arguments, which specify the sense in which the second wave is over and the way in which it is generating a third wave, concern feminist politics, generation change, and the pattern of feminist theorizing.

The argument regarding feminist politics starts from the widespread sense that the second wave is over because the questions and issues it raised have been addressed, or else are exhausted, or cannot at present be solved by second-wave feminist discourse and practice. Furthermore it is said that the clarity which second-wave campaigns had against blatant examples of systematic injustices has become blurred. This is an argument for the third wave emerging through the internal dynamics of feminist *politics*.

The widespread sense that some rights gains have been won, and some gains have been consolidated through legislation, supports the notion that some questions have been at least addressed. In May 1997 over one hundred women MPs were elected to Parliament in Britain, and a number of women have gained promotion to high positions in their professions and careers. These represent only modest achievements, but there is a strong current of popular opinion that considers that as *issues* to be brought to the attention of the popular consciousness, these matters have been addressed.

One example of the view that the second-wave discourse cannot solve all the problems with which it has engaged concerns recent work on the topic of pornography, by Weeks and others from within the discourse on masculinities (Weeks 1985, Horrocks 1995), by writers on lesbian s/m (Lewis, R. 1994), as well as by writers on some aspects of the conception of representation which also make the topic of pornography more complex (Kappeller 1986). These recent contributions to the debate all represent reactions against the orthodoxies established by second-wave feminists like Dworkin and Mackinnon. These reactions are perhaps to be taken most seriously when they challenge the definition of pornography on two counts: through discussion of lesbian s/m and marginalized masculinities. Such writers take issue with the definition of pornography not only as morally wrong, but also as a wrong done by (potentially) all men to all women. Despite the great importance for second-wave feminist politics of Dworkin and Mackinnon's explication of the link between a dominant masculinity and the pornography industry in Western societies, their definition of pornography is now widely regarded as simplistic and as presenting a false universal.

Another aspect of the internal dynamics of feminist politics is the widespread sense that feminism, politically, is no longer radical. It has come to be seen, in contrast to new social movements such as green and roads protests, and in contrast with gay, lesbian and queer demands, as a norm, a way of conforming. The argument here is that the 'gender perspective' has become integrated into mainstream politics, especially in questions of social and welfare policy. One effect of this development, it is argued, is that the energy needed to focus the political force of feminism has been diffused. Lennon and Whitford's observation about feminist epistemology is equally true of second wave feminism in general: 'to the extent to which feminism has moved from its moment of critique to that of construction, it has become implicated within the power network' (Lennon and Whitford 1994: 14).

The decline in high profile political activity, however, is owing as much to the positive move of some second wave campaigns into the mainstream institutional framework, particularly with respect to the welfare state, as to a loss of political energy. Two British examples help to make this point. One of the most distinctive outcomes of the general election of May 1997 was the entry of more women into mainstream politics. Second, the establishment by local councils in Britain of domestic violence units helps to ensure that the problem is tackled more effectively, but also means that the issue has a lower visibility, absorbed into the local government bureaucracy.

A further dimension of the changes that have taken place in the way second-wave feminist politics is refracted, is found in the role of the radical strand of feminism. The second wave increasingly became dominated by the radical strand, and the campaigning spirit which particularly characterized that strand has led to some successes and some ongoing campaigns, but has to some extent been dissipated. The marches and protests that characterized radical feminist politics in the 1970s have become a defining feature of that period. It became increasingly clear during the 1970s and 1980s that liberal feminism was being overtaken by the wider liberal equal opportunities agenda, that Marxist feminism was receding from visibility into sterile debates about the application of Marxist categories, and that Socialist feminism was suffering the decline in popularity experienced by socialism in general in the post-Soviet era. Another aspect of this is the change documented by Sylvia Walby from private to public patriarchy, in the increasing role played by the welfare state in sustaining gender inequalities (Walby 1990; see also Fraser 1987).

These changes in the internal politics of feminism form one aspect of the internal dynamic which has brought about a threshhold at the end of the second wave. A second aspect is the impact of generational change. A new generation of young women have a different agenda for their lives. Many of them do not see the point of, as they see it, angry second-wave feminists, and do not identify with the methods of their call for political action.

Just as second-wave feminists in the 1960s developed a distinctive style of politics from the protest movements of Left politics and from small consciousness-raising groups, so the character of politics for the new generation of young women takes its bearings from protest and civil disobedience actions connected with wider green and environmental politics and alternative life-styles, rather than from activism within established political parties and organizations. Furthermore the current generation, brought up in the context of the radically individualist neo-liberal Thatcherite world of self-interest and job insecurity, self-consciously seek to pursue more individual and less political goals. In addition, though largely unselfconsciously, they are the beneficiaries of the gains made by second-wave feminists.

More widely, second-wave feminism has a generally poor reputation in the popular image of the new generation. Feminism is considered to be idealistic rather than practical, associated with overly serious 1960s New Left politics, and with bra-burning women who thought they could change the world. In an interesting way this development mirrors the 1960s feminists' rejection of their mothers (Freely 1995). A contributory factor to the poor reputation of second-wave feminism among a new generation of young women is that it seems to them to offer, in the important area of sexuality, only the alternatives of lesbianism or guilt (Smart 1996). Second-wave feminism is felt to have failed to provide a clear sense of positive heterosexuality for women.

These points contribute to an argument that developments in feminist politics and current generational dynamics point to the demise of second wave feminism. Works like Natasha Walter's recent book seek to engage more positively, though controversially, with the legacy and future of feminism. In *The New Feminism* (1998), she identifies the shortcomings of second-wave feminism from the perspective of a younger generation, in particular its supposed imposition of a narrow and humourless political correctness and its valuing collective over individual action. But alongside some political naivety and a lack of theoretical understanding, Walter does make the case for the continuing need to address issues such as the female poverty trap and inadequate protection against domestic violence, women's inequality in the workplace, career structures, the home, childcare and motherhood. Her book details some of the practical topics which support the view that there is a future for feminism.

Indications that a third wave of feminism is emerging are also found in the way in which young women, many of whom do not call themselves feminists, are developing another agenda of recognizably feminist issues and concerns to do with areas of inequality and discrimination between men and women. Examples in Britain include highly-publicized cases of sex discrimination involving lack of promotion in the police force and business, and cases of sexual harassment brought by women in the armed forces.

The third element of the argument concerns feminist and related theorizing. It is clear that the internal dynamics of second-wave feminism have not only led to its demise but are producing a third wave. The contention here is that a third wave is being generated under the impact of the fragmentation of the coherence of the second wave.

Two concurrent processes are at work here: supplementation and fracturing. As a result the implicit coherence provided by the dominance of white Western middle-class radical feminists in the second wave has gone. Over the past thirty years the neat tripartite scheme of liberal, Marxist-socialist and radical feminism has been *supplemented* by the proliferation of other feminisms, such as black and other ethnic feminisms, post-colonial feminism, the politics of lesbianism, psychoanalytic feminism, communitarian feminism, postmodern feminism, and ecofeminism. This has resulted in a range of perspectives and positions in which the earlier neat lines of Western theoretical bias are blurred.

Second, feminism has generated further and specific independent ideas, campaigns, awarenesses, and issues, such as developing countries' women's agendas, queer theory, and masculinities theory and practices. These have all gone to challenge and *fracture* the neat division into liberal, Marxist-socialist and radical strands which defined second-wave feminism.

At present there is a lack of distinctness between the three major strands defining second wave feminist theory, and they cannot properly represent or account for the theory being produced under the broad umbrella of feminism. This situation has resulted in the fragmentation of the coherence of second-wave theorizing. This can be interpreted in three ways.

First, it has been negative, in that its effect has been feminism's inability fully to reckon with 'other' differences such as race, class and cultures. There is thus a sense that the logic of 'other' differences such as those expressed by black feminism, by the challenges offered by feminists in other cultures and societies, in the third world, and by lesbian separatists, *has* lethally demonstrated the limits of a second-wave feminism that has been predominantly white, middle class, Eurocentric, and Anglophone or Western. This development has brought to light the way in which white second-wave feminism's real gains have ultimately been directly targeted only at a few. The impact of 'other' differences has left fewer and fewer women in the residual rump, as gay, black, working class, and disabled women assert their difference from the norm established by white second-wave feminism. In addition, the notion of marginalized masculinities problematizes the very notion of the priority claimed by women as the marginalized 'other' in patriarchal society. Furthermore the disavowal of a feminist identity by postmodern feminists has compounded, for some, the question of what comes after the second wave. Walters makes an important point, however, in defence of the important effect that political solidarity amongst women can have. She contends that feminism *does* have a future, as a conceptual and political identity, since 'feminists have been wary of the quick dismissal of "the subject" and political agency [by postmodern theorizing's central critique of identity] just when it seemed that women were getting around to acquiring some' (Walters 1996: 839).

The second interpretation of the fragmentation of the coherence of second wave theorizing is that it has been tragic. Feminism's inability fully to grasp the nettle of difference has resulted in a certain loss of emancipatory status amongst progressive democratic theorists.

In the third view, however, the fragmentation of coherence can be seen as positive, in forcing feminism to regroup into a (sometimes unwieldy and incoherent, and sometimes unwilling) third wave. One example of this is the success of feminists like Grosz and Gatens in laying to rest the essentialist myth (Grosz 1994 :213n20), a myth which was propounded by some feminists and anti-feminists alike. It is important to add that while this development discloses the false theoretical basis on which some feminists proposed and undertook separatist theoretical positions and set up all-women communities, it does not undermine the impetus to organize social practices differently nor the strength gained from solidarity which such undertakings also represent.

Another example of a positive aspect is the development of a greater awareness, and the beginnings of a more complex theorization, of discrimination, in terms of the range of its incidence and the multiple forms it can take. A third example is the development of both the discussion of marginalized masculinities and their relation to the dominant masculinity, and of queer theory. These are developments which in some ways move *beyond* feminism, but could only have happened *through* feminism. As Carver notes, '[h]aving retheorized "woman" as a category incorporating "differences" – self-expressed differences among women – in the context of academic critique, and also in terms of political demands and activity, feminists have prepared the way, perhaps inadvertently, for a retheorization of men' (Carver 1996: 680).

What underpins all these examples, and points to an important way forward for feminism in the third wave, is the realization of the fundamental significance of the mind/body dichotomy in perpetuating social hierarchy on the basis of gender. The aims of feminism can be tackled adequately only when the role that the mind/body dichotomy has played in patriarchal society is fully recognized, and a non-dichotomous, relational set of mind-body connections is developed. Second-wave feminism can be characterized as distinctively working *within* the mind/body dichotomy, and this is part of the reason that the only available options it could offer women were to become honorary men or to retreat into the motherhood of 'natural' sexual difference. In the third wave, the promise of 'difference' can be realized, because the syndrome whereby men are identified with the public 'mind' gender-neutral realm of work and citizenship and autonomy and rationality, and women are associated with the private 'body' realm of reproduction and care, can be seen as resting upon a falsely naturalized dichotomy. Furthermore, viewed non-dichotomously, 'difference' involves much more than disagreement and the status of disagreement, in adversarial terms. It is also about recognition and rights in a context of diversity which is no longer closed-ended by the 'whole' which has been defined by dichotomous thinking.

The meaning of 'difference' within a non-dichotomous mode of thinking can usefully be contrasted with the mainstream liberal view summed up in the term 'justice is blind'. The idea that justice should be blind entailed that in order to arrive at just decisions, decision-makers should ignore difference: that is, they should be blind to matters of gender, race, class, and religion. The idea was to ensure that snobbery and prejudice on the part of decision-makers did not play a role in questions of justice. In other words, when 'blind' in this way a case could be assessed simply in terms of its legal merits and therefore fairness would be the outcome.

This line of reasoning is no longer appropriate in a world in which gender and race ask to be recognized not ignored. The liberal mainstream idea was based on the Lockean model of liberal religious toleration, which held that acceptance into the public world should be independent of views held by private moral conscience in the private world. In this model the public world is taken to be neutral between moral choices. But it has been conclusively demonstrated by feminists and others that the public sphere is not neutral, and that 'the private is political'. Furthermore the development of the welfare state, which straddles the public/private divide, effectively challenges the idea that the liberal public/private distinction can be, or is in practice, maintained.

Moreover feminists challenge the liberal conception of a dichotomy between a pre-social and mind-centred free and rational core of an individual and a set of somehow superimposed differences. The approach to difference developed by feminists and others asks that, rather than being blind to differences, justice should recognize the range of differences in diversity, as a crucial part of what it is to be human, worthy of respect and entitled to political representation. It also requires that such diversity be taken into account in the distribution of political power, constitutions (Tully 1995) and citizenship.

In terms of the academic profession, the move from feminism to 'gender studies', which includes masculinities as a significant feature, has challenged the claim of second-wave feminism to sole ownership of the academic discipline concerned with discrimination and emancipation on gender grounds. Much recent work in the area of masculinities (see Hearn 1992; Morgan 1992), has either implicitly or explicitly sought in part to locate itself by identifying feminism as a form of special pleading, an alleged claim by women which is considered invalid in the light of the history of discrimination against marginalized masculinities.

The useful recent article by Carver, which is exempt from this strategy, demonstrates that the discourse of masculinities does not need to pose itself, as it is tending to do, against feminism (Carver 1996: 678). Furthermore, the discourse of masculinities seeks to replace the role which patriarchal society has played in second-wave feminism, with the notion of a hegemonic masculinity, a single stereotype of macho masculinity. It is *this* stereotype, it is argued, which has had the effect of oppressing other expressions of masculinity, and indeed the plurality not only of heterosexual but especially of homosexual masculinities. As Carver notes, '[t]heorists in sociology of masculinities and "men's studies" have argued that the human "subject" in academic discourse, such as traditional political theory and history, is certainly *not a woman*, but not therefore really a man' (ibid.: 677). However it is pertinent to ask, as Coole does, '[i]s the feminine, too, to be appropriated by men?' (Coole 1994: 133).

The first reactions of feminists to the move from academic feminism to gender studies seem to be either to concede the claims wholesale, in the same way that some did earlier to black feminism, in an effort to maintain a solidarity with other emancipatory movements, or to close ranks in a thoroughly defensive manner. Neither of these panic reactions is particularly helpful to feminism's theoretical integrity. For a start, neither total concession nor defensiveness does away with the need actually to think through the relationship between feminism and gender studies.

There are grounds for arguing that the emergence of the discourse on masculinities is to be welcomed by feminists as increasing the awareness of questions of gender and sexuality, and because some of the arguments run in parallel with feminist arguments. On the other hand, feminism in a third wave retains its integrity as a distinct perspective far better also by recognizing the distance between the two enterprises, and not succumbing, through a misplaced sense of guilt, to the attempt of the masculinities literature to subsume and derogate second wave feminist analyses and ideas.

Among feminists, the attitude toward the strands of second wave feminism and their diversification has also changed. It is no longer necessary to declare a partisan commitment to liberal, socialist or radical principles, or to think in consequence, that one strand is 'right' and the others are somehow competing and 'wrong'. For the attitude that one approach is 'right' and the others 'wrong' is misguided. Most if not all contributions to feminism have something to offer, and many have a great deal to contribute. The range of viewpoints is a positive development which is to be welcomed. At their best, the range of perspectives and theoretical approaches is not in competition. The resulting diversity is a positive outcome, and indeed it would not be persuasive or acceptable for one strand to 'win out'. Such a result would only amount to the triumph of power over ideas. As Rosemary Pringle notes, the 'distinction between liberals, radicals and socialists no longer adequately describes the debates that are taking place within feminism. Perhaps a majority of feminists decline any of these labels and would question why anyone would continue to apply them' (Pringle 1988: 30).

The impact of postmodern ideas has led positively to a diversity of views and an overall consensus on the value of diversity and difference. But it has also led negatively to much ultimately-futile agonising along the lines of, 'is feminism redundant if the category of woman cannot be theoretically sustained?' There is a strong case for reasoning that the problem of 'no woman' is a problem only for postmodern feminism, and not for feminism as a whole. But Coole has argued thoughtfully that this problem leads directly to two further problems for feminism: how can gender be recognized as both material and cultural, and how can a 'concern with inequality and citizenship [which] call[s] for a politics of solidarity predicated on women's shared problems in a structurally and materially unequal world' be reconciled with 'a cultural feminism that is fascinated by the diversity of women's perspectives' (Coole 1994: 134).

The response that this book has sought to give is that these dilemmas are problematic, precisely because they rest upon the attempt to privilege as *independent* one side of dichotomously-presented alternatives of nature/culture and material/ideological, both of which are precisely underpinned by a mind/body dualism. The presentation of these specific pairs of perspectives *as dilemmas* is overcome by a relational mode of thinking which recognizes that material and cultural perspectives only make sense when seen as connected and interdependent.

Feminist theorizing *has* become more fluid and fragmented, but also more vital and flourishing. Its theorizing *is* getting beyond critique to ideas which are distinctively feminist, for example in the work of Grosz and Butler on the body. But if feminism has a future in a third wave then other important theoretical questions facing the third wave include (as well as those cited by

Walter), the reconceptualization of childcare in terms of emotional and 'mental' care (Walzer 1996) as well as of physical and educational care; the further development of the notion of difference to properly account for (and not appropriate) multicultural difference; and the further analysis of the 'modern' dichotomization of the categories of theorizing, the disclosure of its negative effects, and the recognition of the importance of a range of non-dichotomous modes of theorizing.

Another aspect of the growing maturity and range of analysis of feminist theorizing has been the development of more kinds of links with mainstream theorizing (see Okin 1989b, 1994, Elshtain 1981). As feminist theorizing has struggled for and gained a higher profile, so the relationship with the mainstream has been renegotiated. Assertion of a place and a voice to be taken seriously is being gradually replaced by more interventions into the mainstream from the platform established by that place and that voice (see Benhabib 1992, 1996, Nussbaum 1990, Fraser 1989, 1997a, 1997b, 1997c).

### *External dynamics*

The future of feminism does not depend only on internal developments. As Suzanna Walters notes, second-wave feminism has also changed under the impact of external factors: 'feminism and feminist theory are themselves the subject of much critical revision and rethinking, particularly in the light of both structural shifts . . . and ideological developments'. By structural shifts Walters has in mind 'changes in family life, [and] increasing numbers of women in the workforce', and ideological developments refer to 'renewed media attacks on feminism, the backlash phenomenon, the rise of right-wing Christian antifeminism and "family values"' (Walters 1996: 831). The effect of the backlash against feminism, the notion of postfeminism, and the emergence of the idea of 'girl power' are all aspects of these external dynamics.

The backlash against feminism refers to the phenomenon in the 1980s and early 1990s, when an allegedly widespread sense of dissatisfaction among women was blamed on feminism. The second wave is portrayed in the backlash literature as the era of puritanical victim feminism. It is important to note two features of the backlash, namely its predominantly North American character, and its primarily journalistic and popular articulation. Many of the writers included in the backlash discourse are American, and they write within a specifically American context of a popular, largely radical, feminist movement framed by the civil rights movement and its accent on legal redress. Thus, characteristically American factors which have helped to shape the backlash discourse in important ways include the strong tradition of media writing on feminism and other social issues; the legalistic and rights-based language of debates on social matters; the impact on second-wave feminism of specific writers such as Kate Millett, Betty Friedan, and Gloria Steinem; the role of the National Organisation for Women in second-wave feminism; the marginalization of liberal ideas in American politics over the past twenty years; the existence of a large and vocal conservative and religious lobby; and the conflict between radical feminist political campaigns and the mainstream civil rights movement.

Backlash does not refer only to the success or failure of *ideas* such as equality to advance individual goals of self-realization; it also comprehends the effect of public and social policy statements on groups of women. One important expression of the backlash has been the covert and explicit condemnation in Britain of single mothers as welfare claimants under neo-liberal ideas and conservative family values.

In her book *Backlash. The Undeclared War Against Women*, published in 1991, Susan Faludi, expressing a sympathy with feminism, argued against backlash politics that '[w]hat has made women unhappy in the last decade is not their equality – which they don't yet have – but the rising pressure to halt, and even reverse, women's quest for that equality' (Faludi 1991: 12). A recent British contribution edited by Ann Oakley and Juliet Mitchell, *Who's Afraid of Feminism. Seeing Through the Backlash* (1997), contends that the backlash has been generated to counteract the power that feminism has exercised. The contributors identify backlash politics as a reaction against the activism of second-wave feminism, a reaction which is expressed in the reassertion of the primacy of the family, of women's commitment to men and children, and of essentialist 'natural' sexual difference. They contend however, though not wholly convincingly, that rather than viewing backlash as a threat to feminism, it can be considered in a positive light as highlighting precisely the *power* of feminism.

Haste's contribution to the analysis of the backlash is more persuasive. She maintains, on the basis that there is 'an important difference between dissent and backlash', that backlash 'is primarily a *reactive position*'. Backlash involves 'defending something that is perceived either to have been lost, or to be under threat' (Haste 1993: 267). Haste contends that 'the language of backlash asserts the traditional metaphors of gender [that is hierarchy and functional complementarity] – yet with an awareness of change. The metaphors of backlash reflect anxieties about the perceived changes in the rhetoric of gender', expressed in terms of 'the "dire consequences" of changing gender roles, and assertions about "natural" sex differences and relations between the sexes'. Backlash, she argues, thus 'also reveals how far changes have been assimilated into the culture. What is problematic is defined by what is seen to have been lost, whereas for the reformer, what is problematic is defined by what is yet to be achieved' (ibid.: 17).

The populist contributions of Naomi Wolf, Nancy Friday, Katie Roiphe, Kate Fillion, and David Thomas are representative of those who have been critical of feminism from the backlash perspective. In *Fire With Fire: The New Female Power and How It Will Change the Twentyfirst Century,* Wolf (1993) argued that feminism encouraged women to view themselves only as victims, although in her earlier work, *The Beauty Myth* (1990), she was more sympathetic to the perspective of feminism, in criticizing the use of norms of body image and dieting to control women. In *The Power of Beauty,* Friday (1996) accuses feminists of male-bashing. Roiphe, in *The Morning After: Sex, Fear and Feminism* (1993) criticized feminism on the grounds that, by not only highlighting but adding to fears of date rape and sexual harassment, feminism disempowered women by reinvesting in outdated sexual restrictions, prudery and celibacy. In writers such as Wolf, Friday, Roiphe and Fillion, backlash is also closely linked to the way in which the aims of second wave feminism are often regarded as irrelevant to a younger generation's social perspective. Thomas, in *Not Guilty: In Defence of the Modern Man* (1993), has also contributed to the backlash debate, arguing in direct opposition to a fundamental second-wave feminist claim, that the public power of men has been accompanied by their private disadvantage.

Fillion, in *Lip Service: The Myth of Female Virtue in Love, Sex and Friendship* (1997), develops the themes articulated by Wolf and Roiphe. She rehearses the attack on feminist doctrines on the grounds that these ideas have portrayed women as victims and as passive. The 'modern script', written by feminism, does not allow women to recognize the influence of such doctrines, she believes (ibid.: 321). But Fillion shows little understanding of the important role played by collective action in political and social change, in arguing that the problem and its resolution now lie with individual women, who need to be free from feminism. In this spirit she declares that 'self-determination is what women want' (ibid.: 18). Her overall contention is that women (as well as men) are not free of aggressive impulses in their relations with either men or women. Inverting the meaning of women's liberation, she argues that ceasing to pay lip service to the old male/female dualities, promoted by some feminists as well as by the religious right, the political left and the mass media, allows women to be free and honest and liberated.

The main concern of Fillion's book however is with the sexuality of young women. She says that under the influence of second-wave feminism, 'girls are taught defensive sexuality: how to say No, how to use birth control, how to react to *boys* who want sex . . . Telling them that sex may make victims of them' (ibid.: 319). But 'girls need to learn sexual agency as well as self-defence', she maintains (ibid.: 321). Her major programmatic point, one with which many feminists would not disagree, is that 'girls urgently need female role models who are powerful sexual subjects' (ibid.: 320). She also puts forward the interesting idea that having power over one's own life involves making mistakes, and taking responsibility for painful outcomes. She says that often '[a]gency – having some control over one's own life – is confused with happy endings' (ibid.: 18).

In her most recent book, *Promiscuities,* Wolf (1997) also focuses on the lack of a positive identity of young women's sexuality, and also holds feminism responsible. The taboo of women's erotic coming-of-age remains to be confronted after the feminist revolutions initiated in the 1960s, she argues. From the starting-point that our culture still fears and distorts women's desire, she argues that 'women can still be "ruined" by having a sexual past to speak of' (ibid.: 5). On the (not fully justified) grounds that we become adults of our culture through experiencing and recounting stories, Wolf constructs her book through a set of private histories reconstructed from memories. She maintains that, in producing a narrative of the sexual stories of adolescence of a group of women, she is not only mirroring the way sexuality is learned, but is articulating what has not been allowed to be explicit in the culture dominated by second-wave feminism. Wolf contends that 'in spite of the rhetoric of freedom that surrounds us, women's reclamation of the first person sexual is filled with the potential for personal disaster' (ibid.: 5). Her method displays both the strengths and weaknesses of a use of the narrative form which has, ironically, become rampant amongst some feminist sociologists.

Some of the substantive ideas developed by these writers have merit. However, the orientation they take with respect to second-wave feminism is narrow, logically unproven, and unnecessarily rancorous. There are many social practices and social values at play in Western culture that are far more significant than is second wave feminism in accounting for the suppression of a positive identity of women's sexuality. There is thus a logical gap between accounting for the lack of a positive sexual identity for women and the history of second-wave feminism. In this way backlash writers make an unsubstantiated connection between the latter as cause and the former as effect. Indeed these backlash writers overestimate the role that second-wave feminism has played and so, in effect, target a straw woman. They also underestimate the way in which the character of second-wave feminist ideas and theories was shaped by the context in which they occurred, that of a culture and society in which unreflective and uncritical discrimination was widespread. Feminism has been responsible for helping to make the culture and society more reflective and critical about issues of discrimination.

The major criticisms of the backlash literature, however, arise from the way the backlash against feminism has acquired a predominantly North American character and a primarily journalistic articulation and claim to popular appeal. The first of these features has given it a very narrow focus with reference to Western liberal culture, and much less application to the British and other cultural contexts outside the US. The second of these features, more importantly, has resulted in backlash writers demonstrating a notable lack of understanding of the process of political change, and propounding a set of arguments which are acutely under-theorized. The writing of the backlash contains very little understanding of second-wave theorizing and very little attempt to retheorize the social categories at issue.

The term 'postfeminism' was coined in the 1980s, to mean either 'the problems have been solved', or 'nobody's interested any more', or under the impact of the recognition of difference, 'are there women really?' Figures associated with this development include Camille Paglia and the singer Madonna. Both seek to portray women with powerful libidinous impulses, uninhibited by the prudish prohibitions and control of feminism and political correctness. Paglia (1992) also endorses the corresponding view of a dominant biologically-determined testosterone-driven masculinity and considers that second-wave feminists have falsely taught women to fear such a masculinity. In this guise postfeminism bears a striking resemblance to the backlash against feminism, being distinctively North American in tone and populist and unreflective in appeal.

While postfeminism is often associated with the backlash, the term need not necessarily carry a negative resonance, and its ascription is not restricted to anti-feminist writers. Haste distinguishes between backlash as primarily an expression of fear, and a notion of 'rational discussions and the negotiation of new definitions of gender roles' (Haste 1993: 270), and this latter approach may be shared ground among some 'postfeminists' and third-wave feminists, and in some discussions of gender politics and masculinities. 'Postfeminism' also represents a response to the recognition by some feminists that second-wave feminism was losing its coherence.

Patricia Mann's contribution, 'Musing as a Feminist on a Postfeminist Era', rehearses a representative 'postfeminist' argument which is typically overly-optimistic and uncritical in tone. Her perspective is that 'changing gender relations are the most significant social phenomenon of our time' (Mann 1997: 222), but she does not address the question whether all these changes are meaningful in feminist terms, or the point that it will take more than a few gender changes to shift the underlying dichotomization of thinking and its expression in naturalized social practices. Mann's individualistic statement, that 'one outstanding feature of our times is a destabilization of gender-based (as well as sexual, racial and class-based) identities such that individual women and men cannot rely upon these identities as the basis for deciding how to act' (ibid.: 225), seriously underestimates the power of new constructions of conformity faced by young people.

The idea of post-feminism was also fostered by the media fiction that feminism is dead: either because we lost, or because we won. However as Fraser forcefully and convincingly argues in a book which documents the continuing prevalence of social and economic gender inequalities, 'it will not be time to speak of postfeminism until we can legitimately speak of postpatriarchy' (Fraser 1997c: 167).

## The future of feminism: the third wave

It is clear that the settled characterization of second-wave feminism has been radically affected by both internal and external developments, to the extent that the future of feminism is in urgent need of reassessment. The political dynamism of the second wave has become diffused, its strands have lost their coherence, and its theorizing has been fragmented. Furthermore the emancipatory perspective that inspired the second wave has been overtaken and a new generation has different goals. Thus in evaluating the current condition of second-wave feminism, there is a strong case for arguing that the outcome of the internal and external dynamics described above results in the unsustainability of the notion of second-wave feminism.

However there are sound reasons for arguing that what is emerging is a third wave or 'third phase of feminism' (Haste 1993: 283), rather than a post-feminist condition. Recent books suggesting a terminal backlash against feminism are ultimately unconvincing because of the severely under-theorized level of the discussion. They are not in touch with second-wave theory, nor do they advance an alternative theoretical understanding. Moreover the ideas relating to the reform of social practices, especially with respect to a heterogeneous heterosexuality, which these books at their best address, need a secure underpinning by a theoretical perspective.

Three lines of reasoning converge on the argument that feminism now faces a third wave rather than terminal decline or marginalization. While the third wave is distinguished from the second by the sense that, as Coole puts it, the 'grand narrative account formerly offered has become politically suspect' (Coole 1994: 128), it remains the case that, despite Coole's doubts, 'the task of academic feminism' is still, first, 'to render women visible' (ibid.: 129).

First, there remain important issues of gendered social hierarchy in the organization and value attached to social practices, which call for further political activity by feminists. There are still many well-documented areas, in social arrangements and in policy making, of inequality on the basis of gender, of discrimination, of sexism, of misogyny, of subordination of women as women, and of unrepresentation and under-representation in terms of political power. For instance it needs to be remembered that despite the recent unprecedented influx of women MPs, following the British general election of 1997, women still only fill twenty per cent of seats in the House of Commons.

The persistence of social divisions on the basis of gender and other factors requires the combined forces of the social and political recognition of diversity, and a proactive redistributive justice. In two articles in her latest book *Justice Interruptus,* Fraser (1997a, 1997b) makes a spirited case for just this point. The recent Church of England guidelines on the conduct of their ministers *vis-à-vis* parishoners, which warned against 'hysterical women', show that patriarchal culture remains a potent force.

The second reason supporting the idea of a third wave concerns the effect of self-definition. In one sense this refers to the fragmentation of feminist theorizing discussed above. While this fragmentation can be regarded as undermining the coherence of second-wave feminism, there are also sound grounds (necessary for a plausible self-definition) for seeing it in a very positive light, as having led to a rich, dynamic and distinctive diversity within an ongoing discourse.

In this connection the availability of a non-dichotomous mind–body distinction points a fruitful way forward for theorizing difference. A third wave of feminism is offered an open-ended theoretical coherence by the emergence of non-dichotomous forms of theorizing which contain the opportunity of overturning the dominance of dichotomous thinking. One example of how theorizing difference might be developed can be briefly outlined here. Following from Bell's argument (1995), a strong case can be made for the value of recognizing a clear connection between a metaphor and an adequate account of difference. That is, understanding feminism as in a metaphorical relation with the abolitionist, anti-racist, gay, lesbian and queer, and anti-disability struggles, is a fruitful method which recognizes rather than denies their commonality. In other words, rather than seeing the relation of feminism to these struggles through common positioning in master/slave struggles, with the attendent problems involved in ranking such struggles and accommodating the voice of each in political alliances and coalitions, the metaphorical relation operates to recognize difference and not to deny it.

The second, and related, sense of the effect of self-definition concerns second-wave feminism's self-definition. The second wave oriented itself chronologically in relation to a first wave which was taken to be largely liberal in content, and divided itself into the three primary strands. The third wave's self-definition, on the other hand, is constructed (again on sound grounds which endorse its plausibility) on multiple approaches. These approaches are not taken to represent any sense of chronological development, but are all current, representing present alternatives. An important and indeed crucial difference between the self-definitions of second- and third-wave feminisms is that the former aspired to a stipulative definition, whereas in the third wave 'feminism' has acquired the status of an essentially contested concept (Coole 1994: 130).

Third, the new generation, while not necessarily in sympathy with second-wave feminism, is concerned with fostering a non-discriminatory society. In this respect there is a real change occurring in the new generation, which reinforces the argument for a third wave of feminism based on non-dichotomous thinking. It is not that sexist values have disappeared (they have not), nor that men do half the housework and childcare (they do not), but that the *hegemony* of the dichotomous polarization and hierarchy of a heterosexualist definition of male and female is no longer regarded as acceptable. For instance, amongst young people the view that a diversity and range of different expressions of gender and sexuality can co-exist is becoming more and more widely accepted at a meaningful level. There is a widespread conviction that the aspiration to the right to become honorary males in a male-defined public world is inherently unsatisfactory for women, both at a theoretical level and in practice.

However, just as there was a strong continuity of issues and campaigns between the first and second waves (Lovenduski and Randall 1993), so there is much unfinished business from the second wave to be addressed. For example, Segal makes a convincing case that, despite the failure of second-wave feminism to facilitate the development of a positive sexual identity for women, as 'feminists, we play into the hands of our enemies if we downplay, rather than seek fully to strengthen, ideas of women's sexual liberation' (Segal 1994: 312). Feminism has not been transcended and left behind, hollow and empty, but it now exists in a context very different from the one it inhabited in the second wave, at a time of student protest, Vietnam War resistance, New Left politics, the experience by some women of financial independence during World War Two, the development of contraception and the promise of sexual liberation, the dynamism of the Women's Movement's political activism, and technological progress in the development of home appliances. The third wave faces a very different horizon of expectation and perception. Its context includes the success and failure of some second-wave aims and ideals, social practices concerned with political representation and paid as well as unpaid work which continue to express patriarchal power, the backlash against feminism, postmodern theory, gender studies and masculinities, queer theory, AIDS, and gay and lesbian theory and practice. The context of the third wave is also formed by the predominantly nonpolitical culture of many of the new generation, a culture which replaces the aims of collective political emancipation with a preoccupation with the body as a vehicle for individual self-expression through fitness, health, beauty, fashion, music and dancing.

'Feminism', as an area of study, confronts a paradox. Other areas of study such as politics or economics have political activity or economic activity as their object in the present and in the future. 'Feminism' has gender relations, not women, as its present object of study, but the transformation of gender relations as its future. Unlike politics or economics, physics or archaeology, feminism threatens to abolish its specific subject matter, all the more so where it is successful in achieving its aims of overcoming inequalities on the basis of gender, transforming patriarchal to postpatriarchal society, ending sexist values and discriminatory practices. Only the history and sociology of feminism would remain in that event. However, since it is unlikely that in the short term these aims will be accomplished, feminism and its practical objectives are likely to remain. Nevertheless the uncertainty of femininism's future, and its inherent aim of self-destruction, give it as an object of study a peculiarly unsettled character. In consequence, the end of the second wave of feminism raises fundamental questions along these lines which colour the reassessment of the second wave.

The argument of this section of the chapter has been that feminism *does* have a future. The points that have been made indicate not that feminism is over, but that the second wave of feminism is over. The theory and practice of feminism no longer fit neatly into the self-definition of the second wave. However, feminism has a future as long as it continues to combine theory and practice. Ultimately the future of feminism depends upon a continuing recognition that issues arising from oppression on grounds of gender, in the sense of Young's five-fold analysis (1990a), are political and need to be analysed, theorized and acted upon. That is, feminism has a future as long as the dynamics between its political and theoretical dimensions remain rich. So while 'the desire to change the power relations between the sexes in order to create greater equality' (Haste 1993: 100), needs to reinterpreted in a different context in the third wave, the aim remains as important as it was for second-wave feminism.

Just as important is the case that until the strangehold of dichotomous thinking in general, and of the mind/body dichotomy in particular, is overcome, the identity and future of post-second-wave feminism is likely to remain ambiguous, internally-riven and deeply problematic. In order to refocus the future possibilities of feminism, feminism in a third wave, it is important for feminist theory to demonstrate how relational thinking can contribute to our understanding of the discriminatory basis of real social practices such as those associated with sex and gender, reason and emotion, and to begin to think how these social practices can be reinvested with egalitarian aims. There are signs that just such a development is already occurring, based on non-dichotomous ways of thinking. Furthermore it is clear that a third wave which promotes non-dichotomous thinking and practices can also have an inclusivist and validatory attitude rather than an exclusivist one to the variety of feminist movements and strategies in other countries and cultures and contexts such as black feminism, ecofeminism, and women's issues in the developing world.

A catalogue of the damaging effects of the reason/emotion and man/woman dichotomies can be found in the feminist literature. A case has been made in this book not for abolishing or inverting these distinctions, but for a non-dichotomous extended conception of reason and a two-stage process of gender visibility and corporeal subjectivity. A third wave of feminism can be developed with a relational logic and non-dichotomously understood concepts. It also requires a constructionist methodology of the type outlined, which recognizes that a fundamental feature of dichotomous thinking has been the idea that the dichotomies were given and natural. The naturalization of constructed dichotomies, and the priority given to explanations founded upon biological determinism, both disguised as theories of human nature, have been pernicious and deep-seated.

The way forward for a vibrant and theoretically sound third wave of feminism is not down the road of increased gender blindness, nor through feminist separatism. A third wave of feminism as a positive political force is possible through the two-step process of gender visibility and corporeal subjectivity. Increased gender visibility is gained through recognizing examples of gender inequalities as discriminatory. Corporeal subjectivity is delivered when the integral interdependence of mind, body and emotion within all persons, constituted partly through interdependence with others, is recognized in particular persons in the form of differences. Corporeal subjectivity involves the recognition that diversity is expressed in a range of non-dichotomous differenc*es*, such that the significance of a naturalized dichotomous gender difference is no more fixed or important than is a naturalized dichotomous racial difference.

# NOTES

## INTRODUCTION

1 The demonstration of the rich scope of supporting evidence for the argument, in Chapters 1 and 2 especially, has two purposes. It is designed to advertise the availability in the existing literature of rigorous discussion of all the major threads which the argument here brings together. It also aims to provide a comprehensive discussion of components unfamiliar to some parts of mainstream political theory.

## 1 DICHOTOMY

1 Plumwood's central argument is that:

> Western thought has given us a strong human–nature dualism that is part of the set of interrelated dualisms of mind–body, reason–nature, reason–emotion, masculine–feminine and has important interconnected features with these other dualisms. This dualism has been especially stressed in the rationalist tradition. In this dualism what is characteristically and authentically human is defined against or in opposition to what is taken to be natural, nature, or the physical or biological realm . . . The maintenance of sharp dichotomy and polarisation is achieved by the rejection and denial of what links humans to the animal.
>
> (Plumwood 1995: 156)

2 For instance Jenks' use of dichotomy (1998) is informed by the desire to enable students to see the strengths of the argument of both sides, in an open manner. However his contrasting of the 'relatively timeless' dichotomies addressed in the book, with 'constructed', 'divisive' ones such as straight/gay (Jenks 1998: 6), signally fails to recognize the constructed character of the former as abstract, the constructed character of each argument/chapter as containing two sides, and the way that both forms of dichotomy share equally in the negative impact of the tradition of dichotomous thinking.

3 See Hegel (1807), and note Gillian Rose's argument for the importance of using Hegel to orient oneself to post-modernity in a positive and productive way (Rose 1994).

4 Additional evidence for Jay's observation of the alignment of dichotomy and conservatism can be found in an assessment of Janet Radcliffe Richards' argument in 'Separate Spheres' (1986).
5 See also Yeatman (1994).
6 The analysis is not exhaustive; it also explores some aspects of dichotomous thinking different from, but not incompatible with, those developed in accounts given for instance by Jay and Grosz.
7 This section draws upon definitions from the *Shorter Oxford English Dictionary,* Oxford: Clarendon 1973. In the course of her very important article, in which she details the dualistic or dichotomous features of (the dominant) classical logic in the context of a wider range of logics, Plumwood makes a good case for using the term 'dualism' in preference to 'dichotomy', in analysing the matter under discussion here. But there are also good reasons for retaining the term 'dichotomy', notably that dualism implies the oppositional but not necessarily the hierarchical component at issue. Conversely dichotomy suggests a multi-dimensional subject whereas dualism evokes a uni-dimensional subject. Furthermore dichotomy suggests a radical, extreme and fixed form of distinction, whereas dualism can imply no more than a pair of alternatives. Moreover Plumwood's interest in the subject varies from the one which is central here; in the core of the article she is concerned to chart the features of the social oppression which follows from dichotomous or dualistic thinking. As Plumwood herself notes, and this is borne out by the research undertaken here, dualism and dichotomy are used roughly interchangeably in the feminist literature (Plumwood 1993: 446).
8 But it is clear that Wendy Brown's criticism of 'antinomous construction' also refers to dichotomy (Brown 1988: 197; see also 195, 199).
9 See also Fraisse's documentation of the perhaps corresponding nineteenth-century European fear of the confusion of sexual identities, to prevent which a strict definition of sexual difference was felt necessary. (Fraisse 1994: 193).
10 Thanks to Lucy Brookes for reminding me of the importance of this point. Sarah Kofman (1985), in her close analysis of Freud's essay, 'On Femininity', and engaging with the interpretation of Irigaray, confirms the view gained from reading Freud that his theory contains a man/woman dualism which is based on a biologically reductionist distinction between men and women, and that he defended his view against contemporaneous feminists with the bisexuality thesis (women who are 'more masculine than feminine') which he used against women but not men. Kofman's argument also confirms that Freud fervently wanted his work to be regarded as science and not as philosophy or speculation, but that the historical specificity of some of the elements (including his view of women) make his work, despite his use of the method of observation, not science but intelligent speculation.
11 See note 7. While the term 'dualism' emphasises well the oppositional feature, the term 'dichotomy' suggests more adequately the presence of the other features as well.
12 See Prokhovnik (1991) chapters 1 and 2, for a defence of this view.
13 Scott (1988) develops ideas about language and difference similar to those advanced here, through the work of Foucault, Saussure and Derrida.
14 As Lloyd notes, in the 'Romantic movement of the late eighteenth and early nineteenth centuries there was a reaction against the hyperrationalism of the

Enlightenment and the mechanical conception of the universe in the "Newtonian revolution". But even the Romantics could not disagree with the underlying assumption of rationalism – that reason and passions are firmly opposed' (Lloyd 1993: 24).

15 Note also Schmitt's very interesting explicit criticism of 'either/or' thinking (1985: 8, 18, 53).

## 2 REASON AND EMOTION

1 Damasio's neurological explanation cannot be taken as decisive for what is a socially-constructed and necessarily socially-understood practice (that is, the relation of emotion and reason in theorising). However, his evidence is useful in counteracting the convention amongst biologists that the process of reason is quite separate from emotional activity. So while Damasio's work cannot be treated as providing a bedrock explanation any more than can the previous biological paradigm, and while Damasio himself seeks to provide a neurologically and biochemically reductionist account of thinking in rational and social ways which cannot be accepted here, his work nevertheless provides some useful ammunition in undermining the earlier paradigm.

2 There is real potential in the view of emotions held by Spinoza, both because he treats emotions as thoughts, and because his theory does not operate according to a mind/body dichotomy (see Spinoza 1677, Neu 1977, Gatens 1996a, 1996b, Lloyd 1994, 1996, Grosz 1994: 10–13). These aspects of his work, and thus his early rendition of a cognitivist view that is probably more adequate than the contemporary one, make the recovery of Spinoza's theory of emotions an important enterprise. However the current project is not able to do justice to Spinoza's work.

3 Worley (1995), for instance, contends that no serious male bias has been associated with the philosophical and scientific method of objectivity and lack of emotion. However this line of argument does not sufficiently address the question at issue. It fails to acknowledge the serious effects that have followed from the mapping of objective/subjective on to man/woman and reason/emotion, in leaving us with an emaciated and dichotomous view of reason.

4 See also Christine Battersby (1989), Genevieve Fraisse (1994), and Michele Le Doeuff (1977), on philosophical anti-feminism since the eighteenth century.

5 Fraisse notes the 'profound anxiety' of nineteenth-century writers stemming from 'the fear of confusing the sexes' (Fraisse 1994: 193).

6 Putnam's argument rests on his contention that incommensurability is wrong because translatability is possible. He says, '*both* of the two most influential philosophies of science of the twentieth century [positivism and Kuhn's incommensurability] . . . are self-refuting . . . To tell us that Galileo has "incommensurable" notions and *then to go on to describe then at length* is totally incoherent' (Putnam 1981: 114–5).

7 I am not fully persuaded by any one of the theories of emotion. All have strengths and problems and omissions. Most importantly, while the cognitivist theory is able to analyse the interaction between reason and emotion, it is at the expense of entrenching even further a split between mind and body. See Morwenna Griffiths (1995: 97–8). However this book is not the place to come

to a comprehensive theory of the emotions, and is concerned to define emotion (and reason) only for the purposes of explicating the links between emotion and reason in theorising.

Deborah Lupton's *The Emotional Self. A Sociocultural Exploration* (1998) has come to my attention too late for its contents to be systematically incorporated into the discussion of emotion here. However its first chapter contains a clear outline of different disciplinary approaches to emotion, with a thoughtful conclusion positing a well-justified form of social construction, and its fourth chapter usefully addresses the cultural gender-coding of emotions as feminine.

8 As Grosz observes, '[r]eason is surreptitiously defined by claiming it is *not* corporeal, not based on passion, nor madness, nor emotions, rather than described in positive or substantive terms' (Grosz 1988b: 99). See also McMillan (1982: 56) who notes that the whole rationalist enterprise depended upon a spurious contrast between reason and emotion. Okin also endorses the view that there is a 'false dichotomy between reason and feeling' (Okin 1989a: 24).

9 The term 'salience' is used here to refer collectively to what De Sousa calls salience, Crawford *et al.* call appraisal, and Greenspan (1988: 4) calls emotion as propositional feelings.

10 On this point Paul Heelas (1996) usefully identifies a range of cross-cultural differences in understanding emotions. And as Harré puts it, some 'emotions cannot seriously be studied without attention to the local moral order . . . [with] careful attention to the details of local systems of rights and obligations, of criteria of value and so on . . . That moral order is essential to the existence of just those concepts in the cognitive repertoire of the community' (Harré 1986: 6).

## 3 SEX AND GENDER

1 It is important to note that the significance given to embodiedness in the notion of corporeal subjectivity is very different from contemporary youth culture's emphasis on the body. The latter is expressed through physical fitness, health, body shape, music and dancing, and is used as a source of identity, and as an alternative to a concern with political emancipation and radical social goals which are regarded by this generation as earnest and boring.

2 The term 'gender' has further meanings within psychology (see for instance a recent contribution by Chodorow, 1995) and so is subject to further ambiguities. However the argument of this chapter is primarily concerned with political theory, and the focus of the investigation remains within that discipline and the related one of sociology.

3 Queer theory is also indebted to ideas about regulation and the repressive character of all norms derived from Foucault (1981).

4 Only part of Butler's argument is addressed here. Butler develops different aspects of her thinking in different texts, so that one is always necessarily selecting parts of her work, and these parts may not be systematically consistent with points she makes or highlights elsewhere.

5 A potential problem with this view, however, is that we still need to account for the source which supplies significance to those organs, that principle of composition, and that content of the composition. All of this would seem to be drawn from outside the substantive subject at hand.

6 While the force of the logic Butler follows here is persuasive, it is possible to arrive at the same conclusion without the reliance on Foucault and without her subscription to the ontological primacy of 'discursive practices'.

7 Another sympathetic version of compatibility, framed in different terms, is outlined by Sara Ahmed (1996).

# BIBLIOGRAPHY


Addelson, K. P. (1983) 'The Man of Professional Wisdom', in S. Harding and M. Hintikka (eds) *Discovering Reality. Feminist Perspectives on Epistemology, Metaphysics, Methodology, and Philosophy of Science,* Dordrecht: Reidel.

Ahmed, S. (1996) 'Beyond Humanism and Postmodernism: Theorizing a Feminist Practice', *Hypatia* 11.

Alcoff, L. (1995) 'Democracy and Rationality: A Dialogue with Hilary Putnam', in M. Nussbaum and J. Glover (eds) *Women, Culture, and Development. A Study of Human Capabilities,* Oxford: Clarendon Press.

Allen, J. (1990) 'Does Feminism Need a Theory of the State?', in S. Watson (ed.) *Playing the State,* London: Verso.

Andersen, J. (1996) *On the Track of Contemporary Youth. Youth Cultures and Reflexive Strategies*, Aalborg, Denmark: Aalborg University.

Anderson, E. (1995) 'Feminist Epistemology: An Interpretation and a Defense', *Hypatia* 10.

Antony, L. (1995) 'Is Psychological Individualism a Piece of Ideology?', *Hypatia* 10.

Arendt, H. (1958) *The Human Condition,* Chicago: University of Chicago Press.

Armon-Jones, C. (1986) 'The Thesis of Construction' in R. Harré (ed.) *The Social Construction of Emotions*, Oxford: Blackwell.

Arnold, M. (1968) *The Nature of Emotion*, Harmondsworth: Penguin.

Aronovitch, H. (1997) 'The Political Importance of Analogical Argument', *Political Studies* 45.

Averill, J. (1996) 'Intellectual Emotions', in R. Harré and G. Perrott (eds) *The Emotions. Social, Cultural and Biological Dimensions*, London: Sage.

Babbitt, S. (1993) 'Feminism and Objective Interests: The Role of Transformation Experiences in Rational Deliberation', in L. Alcoff and E. Potter (eds) *Feminist Epistemologies*, London: Routledge.

Babich, B. (1996) 'The Metaphor of Woman as Truth in Nietzsche: The Dogmatist's Reverse Logic', *Journal of Nietzsche Studies* 12.

Bader, V. (1995) 'Citizenship and Exclusion. Radical Democracy, Community, and Justice. Or, What is Wrong with Communitarianism?', *Political Theory* 23.

Baehr, A. (1996) 'Toward a New Feminist Liberalism: Okin, Rawls, and Habermas', *Hypatia* 11.

Baier, A. (1980) 'Master Passions', in A. Rorty (ed.) *Explaining Emotions*, Berkeley: University of California Press.

—— (1985a) 'Actions, Passions, and Reasons', in A. Baier, *Postures of the Mind. Essays on Mind and Morals,* London: Methuen.

—— (1985b) *Postures of the Mind. Essays on Mind and Morals,* London: Methuen.

—— (1995) 'A Note on Justice, Care, and Immigration Policy', *Hypatia* 10.

Bar On, B.-A. (1993) 'Marginality and Epistemic Privilege', in L. Alcoff and E. Potter (eds) *Feminist Epistemologies*, London: Routledge.

Barrett M. and Phillips A. (1992) 'Introduction', in M. Barrett and A. Phillips (eds) *Destabilizing Theory*, Cambridge: Polity.

Barry, B. (1995) *Justice as Impartiality,* Oxford: Clarendon.

Battersby, C. (1989) *Gender and Genius. Towards a Feminist Aesthetics*, London: Women's Press.

Beiner, R. (1983) *Political Judgment*, London: Methuen.

—— (1992) *What's the Matter with Liberalism?*, Berkeley, University of California Press.

—— (ed.) (1995) *Theorizing Citizenship,* New York: State University of New York Press.

Bell, V. (1995) 'On Metaphors of Suffering: Mapping the Feminist Political Imagination', *Economy and Society* 24.

Bellamy, R. and Castiglione, D. (1997) 'Constitutionalism and Democracy - Political Theory and the American Constitution', *British Journal of Political Science* 27.

Benhabib, S. (1990) 'Epistemologies of Postmodernism: A Rejoinder to Jean-Francois Lyotard', in L. Nicholson (ed.) *Feminism/Postmodernism*, London: Routledge.

—— (1992a) 'Models of Public Space', in S. Benhabib, *Situating the Self*, Cambridge: Polity.

—— (1992b) 'Judgment and the Moral Foundation of Politics in Hannah Arendt's Thought', in S. Benhabib, *Situating the Self,* Cambridge: Polity.

—— (1995) 'Cultural Complexity, Moral Interdependence, and the Global Dialogical Community', in M. Nussbaum and J. Glover (eds) *Women, Culture, and Development. A Study of Human Capabilities,* Oxford: Clarendon Press.

—— (1996) *Democracy and Difference,* Princeton: Princeton University Press.

Ben-Ze'ev, A. and Oatley, K. (1996) 'The Intentional and Social Nature of Human Emotions: Reconsideration of the Distinction Between Basic and Non-Basic Emotions', *Journal for the Theory of Social Behaviour* 26.

Berlin, I. (1969) 'Two Concepts of Liberty', in I. Berlin, *Four Essays on Liberty*, Oxford: Oxford University Press.

Bernstein, J. (1994) 'Conscience and Transgression: The Persistence of Misrecognition', *Bulletin of the Hegel Society of Great Britain* 29.

Berry, C. (1988) *Human Nature*, London: Macmillan.

Bordo, S (1988) 'Anorexia Nervosa: Psychopathology as the Crystallization of Culture', in I. Diamond and L. Quinby (eds) *Feminism and Foucault. Reflections on Resistance*, Boston: Northeastern University Press.

—— (1989) 'The Body and the Reproduction of Femininity: A Feminist Appropriation of Foucault', in A. Jaggar and S. Bordo (eds) *Gender/Body/Knowledge. Feminist Reconstructions of Being and Knowing*, New Brunswick: Rutgers University Press.

—— (1990), 'Feminism, Postmodernism, and Gender-Scepticism', in L. Nicholson (ed.), *Feminism/Postmodernism*, London: Routledge.

—— (1993) *Unbearable Weight. Feminism, Western Culture, and the Body,* Berkeley, University of California Press.

Braidotti, R. (1986) 'Ethics Revisited: Women and/in Philosophy', in C. Pateman and E. Gross (eds) *Feminist Challenges. Social and Political Theory*, London: Allen & Unwin.

—— (1991) *Patterns of Dissonance*, Oxford: Blackwell.

—— (1992) 'On the Female Feminist Subject, or: From 'She-Self' to 'She-Other', in G. Bock and S. James (eds) *Beyond Equality and Difference*, London: Routledge.

Brennan, T. (1992) *The Interpretation of the Flesh*, London: Routledge.

Brown, W. (1987) 'Where Is the Sex in Political Theory?', *Women and Politics* 7.

—— (1988) *Manhood and Politics. A Feminist Reading of Political Theory*, Totowa Pa.: Rowman & Littlefield.

—— (1991) 'Feminist Hesitation, Postmodern Exposures', *Differences* 3.

—— (1995) *States of Injury. Power and Freedom in Late Modernity*, Princeton: Princeton University Press.

Butler, J. (1987) 'Variations on Sex and Gender. Beauvoir, Wittig and Foucault', in S. Benhabib and D. Cornell (eds) *Feminism as Critique. Essays on the Politics of Gender in Late-Capitalist Societies*, Cambridge: Polity.

—— (1989) 'Gendering the Body: Beauvoir's Philosophical Contribution', in A. Garry and M. Pearsall (eds) *Women, Knowledge and Reality. Explorations in Feminist Philosophy*, New York: Routledge.

—— (1990a) 'Gender Trouble, Feminist Theory, and Psychoanalytic Discourse', in L. Nicholson (ed.) *Feminism/Postmodernism*, London: Routledge.

—— (1990b) *Gender Trouble*, New York: Routledge.

—— (1993) *Bodies That Matter*, New York: Routledge.

—— (1997) 'Critically Queer', in S. Phelan (ed.) *Playing with Fire*, New York: Routledge.

Byrne, L. (1994) 'Reason and Emotion in Spinoza's "Ethics": The Two Infinities', in G. Hunter (ed.) *Spinoza – the Enduring Questions*, Toronto: University of Toronto Press.

Calhoun, C. (1995) 'The Gender Closet: Lesbian Disappearance Under the Sign "Women"', *Feminist Studies* 21.

Carter, E., Donald, J., and Squires, J. (1995) *Cultural Remix. Theories of Politics and the Popular*, London: Lawrence & Wishart.

Carter M. and Carter S. B. (1981) 'Women's Recent Progress in the Professions or, Women Get a Ticket to Ride After the Gravy Train has Left the Station', *Feminist Studies* 7.

Carver, T. (1996) '"Public Man" and the Critique of Masculinities', *Political Theory* 24.

Cavarero, A. (1992) 'Equality and Sexual Difference: Amnesia in Political Thought', in G. Bock and S. James (eds), *Beyond Equality and Difference. Citizenship, Feminist Politics and Female Subjectivity*, London: Routledge.

—— (1996) 'Rethinking Oedipus: Stealing a Patriarchal Text', paper presented to the 1996 Society of Women in Philosophy Conference, 'Women and Philosophy', Canterbury, December 1996.

Charles, N. (1993) *Gender Divisions and Social Change*, Hemel Hempstead: Harvester Wheatsheaf.

Chodorow, N. (1995) 'Gender as a Personal and Cultural Construction', *Signs* 20.

Cixous, H. (1981) 'The Laugh of the Medusa', in E. Marks and I. de Courtivron (eds) *New French Feminisms*, New York: Schocken Books.

Clough, P. T. (1994) *Feminist Thought*, Oxford: Blackwell.

Cocks, J. (1984) 'Wordless Emotions: Some Critical Reflections on Radical Feminism', *Politics and Society* 13.

—— (1989) *The Oppositional Imagination. Feminism, Critique and Political Theory*, London: Routledge.

Condren, C. (1985) *The Status and Appraisal of Classic Texts. An Essay on Political Theory, Its Inheritance, and the History of Ideas*, Princeton: Princeton University Press.

Connolly, W. (1993) *The Terms of Political Discourse*, 2nd ed., Oxford: Blackwell.

Coole, D. (1988) *Women in Political Theory. From Ancient Misogyny to Contemporary Feminism*, Hemel Hempstead: Harvester Wheatsheaf.

—— (1994) 'Whither Feminisms?', *Political Studies* 42.

Cornell, D. and Thurschwell, A. (1987) 'Feminism, Negativity, Intersubjectivity', in S. Benhabib and D. Cornell (eds) *Feminism as Critique. Essays on the Politics of Gender in Late-Capitalist Societies*, Cambridge: Polity.

Craib, I. (1995) 'Some Comments on the Sociology of the Emotions', *Sociology* 29.

Crawford, J., Kippax, S., Onyx, J., Gault, U., and Benton, P., (1992) *Emotion and Gender. Constructing Meaning from Memory*, London: Sage.

Daly, M. (1978) *Gyn/Ecology*, Boston: Beacon.

Damasio, A. (1994) *Descartes' Error*, New York: Putnam.

Davis, K. (1992) 'Toward a Feminist Rhetoric: The Gilligan Debate Revisited', *Women's Studies International Forum* 15.

De Beauvoir, S. (1952) *The Second Sex*, trans. H. M. Parshley, New York: Vintage.

Derrida, J. (1972) *Positions*, trans. A. Bass, London: Athlone.

De Sousa R., (1980) 'The Rationality of Emotions', in A. Rorty (ed.) *Explaining Emotions*, Berkeley: University of California Press.

—— (1987) The Rationality of Emotion, Cambridge, Mass.: MIT Press.

Deveaux, M. (1995) 'Shifting Paradigms: Theorizing Care and Justice in Political Theory', *Hypatia* 10.

Diamond, J. (1997) *Why is Sex Fun?*, London: Weidenfeld.

Dimen, M. (1989) 'Power, Sexuality, and Intimacy', in A. Jaggar and S. Bordo (eds) *Gender/Body/Knowledge. Feminist Reconstructions of Being and Knowing*, New Brunswick: Rutgers University Press.

Diprose, R. (1994) *The Bodies of Women. Ethics, Embodiment and Sexual Difference*, London: Routledge.

Dolar, M. (1995) 'The Legacy of the Enlightenment: Foucault and Lacan', in E. Carter, J. Donald and J. Squires (eds) *Cultural Remix. Theories of Politics and the Popular*, London: Lawrence & Wishart.

Dworkin, A. (1989) *Pornography. Men Possessing Women*, New York: Dutton.

Eisenstein, Z. (1981) 'Antifeminism in the Politics and Election of 1980', *Feminist Studies* 7.

Elliott, T. (1994) 'Making Strange What Had Appeared Familiar', *The Monist* 77.

Elshtain, J. (1981) *Public Man, Private Woman*, Princeton: Princeton University Press.

—— (1983) 'On "the Family Crisis"', *Democracy* 3.

—— (1987) 'Against Androgyny', in A. Phillips (ed.) *Feminism and Equality*, Oxford: Blackwell.

Ernst, W. (1996) 'European Madness and Gender in Nineteenth-Century British India', *Social History of Medicine* 9.

Evans J., Hills J., Hunt K., Meehan E., ten Tusscher T., Vogel U. and Waylen G. (1986) *Feminism and Political Theory*, London: Sage.

Faludi, S. (1991) *Backlash. The Undeclared War Against Women*, London: Chatto & Windus.

Fillion, K. (1997) *Lip Service. The Myth of Female Virtue in Love, Sex and Friendship*, London: Pandora.

Flax, J. (1983) 'Political Philosophy and the Patriarchal Unconscious: A Psychoanalytic Perspective on Epistemology and Metaphysics', in S. Harding and M. Hintikka (eds) *Discovering Reality. Feminist Perspectives on Epistemology, Metaphysics, Methodology, and Philosophy of Science*, Dordrecht: Reidel.

—— (1990) 'Postmodernism and Gender Relations in Feminist Theory', in L. Nicholson (ed.) *Feminism/Postmodernism*, London: Routledge. Also in J. Butler and J. Scott (eds) (1992) *Feminists Theorise the Political*, London: Routledge.

—— (1992) 'Beyond Equality: Gender, Justice and Difference', in G. Bock and S. James (eds), *Beyond Equality and Difference. Citizenship, Feminist Politics and Female Subjectivity*, London: Routledge.

Fontana, B. (ed.) (1994) *The Invention of the Modern Republic*, Cambridge: Cambridge University Press.

Foucault, M. (1981) *History of Sexuality* vol. 1, Harmondsworth: Penguin.

Fox Keller, E. (1985) *Reflections on Gender and Science*, New Haven: Yale Universitry Press.

Fraisse, G. (1994) *Reason's Muse. Sexual Difference and the Birth of Democracy*, trans. J. Todd, Chicago: University of Chicago Press.

Frank, R. (1988) *Passions within Reason. The Strategic Role of the Emotions*, New York: Norton & Co.

Fraser, N. (1987) 'Women, Welfare and the Politics of Need Interpretation', *Hypatia* 2.

—— (1989) *Unruly Practices. Power, Discourse and Gender in Contemporary Social Theory*, Cambridge: Polity.

—— (1994) 'After the Family Wage. Gender Equity and the Welfare State', *Political Theory* 22.

—— (1995) 'False Antitheses', in S. Benhabib, J. Butler, D. Cornell and N. Fraser, *Feminist Contentions. A Philosophical Exchange*, New York: Routledge.

—— (1997a) 'From Redistribution to Recognition?', in N. Fraser, *Justice Interruptus. Critical Reflections on the 'Postsocialist' Condition*, New York: Routledge.

—— (1997b) 'Multiculturalism, Antiessentialism, and Radical Democracy: A Genealogy of the Current Impasse in Feminist Theory', in N. Fraser, *Justice Interruptus. Critical Reflections on the 'Postsocialist' Condition*, New York: Routledge.

—— (1997c) 'Structuralism or Pragmatics? On Discourse Theory and Feminist Politics', in *N. Fraser, Justice Interruptus. Critical Reflections on the 'Postsocialist' Condition*, New York: Routledge.

Frazer, E. (1997) 'Method Matters: Feminism, Interpretation and Politics', in A. Vincent (ed.) *Political Theory. Tradition and Diversity*, Cambridge: Cambridge University Press.

Freely, M. (1995) *What About Us? An Open Letter to the Mothers Feminism Forgot*, London: Bloomsbury

Freud, S. (1986) *The Essentials of Psycho-Analysis*, selected by A. Freud, trans. J. Strachey, Harmondsworth: Penguin.

Fricker, M. (1994) 'Knowledge as Construct. Theorising the Role of Gender in Knowledge', in K. Lennon and M. Whitford (eds) *Knowing the Difference. Feminist Perspectives in Epistemology*, London: Routledge.

Friday, N. (1996) *The Power of Beauty*, London: Hutchinson.

Friedan, B. (1963) *The Feminine Mystique*, London: Penguin.

Frye, M. (1993) 'The Body Philosophical', in C. Kramarae and D. Spender (eds) *The Knowledge Explosion. Generations of Feminist Scholarship*, Hemel Hempstead: Harvester Wheatsheaf.

Garry, A. (1995) 'A Minimally Decent Philosophical Method? Analytic Philosophy and Feminism', *Hypatia* 10.

Gatens, M. (1991) *Feminism and Philosophy. Perspectives on Difference and Equality*, Cambridge: Polity.

—— (1992) 'Power, Bodies and Difference', in M. Barrett and A. Phillips (eds) *Destabilizing Theory*, Cambridge: Polity.

—— (1996a) *Imaginary Bodies. Ethics, Power and Corporeality*, London: Routledge.

—— (1996b) 'Through a Spinozist Lens: Ethology, Difference, Power', in P. Patton (ed.) *Deleuze: A Critical Reader*, Oxford: Blackwell.

Gilligan, C. (1993) *In a Different Voice*, Cambridge, Mass.: Harvard University Press.

—— (1995) 'Hearing the Difference: Theorizing Connection', Hypatia 10.

Glennon, L. (1979) *Women and Dualism. A Sociology of Knowledge Analysis*, New York: Longman.

Goleman, D. (1995) *Emotional Intelligence*, London: Bloomsbury.

Gould, C. (1993), 'Feminism and Democratic Community Revisited', in J. Chapman and I. Shapiro (eds) *Democracy and Community. Nomos XXXV*, New York: New York University Press.

Grant, J. (1993) *Fundamental Feminism. Contesting the Core Concepts of Feminist Theory*, New York: Routledge.

Green, K. (1993) 'Reason and Feeling: Resisting the Dichotomy', *Australasian Journal of Philosophy* 71.

—— (1995) *The Woman of Reason. Feminism, Humanism and Political Thought*, Cambridge: Polity.

Greenspan, P. (1988) *Emotions and Reasons. An Inquiry into Emotional Justification*, New York: Routledge.

Griffiths, M. (1995) *Feminisms and the Self. The Web of Identity*, London: Routledge.

Grimshaw, J. (1986) *Feminist Philosophers. Women's Perspectives on Philosophical Traditions*, Brighton: Wheatsheaf.

—— (1996) 'Philosophy and the Feminist Imagination', paper presented to 1996 Society of Women in Philosophy Conference, 'Women and Philosophy', Canterbury, December 1996.

Gross, E. (1986) 'Conclusion: What is Feminist Theory?', in C. Pateman and E. Gross (eds) *Feminist Challenges. Social and Political Theory*, Sydney: Allen & Unwin.

Grosz, E. A. (1988a) 'Introduction', in B. Caine, E. Grosz and M. Lepervanche (eds) *Crossing Boundaries: Feminisms and the Critique of Knowledges*, Sydney: Allen & Unwin.

—— (1988b) 'The In(ter)vention of Feminist Knowledges', in B. Caine, E. Grosz and M. Lepervanche (eds) *Crossing Boundaries: Feminisms and the Critiques of Knowledges*, Sydney: Allen & Unwin.

—— (1989) *Sexual Subversions. Three French Feminists*, Sydney: Allen & Unwin.

—— (1990a) 'Philosophy', in S. Gunew (ed.) *Feminist Knowledge. Critique and Construct*, London: Routledge.

—— (1990b) *Jacques Lacan. A Feminist Introduction*, London: Routledge.

—— (1990c) 'A Note on Essentialism and Difference', in S. Gunew (ed.) *Feminist Knowledge*, London: Routledge.

—— (1993) 'Bodies and Knowledges: Feminism and the Crisis of Reason', in L. Alcoff and E. Potter (eds) *Feminist Epistemologies*, London: Routledge.

—— (1994) *Volatile Bodies. Towards a Corporeal Feminism*, Bloomington: Indiana University Press.

Hale, J. (1996) 'Are Lesbians Women?', *Hypatia* 11.

Haraway, D. (1991) '"Gender" for a Marxist Dictionary: The Sexual Politics of a Word', in D. Haraway, *Simians, Cyborgs and Women*, New York: Routledge.

Harré, R. (1986) 'An Outline of the Social Constructionist Viewpoint', in R. Harré (ed.) *The Social Construction of Emotions*, Oxford: Blackwell.

Hartsock, N. (1990) 'Foucault on Power: A Theory for Women?', in L. Nicholson (ed.) *Feminism/Postmodernism*, London: Routledge.

Haste, H. (1993) *The Sexual Metaphor*, Hemel Hempstead: Harvester Wheatsheaf.

Hawkesworth, M. (1997) 'Confounding Gender', *Signs* 22.

Hearn, J. (1992) *Men in the Public Eye: The Construction and Deconstruction of Public Men and Public Patriarchies*, London: Routledge.

Heelas, P. (1996) 'Emotion Talk Across Cultures', in R. Harré and G. Parrott (eds) *The Emotions. Social, Cultural and Biological Dimensions*, London: Sage.

Hekman, S. (1990) *Gender and Knowledge. Elements of a Postmodern Feminism*, Cambridge: Polity.

—— (1995) *Moral Voices, Moral Selves. Carol Gilligan and Feminist Moral Theory*, Cambridge: Polity.

Hegel, G. W. F. (1807) [1971] *The Phenomenology of Mind*, trans. J. B. Baillie, London: Allen & Unwin.

Held, V. (1995) 'The Meshing of Care and Justice', *Hypatia* 10.

Hobbes, T. (1651) [1946] *Leviathan*, ed. M. Oakeshott, Oxford: Blackwell.

Hollis, M. and Lukes, S. (eds) (1982) *Rationality and Relativism*, Oxford: Blackwell.

Honneth, A. (1995) *The Struggle for Recognition. The Moral Grammar of Social Conflicts*, Cambridge: Polity.

Hood-Williams, J. (1996) 'Goodbye to Sex and Gender', *Sociological Review* 44.

Horrocks, R. (1995) *Male Myths and Icons. Masculinity in Popular Culture*, London: Macmillan.

Hubbard, R. (1983) 'Have Only Men Evolved?', in S. Harding and M. Hintikka (eds) *Discovering Reality. Feminist Perspectives on Epistemology, Metaphysics, Methodology, and Philosophy of Science,* Dordrecht: Reidel.

Irigaray, L. (1993) *Je, Tu, Nous. Towards a Culture of Difference*, trans. A. Martin, New York: Routledge.

Jaggar, A. (1989) 'Love and Knowledge: Emotion and Feminist Epistemology', in A. Garry and M. Pearsall (eds) *Women, Knowledge and Reality. Explorations in Feminist Philosophy*, New York: Routledge.

Jay, N. (1981) 'Gender and Dichotomy', *Feminist Studies* 7.

Jeffreys, S. (1994) 'Creating the Sexual Future', in M. Evans (ed.) *The Woman Question*, London: Sage.

Jenks, C. (ed.) (1998) *Core Sociological Dichotomies*, London: Sage.

Johnson, P. (1993) 'Feminism and Enlightenment', *Radical Philosophy* 63.

—— (1994) *Feminism as Radical Humanism*, Sydney: Allen & Unwin.

Jones, A. (1981) 'Writing the Body: Towards an Understanding of "L'Ecriture Feminine"', *Feminist Studies* 7.

Jones, Adam (1996) 'Does "Gender" Make the World Go Round? Feminist Critiques of International Relations', *Review of International Studies* 22.

Jones, K. (1990) 'Citizenship in a Woman-Friendly Polity', *Signs* 15.

Kaplan G. and Rogers, L. (1990) 'The Definition of Male and Female: Biological Reductionism and the Sanctions of Normality', in S. Gunew (ed.) *Feminist Knowledge. Critique and Construct*, London: Routledge.

Kappeller, S. (1986) *The Pornography of Representation*, Cambridge: Polity.

Kelley, D. (1994) *The Art of Reasoning*, New York: W. W. Norton.

Kennedy E. and Mendus S. (eds) (1987) *Women in Western Political Philosophy. Kant to Nietzsche*, Brighton: Wheatsheaf Books.

King, Y. (1989) 'Healing the Wounds: Feminism, Ecology, and Nature/Culture Dualism', in A. Jaggar and S. Bordo (eds) *Gender/Body/Knowledge. Feminist Reconstructions of Being and Knowing*, New Brunswick: Rutgers University Press.

Kofman, S. (1985) *The Enigma of Woman. Woman in Freud's Writings*, trans. C. Porter, Ithaca: Cornell University Press.

Kroon, F. (1996) 'Deterrence and the Fragility of Rationality', *Ethics* 106.

Kruks, S. (1995) 'Identity Politics and Dialectical Reason: Beyond an Epistemology of Provenance', *Hypatia* 10.

Lacan, J. (1977) *Ecrits: A Selection*, trans. A. Sheridan, New York: W. W. Norton.

Le Doeuff, M. (1977) 'Women and Philosophy', *Radical Philosophy* 17.

—— (1989) *The Philosophical Imaginary*, trans. C. Gordon, London: Athlone.

—— (1990) 'Women, Reason, etc.', *Differences: A Journal of Feminist Cultural Studies* 2.

—— (1991) *Hipparchia's Choice. An Essay Concerning Women, Philosophy, etc.*, trans. T. Selous, Oxford: Blackwell.

Lee-Lampshire, W. (1995) 'Decisions of Identity: Feminist Subjects and Grammars of Sexuality', *Hypatia* 10.

Lennon, K. and Whitford, M. (1994) 'Introduction', in K. Lennon and M. Whitford (eds) *Knowing the Difference. Feminist Perspectives in Epistemology*, London: Routledge.

Lewis, R. (1994) 'Dis-Graceful Images: Della Grace and Lesbian Sado-Masochism', *Feminist Review* 46.

Little, M. O. (1995) 'Seeing and Caring: The Role of Affect in Feminist Moral Epistemology', *Hypatia* 10.

Lloyd, G. (1989) 'Woman as Other: Sex, Gender and Subjectivity', *Australian Feminist Studies* 10.

—— (1993) *The Man of Reason. 'Male' and 'Female' in Western Philosophy*, 2nd ed., Minneapolis: University of Minnesota Press.

—— (1994) *Part of Nature. Self-Knowledge in Spinoza's 'Ethics'*, Ithaca, Cornell University Press.

—— (1996) *Spinoza and the 'Ethics'*, London: Routledge.

Lloyd, M. (1996) 'Feminism, Aerobics and the Politics of the Body', *Body and Society* 2.

Longino, H. (1995) 'To See Feelingly: Reason, Passion, and Dialogue in Feminist Philosophy', in D. Stanton and A. Stewart (eds) *Feminisms in the Academy*, Ann Arbor: University of Michigan Press.

Lovenduski, J. and Randall, V. (1993) *Contemporary Feminist Politics*, Oxford: Oxford University Press.

Lovibond, S. (1989) 'Feminism and Postmodernism', *New Left Review* 178.

—— (1994) 'The End of Morality?', in K. Lennon and M. Whitford (eds) *Knowing the Difference. Feminist Perspectives in Epistemology*, London: Routledge.

Lupton, D. (1998) *The Emotional Self. A Sociocultural Exploration*, London: Sage.

Lutz, C. (1996) 'Engendered Emotion: Gender, Power, and the Rhetoric of Emotional Control in American Discourse', in R. Harré and G. Parrott (eds) *The Emotions. Social, Cultural and Biological Dimensions*, London: Sage.

MacIntyre, A. (1985) *After Virtue. A Study in Moral Theory*, London: Duckworth.

McKenna, W. and Kessler, S. (1997) 'Comment on Hawkesworth's "Confounding Gender": Who Needs Gender Theory?', *Signs* 22.

MacKinnon, C. (1989) *Towards a Feminist Theory of the State*, Harvard: Harvard University Press.

McMillan, C. (1982) *Women, Reason and Nature. Some Philosophical Problems with Feminism*, Princeton: Princeton University Press.

Macmurray J. (1962) *Reason and Emotion*, London: Faber & Faber.

McNay, L. (1992) *Foucault and Feminisms: Power, Gender and the Self*, Cambridge: Polity.

Mangena, O. (1994) 'Against Fragmentation: The Need for Holism', in K. Lennon and M. Whitford (eds) *Knowing the Difference. Feminist Perspectives in Epistemology*, London: Routledge.

Mann, P. (1997) 'Musing as a Feminist on a Postfeminist Era', in J. Dean (ed.) *Feminism and the New Democracy. Re-Siting the Political*, London: Sage.

Mansbridge, J. (1993) 'Feminism and Democratic Community', in J. Chapman and I. Shapiro (eds) *Democracy and Community. Nomos XXXV*, New York: New York University Press.

—— (1996) 'Using Power/Fighting Power: The Polity', in S. Benhabib (ed.) *Democracy and Difference. Contesting the Boundaries of the Political*, Princeton: Princeton University Press.

Marcil-Lacoste, L. (1983) 'The Trivialization of the Notion of Equality', in S. Harding and M. Hintikka (eds) *Discovering Reality. Feminist Perspectives on Epistemology, Metaphysics, Methodology, and Philosophy of Science*, Dordrecht: Reidel.

Marks E. and de Courtivron I. (eds) (1980) *New French Feminisms*, Brighton: Harvester.

Marshall, B. (1994) *Engendering Modernity*, Cambridge: Polity.

Marshall, T. H. (1950) *Citizenship and Social Class*, Cambridge: Cambridge University Press.

Mendus, S. (1996) 'Some Mistakes about Impartiality', *Political Studies* 44.

Merchant, C. (1983) *The Death of Nature. Women, Ecology, and the Scientific Revolution*, Harper: San Francisco.

Miller, M. (1993) 'Canons and the Challenge of Gender', *The Monist* 76.

Miller, R. (1995) 'The Norms of Reason', *The Philosophical Review* 104.

Millett, K. (1977) *Sexual Politics*, London: Virago.

Minh-ha, T. (1989) *Woman, Native, Other*, Bloomington: Indiana University Press.

Minow, M. and Shanley, M. L. (1996) 'Relational Rights and Responsibilities: Revisioning the Family in Liberal Political Theory and Law', *Hypatia* 11.

Molloy, M. (1995) 'Imagining (the) Difference: Gender, Ethnicity and Metaphors of Nation', *Feminist Review* 51.

Moore, H. (1988) *Feminism and Anthropology*, Cambridge: Polity.

—— (1994) '"Divided We Stand": Sex, Gender and Sexual Difference', *Feminist Review* 47.

Morgan, D. (1992) *Discovering Men*, London: Routledge.

Morgan, L. (1996) 'Fetal Relationality in Feminist Philosophy: An Anthropological Critique', *Hypatia* 11.

Moulton, J. (1989) 'A Paradigm of Philosophy: The Adversary Method', in A. Garry and M. Pearsall (eds) *Women, Knowledge, and Reality: Explorations in Feminist Philosophy*, New York: Routledge.

Mulhall S. and Swift, A. (1996) *Liberals and Communitarians*, 2nd ed., Oxford: Blackwell.

Mullin, A. (1995) 'Selves, Diverse and Divided: Can Feminists Have Diversity without Multiplicity?', *Hypatia* 10.

Narayan, U. (1995) 'Colonialism and Its Others: Considerations on Rights and Care Discourses', *Hypatia* 10.

Nash, K. (1994) 'The Feminist Production of Knowledge: Is Deconstruction a Practice for Women?', *Feminist Review* 47.

Neu, J. (1977) *Emotion, Thought and Therapy. A Study of Hume and Spinoza and the Relationship of Philosophyical Theories of the Emotions to Psychological Theory of Therapy*, London: Routledge.

Nozick, R. (1989) *The Examined Life*, New York: Simon & Schuster.

—— (1993) *The Nature of Rationality*, Princeton: Princeton University Press.

Nussbaum, M. (1990) *Love's Knowledge. Essays on Philosophy and Literature*, Oxford: Oxford University Press.

—— (1995a) 'Human Capabilities, Female Human Beings', in M. Nussbaum and J. Glover (eds) *Women, Culture, and Development. A Study of Human Capabilities*, Oxford: Clarendon Press.

—— (1995b) 'Emotions and Women's Capabilities', in M. Nussbaum and J. Glover (eds) *Women, Culture, and Development. A Study of Human Capabilities*, Oxford: Clarendon Press.

Nye A. (1988) *Feminist Theory and the Philosophies of Man*, London: Croom Helm.

Oakeshott, M. (1933) *Experience and Its Modes*, Cambridge: Cambridge University Press.

—— (1975) *On Human Conduct*, Oxford: Clarendon.

Oakley, A. and Mitchell, J. (1997) *Who's Afraid of Feminism. Seeing Through the Backlash*, London: Hamish Hamilton.

Oakley, J. (1992) *Morality and the Emotions*, London: Routledge.

O'Brien, M. (1981) *The Politics of Reproduction*, London: Routledge.

O'Driscoll, S. (1996) 'Outlaw Reading: Beyond Queer Theory', *Signs* 22.

Okin, S. M. (1979) *Women in Western Political Thought*, Princeton: Princeton University Press.

—— (1989a) 'Reason and Feeling in Thinking about Justice', *Ethics* 99.

—— (1989b) *Justice, Gender, and the Family*, New York: BasicBooks.

—— (1994) 'Political Liberalism, Justice and Gender', *Ethics* 105.

—— (1995) 'Inequalities Between the Sexes in Different Cultural Contexts', in M. Nussbaum and J. Glover (eds) *Women, Culture, and Development. A Study of Human Capabilities*, Oxford: Clarendon Press.

—— (1996) 'Sexual Orientation, Gender, and Families: Dichotomizing Differences', *Hypatia* 11.

O'Neill O. (1995) 'Justice, Capabilities, and Vulnerabilities', in M. Nussbaum and J. Glover (eds) *Women, Culture, and Development. A Study of Human Capabilities*, Oxford: Clarendon Press.

Orbach, S. (1998) in *Guardian Weekend*, February 7.
Ortner, S. (1982) 'Is Female to Male as Nature is to Culture?', in M. Evans (ed.) *The Woman Question*, London: Fontana.
Ortner, S. and Whitehead, H. (1981) *Sexual Meanings. The Cultural Construction of Gender and Sexuality*, Cambridge: Cambridge University Press.
Ortony, A. (1979) 'Metaphor: A Multidimensional Problem', in A. Ortony (ed.) *Metaphorical Thought*, Cambridge: Cambridge University Press.
Paglia, C. (1992) *Sex, Art, and American Culture*, Harmondsworth: Penguin.
Parrott, W. and Harré, R. (1996) 'Introduction: Some Complexities in the Study of Emotions. Overview', in R. Harré and W. Gerrod Parrott (eds) *The Emotions. Social, Cultural and Biological Dimensions*, London, Sage.
Pateman, C. (1980) 'Women and Consent', *Political Theory*
—— (1987) 'Feminist Critiques of the Public/Private Dichotomy', in A. Phillips (ed.) *Feminism and Equality*, Oxford: Blackwell.
—— (1988) *The Sexual Contract*, Stanford: Stanford University Press.
Patton, P. (1997) 'The Political Philosophy of Deleuze and Guattari', in A. Vincent (ed.) *Political Theory. Tradition and Diversity*, Cambridge: Cambridge University Press.
Phelan, S. (1997) *Playing with Fire*, New York: Routledge.
Phillips, Adam (1998) *The Beast in the Nursery*, London: Faber.
Phillips, Anne (1987) 'Introduction', in A. Phillips (ed.) *Feminism and Equality*, Oxford: Blackwell.
—— (1992) 'Universal Pretentions in Political Thought', in M. Barrett and A. Phillips (eds) *Destabilizing Theory*, Cambridge: Polity.
Pinker, S. (1998) *How the Mind Works*, London: Allen Lane.
Plant, R. (1991) *Modern Political Thought*, Oxford: Blackwell.
Plumwood, V. (1993) 'The Politics of Reason: Towards a Feminist Logic', *Australasian Journal of Philosophy* 71.
—— (1995) 'Nature, Self, and Gender: Feminism, Environmental Philosophy, and the Critique of Rationalism', in R. Elliot (ed.) *Environmental Ethics*, Oxford: Oxford University Press.
Poole, R. (1991) 'The Private Sphere: Virtue Regained?', in R. Poole (ed.) *Morality and Modernity*, London: Routledge.
Popper, K. (1966) *The Open Society and Its Enemies*, 5th ed., London: Routledge.
Pringle, R. (1988) 'Socialist Feminism in the Eighties', *Australian Feminist Studies* 6.
Pringle, R. and Watson, S. (1992) '"Women's Interests" and the Post-Structuralist State', in M. Barrett and A. Phillips (eds.) *Destabilizing Theory*, Cambridge: Polity.
Prokhovnik, R. (1991) *Rhetoric and Philosophy in Hobbes's 'Leviathan'*, New York: Garland.
—— (1998) 'Public and Private Citizenship: From Gender Invisibility to Feminist Inclusiveness', *Feminist Review* 60.
Putnam, H. (1981) *Reason, Truth and History*, Cambridge: Cambridge University Press.

Radcliffe Richards, J. (1986) 'Separate Spheres', in P. Singer (ed.) *Applied Ethics*, Oxford: Oxford University Press.

Radden, J. (1996) 'Relational Individualism and Feminist Therapy', *Hypatia* 11.

Rawls, J. (1973) *A Theory of Justice*, Oxford: Oxford University Press.

—— (1993) *Political Liberalism*, New York: Columbia University Press.

Rich, A. (1979) *On Lies, Secrets, and Silence*, New York: W. Norton.

Rogers, L. (1988) 'Biology, the Popular Weapon: Sex Differences in Cognitive Function', in B. Caine, E. Grosz and M. Lepervanche (eds) *Crossing Boundaries: Feminisms and the Critique of Knowledges*, Sydney: Allen & Unwin.

Roiphe, K. (1993) *The Morning After. Sex, Fear and Feminism*, London: Hamish Hamilton.

Rorty, A. (1980) 'Explaining Emotions', in A. Rorty (ed.) *Explaining Emotions*, Berkeley: University of California Press.

—— (1994) 'The Hidden Politics of Cultural Identification', *Political Theory* 22.

Rose, G. (1994) 'The Comedy of Hegel and the Trauerspiel of Modern Philosophy', *Bulletin of the Hegel Society of Great Britain* 29.

Rosner, M. and Johnson, T. (1995) 'Telling Stories: Metaphors of the Human Genome Project', *Hypatia* 10.

Rubin, G. (1975) 'The Traffic in Women. Notes on the "Political Economy" of Sex', in Reiter, R. (ed.) *Towards an Anthropology of Women*, New York: Monthly Review.

Sanders, K. (1993) 'Michele Le Doeuff: Reconsidering Rationality', *Australasian Journal of Philosophy* 71.

Sawer, M. (1996) 'Gender, Metaphor and the State', *Feminist Review* 52.

Schmitt, C. (1985) *Political Theology. Four Chapters on the Concept of Sovereignty*, trans. G. Schwab, Cambridge, Mass.: MIT Press.

Scott, J. (1988) 'Deconstructing Equality-versus-Difference: Or, the Uses of Poststructuralist Theory for Feminism', *Feminist Studies* 14.

—— (1992) '"Experience"', in J. Butler and J. Scott (eds) *Feminists Theorise the Political*, London: Routledge.

Scruton, R. (1980) 'Emotion, Practical Knowledge and Common Culture', in A. Rorty (ed.) *Explaining Emotions*, Berkeley: University of California Press.

Sedgwick, E. (1990) *Epistemology of the Closet*, Berkeley: University of California Press.

—— (1993) *Tendencies*, Durham, NC: Duke University Press.

Segal, L. (1994) *Straight Sex*, London: Virago.

Sellers S. (1994) *The Helene Cixous Reader*, London: Routledge.

Sevenhuijsen, S. (1995) Symposium on Care and Justice, *Hypatia* 10.

Shanley M. and Pateman C. (eds) (1991) *Feminist Interpretations and Political Theory*, Cambridge: Polity.

Skinner, Q. (1996) *Reason and Rhetoric in the Philosophy of Hobbes*, Cambridge, Cambridge University Press.

Smart, C. (1996) 'Desperately Seeking Post-Heterosexual Woman', in J. Holland and L. Adkins (eds) *Sex, Sensibility and the Gendered Body*, Basingstoke: Macmillan.

Soble, A. (1994) 'Gender, Objectivity, and Realism', *The Monist* 77.

Solomon, R. (1976) *The Passions: The Myth and Nature of Human Emotions*, New York: Doubleday.

Spelman, E. (1989) 'Anger and Insubordination', in A. Garry and M. Pearsall (eds) *Women, Knowledge and Reality. Explorations in Feminist Philosophy*, New York: Routledge.

—— (1990) *Inessential Woman. Problems of Exclusion in Feminist Thought*, London: Women's Press.

Spinoza, B. (1982) [1677] *The Ethics* ed. S. Feldman, trans. S. Shirley, Indianapolis: Hackett.

Steinberg, D. L. (1994) 'Power, Positionality and Epistemology: an Anti-Oppressive Feminist Standpoint Approach', *Women: A Cultural Review* 5.

Steuernagel, G. (1979) *Political Theory and Psychotherapy. Marcuse Reconsidered*, Westport, Conn.: Greenwood Press.

Stocker, M. (1980) 'Intellectual Desire, Emotion, and Action', in A. Rorty (ed.) *Explaining Emotions*, Berkeley: University of California Press.

Stoller, R. (1968) *Sex and Gender*, London: Hogarth Press.

Symposium on Care and Justice (1995), *Hypatia* 10.

Tapper, M. (1986) 'Can a Feminist be a Liberal?', *Australasian Journal of Philosophy* 64.

Tavor Bannet, E. (1992) 'The Feminist Logic of Both/And', *Genders* 15.

Taylor, C. (1982) 'Rationality', in M. Hollis and S. Lukes (eds) *Rationality and Relativism*, Oxford:Blackwell.

—— (1989) 'Cross-Purposes: The Liberal Communitarian Debate', in N. Rosenblum (ed.) *Liberalism and the Moral Life*, Cambridge, Mass.: Harvard University Press.

—— (1992) 'The Politics of Recognition', in C. Taylor and A. Gutmann (eds) *Multi-Culturalism and the Politics of Recognition*, Princeton, Princeton University Press.

Thalos, M. (1994) 'The Common Need for Classical Epistemological Foundations: Against a Feminist Alternative', *The Monist* 77.

Thiele, B. (1986) 'Vanishing Acts in Social and Political Thought: Tricks of the Trade', in C. Pateman and E. Gross (eds) *Feminist Challenges. Social and Political Theory*, Sydney: Allen & Unwin.

Thomas, D. (1993) *Not Guilty. In Defence of the Modern Man*, London: Weidenfeld & Nicolson.

Thompson, D. (1989) 'The "Sex/Gender" Distinction: A Reconsideration', *Australian Feminist Studies* 10.

Tronto, J. (1993) *Moral Boundaries. A Political Argument for an Ethic of Care*, New York: Routledge.

—— (1995) 'Care as a Basis for Radical Political Judgments', *Hypatia* 10.

Tully, J. (1989) 'Wittgenstein and Political Philosophy. Understanding Practices of Critical Reflection', *Political Theory* 17.

—— (1995) *Strange Multiplicity. Constitutionalism in an Age of Diversity*, Cambridge: Cambridge University Press.

Turner, J. (1996) 'The Evolution of Emotions in Humans: A Darwinian-Durkheimian Analysis', *Journal for the Theory of Social Behaviour* 26.

Vance C. (1992) 'Social Construction Theory: Problems in the History of Sexuality', in H. Crowley and S. Himmelweit (eds) *Knowing Women. Feminism and Knowledge*, Cambridge: Polity.

Velleman, D. (1996) 'The Possibility of Practical Reason', *Ethics* 106.

Velody, I. and Williams R. eds. (1998) *The Politics of Construction*, London: Sage.

Visser, I. (1996) 'The Prototypicality of Gender. Contemporary Notions of Masculine and Feminine', *Women's Studies International Forum* 19.

Waerness, K. (1987) 'On the Rationality of Caring', in A. Showstack Sassoon (ed.), *Women and the State*, London: Hutchinson.

Walby, S. (1990) *Theorizing Patriarchy*, Oxford: Blackwell.

Walker, M. (1993) 'Silence and Reason: Women's Voice in Philosophy', *Australasian Journal of Philosophy* 71.

Walker, R. (1993) *Inside/Outside. International Relations as Political Theory*, Cambridge: Cambridge University Press.

Walter, N (1998) *The New Feminism*, New York: Little, Brown.

Walters, S. (1996) 'From Here to Queer: Radical Feminism, Postmodernism, and the Lesbian Menace (Or, Why Can't a Woman be More like a Fag?)', *Signs* 21.

Walzer, S. (1996) 'Thinking About the Baby: Gender and Divisions of Infant Care', *Social Problems* 43.

Warner, M. (1993) *Fear of a Queer Planet*, Minneapolis: University of Minnesota Press.

Warnock M. (1996) *Women Philosophers*, London: Everyman.

Weeks, J. (1985) *Sexuality and Its Discontents. Meaning, Myths and Modern Sexualities*, London: Routledge & Kegan Paul.

Weir, A. (1996) *Sacrificial Logics*, New York: Routledge.

Weiss, G. (1995) 'Sex-Selective Abortion: A Relational Approach', *Hypatia* 10.

Wenzel, H. (1981) 'The Text as Body/Politics: An Appreciation of Monique Wittig's Writings in Context', *Feminist Studies* 7.

Whelehan, I. (1995) *Modern Feminist Thought. From the Second Wave to 'Post-Feminism'*, Edinburgh: Edinburgh University Press.

Whitbeck, C. (1989) 'A Different Reality: Feminist Ontology', in A. Garry and M. Pearsall (eds), *Women, Knowledge and Reality: Explorations in Feminist Philosophy*, New York: Routledge.

Whitford, M. (1991) *The Irigaray Reader*, Oxford: Blackwell.

Williams, S. and Bendelow, G. (1996) 'Emotions and "Sociological Imperialism": a Rejoinder to Craib', *Sociology* 30.

Wilson, J. (1995) *Love Between Equals. A Philosophical Study of Love and Sexual Relationship*, Basingstoke: Macmillan.

Winch, P. (1970) 'Understanding a Primitive Society', in B. Wilson (ed.) *Rationality*, Oxford: Blackwell.

Wittig, M. (1980) 'The Straight Mind', *Feminist Issues* 1.

—— (1981) 'One is Not Born a Woman', *Feminist Issues* 1.

—— (1985) 'The Marks of Gender', *Feminist Issues* 5.

—— (1992) *The Straight Mind and Other Essays*, Boston: Beacon.

Wolf, N. (1990) *The Beauty Myth*, London: Vintage.
—— (1993) *Fire with Fire. The New Female Power and How it will Change the Twentyfirst Century*, London: Chatto & Windus.
—— (1997) *Promiscuities*, London: Chatto & Windus.
Worley, S. (1995) 'Feminism, Objectivity, and Analytic Philosophy', *Hypatia* 10.
Worrall, I. (1990) *Offending Women: Female Law Breakers and the Criminal Justice System*, London: Routledge.
Xu, P. (1995) 'Irigaray's Mimicry and the Problem of Essentialism', *Hypatia* 10.
Yeatman A. (1986) 'Women, Domestic Life and Sociology', in C. Pateman and E. Gross (eds) *Feminist Challenges, Social and Political Theory*, Sydney: Allen and Unwin.
—— (1994) 'Postmodern Epistemological Politics and Social Science', in K. Lennon and M. Whitford (eds) *Knowing the Difference. Feminist Perspectives in Epistemology*, London: Routledge.
Young, I. M. (1990a) *Justice and the Politics of Difference*, Princeton: Princeton University Press.
—— (1990b) 'The Ideal of Community and the Politics of Difference', in L. Nicholson (ed.) *Feminism/Postmodernism*, London: Routledge.
Zemon Davis, N. (1994) 'Gender and Sexual Temperament', in *The Polity Reader in Gender Studies*, Cambridge: Polity.
Zita, J. (1993) 'The Future of Feminist Sex Inquiry', in C. Kramarae and D. Spender (eds) *The Knowledge Explosion. Generations of Feminist Scholarship*, Hemel Hempstead: Harvester Wheatsheaf

# INDEX